David James Burrell

The Wondrous Cross, and Other Sermons

Vol. 1

David James Burrell

The Wondrous Cross, and Other Sermons
Vol. 1

ISBN/EAN: 9783337254636

Printed in Europe, USA, Canada, Australia, Japan

Cover: Foto ©Lupo / pixelio.de

More available books at **www.hansebooks.com**

The Wondrous Cross

The Wondrous Cross

and Other Sermons

BY

DAVID JAMES BURRELL, D.D.

*Pastor of the Collegiate Church at Fifth Avenue and 29th Street
New York*

NEW YORK
WILBUR B. KETCHAM
7 and 9 West Eighteenth Street

CONTENTS

	PAGE
THE WONDROUS CROSS	5
THE EASY YOKE	18
AN UNFINISHED LETTER	30
THE STEPS TO THE IVORY THRONE	41
SELAH	51
ONE CHURCH	60
THE LOGIA	73
EVERYBODY'S PREACHER	84
WHAT THE LAW COULD NOT DO	95
I THIRST	105
KNEELING AT OPEN WINDOWS	114
IN THE DAYS OF HEROD, THE KING	124
THE PASSOVER PILGRIMS	135
EUODIA AND SYNTYCHE	145
THE IMMEASURABLE GOD	154
HOW THE WORLDS WERE FRAMED	165
AS A REFINER OF SILVER	177
ONE RELIGION: ALL OTHERS FALSE	187
THE GLORY IN THE FACE OF JESUS	202
THE DIGNITY OF LABOR	213
A PLEA FOR FANATICISM	224

CONTENTS

	PAGE
THE WITHERED HAND	236
THE BEACON ON BETH-HACCEREM	247
A CERTAIN NOBLEMAN	259
THE FORTUNATE ANGEL	269
THE PRIDE OF NAAMAN	279
THE HANDS OF JESUS	289
THE STRENGTH OF A YOUNG MAN	299
THE SWORD OF GOLIATH	309
THE GOSPEL OF CERTAINTY	320
THE TOWER OF BABEL	331
THE RENDING OF THE VEIL	341

THE WONDROUS CROSS.

"From that time forth began Jesus to shew unto his disciples, how that he must go unto Jerusalem, and suffer many things of the elders and chief priests and scribes, and be killed, and be raised again the third day. Then Peter took him, and began to rebuke him, saying, Be it far from thee, Lord: this shall not be unto thee. But he turned, and said unto Peter, Get thee behind me, Satan: thou art an offence unto me: for thou savourest not the things that be of God, but those that be of men."—Matt. xvi. 21-23.

In the religion of the Parsees there are two supreme beings: Ormuzd, "the Good," creator and sustainer of all things bright and helpful; and Ahriman, "the Black," who presides over the regions of darkness, evokes the malignant passions, and stands sponsor for war and sorrow, disease and death. These two are perpetually arrayed against each other, the gage of conflict being the dominion of this world. It is like a stupendous game of chess, in which wars and truces, the convulsions of nature, and the ups and downs of history, are as the moves of pawns and castles upon the board. It is impossible to say how long the game will continue, or what the issue will be, inasmuch as the contestants are coeval and coequal. Perhaps it will go on forever.

We also believe in two great powers who contend for the sovereignty of this world, but they are not coequal. One is infinite; the other—though of immense guile and resource—is finite. And the end is to be seen from the beginning. God is always and everywhere getting the upper hand of Satan. The world grows constantly and cumulatively better from century to century, from year to year, from day to day. Every time our old world rolls around, it rolls a little farther into the light.

> "The eternal step of progress beats
> To that great anthem, calm and slow,
> Which God repeats.
> God works in all things; all obey
> His first propulsion from the night.
> Wake thou and watch! The world is gray
> With morning light!"

There never was a moment, from the beginning of the eternal ages, when God did not intend to save this world. All things were included in his fore-knowledge. Sin, suffering, salvation, the casting down of iniquity, and the restitution of all things in the fullness of time, were from eternity present before him.

In one of the boldest and most picturesque portions of Scripture we are introduced into the councils of the ineffable Trinity. The three Persons are represented as in solemn conference respecting the deliverance of our sin-stricken race. The cry of the erring and perishing has come up into their ears. The inquiry is heard, "Whom shall we send, and who will go for us?" Then the only-begotten Son offers himself: "Here am I; send me!" He girds himself with omnipotence, binds upon his feet the sandals of salvation, and goes forth as a knight-errant to vindicate and rescue the children of men. When next we behold him, he is a child, wrapped in swaddling-clothes and lying in a manger. The incarnation is the first chapter in his great undertaking, and a necessary part of it. As Anselm says in *Cur Deus Homo*—"He must become man in order to suffer, and he must continue to be God in order that he may suffer enough for all." In thus assuming our nature he laid aside the form of his Godhood and "the glory which he had with the Father before the world was"; but he never lost sight of his beneficent purpose. He realized constantly that he had come to redeem the world by dying for it.

In one of the earliest pictures of the nativity he is represented as lying in the manger, while just above him, on the wall of the stable, is the shadow of a cross. Holman Hunt paints him in the carpenter shop: the day's work is over; the spent toiler lifts his arms in an attitude of utter weariness, and the level rays of the setting sun cast upon the wall yonder again the shadow of a cross. The suggestion is true: he was born under that shadow and lived under it. He knew that he had come to die. He knew that, inasmuch as the penalty had been passed upon the race, "The soul that sinneth, it shall die," there could be no deliverance but by death. *Mors janua vitæ.*

A company of Greeks, on one occasion, came, saying, "We would see Jesus." He kept them waiting while he uttered those apparently inconsequential words, "Now is my soul troubled." Why should his soul be troubled? Because he saw in those waiting Greeks the vanguard of a great multitude who were to come to him as the fruit of the travail of his soul. At that moment he felt himself passing under the shadow of the cross—deeper, darker than ever—

to pay ransom for these seeking ones. He shrank from the bitterness of his approaching death, yet knew it to be necessary for the success of his errand: "Now is my soul troubled; and what shall I say? *Father, save me from this hour?* Nay, but for this cause came I unto this hour. *Father, glorify thy name!*" He had come to die for sinners. It must needs be. He knew that without his vicarious death the guilty race was without hope. He must give "his soul an offering for sin."

It could not be supposed, however, that Satan, the prince of this world, would suffer his power to slip away without a desperate effort to retain it. He would put forth every energy and use every means to thwart the beneficent purpose of Christ. Thus we account for those extraordinary manifestations of malignant energy, during the years of Christ's ministry, known as "demoniacal possession." Wherever a soul was open and willing to be used, there the adversary entered in. The plans of Jesus must be overturned; he must not be permitted to ransom the world; he must not die for it.

Out in the wilderness, after the forty days of fasting, the adversary met Jesus and presented to his weak and suffering soul the great temptation. He led him to a high place, and with a wave of the hand, directed his thought to all the kingdoms of this world, saying, "All these are mine. I know thy purpose: thou art come to win this world by dying for it. Why pay so great a price? I know thy fear and trembling—for thou art flesh—in view of the nails, the fever, the dreadful exposure, the long agony. *Why pay so great a price?* I am the prince of this world. One act of homage, and I will abdicate! Fall down and worship me!" Never before or since has there been such a temptation, so specious, so alluring. But Jesus had covenanted to die for sinners. He knew there was really no other way of accomplishing salvation for them. He could not be turned aside from the work which he had volunteered to do. Therefore he put away the suggestion with the word, "Get thee behind me, Satan! I cannot be moved. I know the necessity that is laid upon me. I know that my way to the kingdom is only by the cross. I am therefore resolved to suffer and die for the deliverance of men."

The stress of this temptation was over; but once and again it returned, as when, after a memorable day of preaching and wonder-working, his followers proposed to lead him to Jerusalem and place him upon the throne of David (John vi. 15); and he "departed into a mountain alone." He could not accept the kingdom in that way.

We now come to the immediate occasion of our context. Jesus, with his disciples, was on his last journey to Jerusalem—that memorable journey of which it is written, "He set his face steadfastly" toward the cross. He had been with his disciples now three years, but had not been able to fully reveal his mission, because they were not strong enough to bear it. A man with friends, yet friendless, lonely in the possession of his great secret, he had longed to give them his full confidence, but dared not venture. Now, as they journeyed southward through Cæsarea Philippi, he asked them, "Who do men say that I am?" And they answered, "Some say John the Baptist; some, Elias: others, Jeremias, or one of the prophets." And he saith, "But who say ye that I am?" Then Peter—brave, impulsive, glorious Peter—witnessed his good confession: "Thou art the Christ, the Son of the living God." The hour had come! His disciples were beginning to know him. He would give them his full confidence. So as they journeyed toward Jerusalem he told them all—how he had come to redeem the world by bearing its penalty of death; "he began to show them, how he must suffer many things of the elders and chief priests and scribes, and be killed." At that point Peter could hold his peace no longer, but began to rebuke him, saying, "Be it far from thee, Lord! To suffer? To die? Nay, to reign in Messianic splendor!" And Jesus turning, said unto Peter, "Get thee behind me, Satan!"—the very words with which he had repelled the same suggestion in the wilderness. As he looked on his disciple he saw not Peter, but Satan—perceived how the adversary had for the moment taken possession, as it were, of this man's brain and conscience and lips. "Get thee behind me, Satan! I know thee; I recognize thy crafty suggestion; but I am not to be turned aside from my purpose. Get thee behind me! Thou art an offence unto me. Thy words are not of divine wisdom, but of human policy. Thou savorest not the things that be of God, but those that be of men!"

We are now ready for our proposition, which is this: *The vicarious death of Jesus is the vital centre of the whole Christian system; and any word which contravenes it is in the nature of a satanic suggestion.* There is one truth before which all other truths whatsoever dwindle into relative insignificance, to wit, that our Lord Jesus Christ was wounded for our transgressions and bruised for our iniquities, that by his stripes we might be healed. The man who apprehends this by faith is saved by it.

And contrariwise, any denial of this truth is mortal heresy. The first satanic suggestion made to man was a denial of the law, when the tempter said to Adam, "Thou shalt not surely die." The last satanic suggestion is a denial of grace: "It is not necessary that Christ should die for thee." The first ruined the race, and the last will destroy any man who entertains it.

The suggestion comes in various ways, as when it is said that the gospel is not the only religion that saves: "If a man is sincere, what difference does it make?

'For forms of faith let canting bigots fight,
His faith cannot be wrong whose life is right.'

Here is a Confucianist bowing before his ancestral tablets; here is a Brahman bathing in his sacred river; and here an African kneeling before his fetish. All these are sincere; shall they not be saved with us?" If so, then the death of the Lord Jesus Christ, the only-begotten Son of the Father, was an incomprehensible waste of divine resource, and there is no significance in the word that is written: "There is none other name under heaven given among men, whereby we must be saved."

It is said again, that we are saved by the life of the Lord Jesus Christ as an example of holiness, leading us on to self-culture and character-building, and his death has practically nothing to do with our entrance into life. If that is true, then Christ did but mock our infirmity in setting up such an ideal. He did indeed come into the world to tell us how men ought to live, what a true man ought to be, what character means. That was incidental to his great redemptive mission, leading us on from deliverance to holiness. But if that were all, then I say he mocked our infirmity. For there is not an earnest man who does not kneel down beside his bed at night, after his most strenuous effort to imitate Christ, and say, "Have mercy upon me, O Lord, for I have sinned." We have all sinned and come short of the glory of God.

Again, it is said that Christ did not die vicariously, under the burden of sin, taking our place before the offended law, but died as all martyrs die. "He came into the world as a reformer, to overthrow the evil condition of things, and suffered the fate of all earnest souls. He gathered into his devoted heart the shafts of the adversary, and fell." If that be so, what is the meaning of the constant statement that the death of Jesus Christ was a voluntary death? The Father gave him, he gave himself, an offering for sin. "I have power to lay down my life, and I have power to take it again; no man taketh my life from me." Life was his; he made it; he played with it as little children play with their toys.

1. *To deny this doctrine of the vicarious atonement, in any of these ways or otherwise, is to set one's self athwart the whole trend of Scripture.* For from Genesis to Revelation there is a thoroughfare stained with the blood that cleanseth from sin. No sooner had man sinned than the protevangel spoke of the

"Seed of the woman" suffering for sin. The first altar, reared by the closed gate of paradise, prophesied of the slain Lamb of God. As the years passed, the prophets declared, with ever-increasing clearness and particularity, the coming sacrifice. David sang of it in his Messianic psalms. Isaiah drew the portrait of the agonizing Christ as if he had gazed on the cross: "He is a man of sorrows, and acquainted with grief . . . Surely he hath borne our griefs, and carried our sorrows. . . . And the Lord hath laid on him the iniquity of us all." The same truth was emphasized by Moses, Daniel, Zechariah, all the prophets down to Malachi, who, waving his torch in the twilight of the long darkness which closed the old economy, said, "The sun of righteousness shall arise with healing in his wings." Open the Book where you will, the face of Jesus, "so marred more than any man's," yet divinely beautiful, looks out upon you.

The rites and symbols of the Old Testament all find their fulfilment in Christ crucified. Their centre was the tabernacle. Enter it and observe how it is everywhere sprinkled with blood. Here is blood flowing down the brazen altar, blood on the ewer, the golden candlestick, the table of showbread, the altar of incense; blood on the floor, the ceiling, on posts and pillars, on knops and blossoms, everywhere. Lift the curtain and pass into the holiest of all—but not without blood on your palms. Here is blood on the ark of the covenant, blood on the mercy-seat—blood, blood everywhere. What does it mean? Nothing, absolutely nothing, unless it declares the necessity of the cross. It is an empty dumb-show, except as it points the worshiper to Him whose vicarious death is the only means of our salvation.

Wherefore I say, the man who denies this truth must set himself against the sum and substance of the Scriptures. For if the atoning death of Christ be taken out of that blessed Book it is, as a solution of the great problem of life, of no more value than a last year's almanac.

2. Again, *a denial of this doctrine involves a downright rejection of the philosophy of history.*

The world has been growing better ever since the cross first cast its luminous shadow over it. Progress is a fact—a fact that must be accounted for. Hume undertook to write history without Christ, and found it a labyrinth without a clue. So did Gibbon. They saw civilization advancing through the centuries; but, rejecting Christ, they could perceive no reason for it. The "logic of events" was nothing to them. There can, indeed, be no "philosophy of history" for a man who refuses to see Constantine's cross in the heavens, with its great prophecy, "*In hoc signo.*" It is a miraculous coincidence that the limits of civilization on earth to-day are coextensive with the charmed circle known as *Christendom.* "The world before Christ," says Luthardt, "was a world without love." The church with the proclamation of Christ, and him crucified, has come down through the centuries, like Milton's angel with the torch; and all along the way have sprung up institutions of learning and charity and righteousness. The cross is the vital power of civilization. "All the light of sacred" and of secular story as well "gathers round its head sublime." If the world grows better, it is because Christ died for it.

3. Still further, *to deny the vital importance of the vicarious death of Jesus is to contradict the universal instinct of mankind.*

The doctrine of the redemptive power of substitutionary pain is not our exclusive property. It has, indeed, a place in all, or nearly all, the false religions. It may be dimly seen in the hammer of Thor; in the wounded foot of Brahma treading on the serpent; in the fable of Prometheus, bound to the Caucasus with a vulture at his vitals, and lamenting, "I must endure this until one of the gods shall bear it for me." It is still more evident in the institution of the sacrifice. Wherever a living thing is slain upon the altar, it means vicarious expiation, or else it means nothing at all.

And why should it be thought strange that God should send his only-begotten Son to suffer in our stead? Is not *sympathy* the noblest as well as the commonest thing in human experience? Men are suffering everywhere and always for other men. Parents are suffering for their children. The pains which we all endure are, for the most part, not the consequence of our own acts. At this point of sympathy our nature reaches its noblest and best. We esteem above all the unselfish man who voluntarily bears the burdens of others. Should we not, then, expect something of the same sort in our Father? He made us in his likeness. It would be monstrous if God did not sympathize with his children who have fallen into trouble. The cross is the very highest expression of sympathy in the universe. The atonement is what we should expect. It is just like God.

And it is God's exact response to the universal

need. It fits our circumstances. As Coleridge said, "The gospel finds me." It answers the deepest longing of earnest souls. Dr. Chamberlain relates, that among those converted by his preaching at the sacred city of Benares was a devotee who had dragged himself many miles upon his knees and elbows to bathe in the Ganges. He had at the bottom of his heart the common conviction of sin and desire of cleansing. "If I can but reach the Ganges," he thought, "this shame and bondage and fear will be taken away." Weak and emaciated from his long pilgrimage, he dragged himself down to the river's edge and, praying to Gunga, crept into it; then withdrawing, he lay upon the river's bank and moaned, "The pain is still here!" At that moment he heard a voice from the shadow of a banyan-tree near by. It was the missionary telling the story of the cross. The devotee listened, and drank it in, rose to his knees, then to his feet; then, unable to restrain himself, he clapped his hands and cried, "That's what I want! That's what I want!" It is what we all want; the whole creation has from time immemorial groaned and travailed for it.

And it is our only hope. There are other religions and other philosophies, but none that suggests a rational plan of pardon for sin. *Spes unica.* I remember an old crucifix, in the public square of a Brittany village, which no one passed without bending the knee. Workmen on their way to the fields, little children going to school, all bowed before that stone figure of the Christ, which the storms of centuries had worn almost out of human semblance. The last night, as I was leaving the village in the twilight, I saw an old woman bent almost prostrate before it. Her hands were clasped; her uplifted face bore the marks of suffering. I could not know the bitterness of that poor heart, but her eyes were turned toward the infinite Source of help and consolation. The dear hand upon the cross lifts every burden, heals every wound, and saves us from the penalty, the shame, and the bondage of sin.

And this is why we preach Christ, and him crucified. "There is none other name under heaven given among men, whereby we must be saved." "He was wounded for our transgressions, he was bruised for our iniquities; and with his stripes we are healed." He is thus made unto us wisdom and righteousness and sanctification and redemption. He is first, last, midst, and all in all.

Preached in Battell Chapel of Yale University, and here reprinted, by courtesy of Fleming H. Revell Co., from "The Culture of Christian Manhood."

THE EASY YOKE

"My yoke is easy."—Matt. xi. 30.

Capernaum had a triple fame. It was beautiful for situation, and was known as "the Pearl of Gennesaret"; as if it were a gem cast up by the waters of that pleasant inland sea. It was known also far and wide for its fishing industry. Zebedee and his sons, with other fishermen, moored their fleets and dragged their nets along its shores. Its chief renown, however, is due to the fact that Jesus dwelt there. It was called "his own city." The only perfect man who ever lived, walked among its people and gave them to know the full meaning of manhood and character. He preached to them the great truths; "burning thoughts in breathing words." He wrought miracles of healing there; opening the eyes of the blind, cleansing lepers, and raising the dead. Surely the people of Capernaum should have been righteous above those of all the neighboring towns.

But, alas! the Scotch proverb is too often true, "Anear the kirk, afar frae God." The miracles of Jesus were a nine-days' wonder in Capernaum. His sermons were as water poured upon the ground, which cannot be gathered up again. The example of his perfect life was of no avail. The light shone in the darkness, and the darkness comprehended it not.

At last the patience of Jesus was worn out, and an admonition fell from his lips as terrible as the lightning of Sinai: "Woe unto thee, Capernaum! Thou hast been exalted unto heaven; thou shalt be brought down to hell!" Then straightway his voice fell and became as gentle as a mother's lullaby; and he stretched forth his hands, saying, "Come unto me, all ye that labor and are heavy laden, and I will give you rest. Take my yoke upon you, and learn of me; for I am meek and lowly in heart: and ye shall find rest unto your souls. For my yoke is easy, and my burden is light."

"Come!" It is a wonderful word—a great word— with the heart of the Infinite throbbing through it. It rings through the Scriptures like a morning greeting echoing down a ravine amid the mountains. The Old Book opens with it: "Come thou and all thy house into the ark." It is resonant everywhere: "Come now, and let us reason together, saith the Lord: though your sins be as scarlet, they shall be as white as snow; though they be red like crimson, they shall be as wool"; "Ho, every one that thirsteth, come ye to the waters, and he that hath no money; come ye, buy, and eat; yea, come, buy wine and milk without money and without price." And the closing of the seals shows heaven and earth in vociferous accord: "The Spirit and the bride say, Come! And let him that heareth say, Come! And let him that is athirst come. And whosoever will, let him take the water of life freely." The patriarchs passed the sweet invitation on to the prophets; the prophets to the apostles and evangelists; and they, through a multitude of ambassadors, down to me, who, as a minister of Jesus, in his stead beseech you in his words, "Come unto me, all ye that labor and are heavy laden, and I will give you rest."

If you, my good friend, do not enter into the fulness of the inheritance of Christ, it will not be because he has not invited you.

But let there be no mistake. Christ wants followers, but they must come advisedly, and in full recognition of the fact that his service is no sinecure. He was the frankest teacher that ever spake to the children of men. He had come all the way from heaven to win them, and was ready to give his life in their behalf; but he must tell them the whole truth. Once when a company of these same people of Capernaum came trooping after him, he turned and said, "Come, but count the cost. See yonder ruined tower! A certain man began to build, and was not able to finish; and, behold, all that pass by point their fingers at him." And it is written, "Many turned back and followed him no more." It means something to be a Christian. "If any man would come after me, let him deny himself, and take up his cross daily, and follow me."

Our text is bi-frontal: it looks two ways. One of its faces is stern and forbidding; the other is as bright as a May morning.

I. *On the one hand the Christian life is set forth as a Yoke.* No more repellent figure could have been found. The service of Christ is elsewhere characterized in other ways, but there is always inspiration in the metaphor. Not so here.

For example, it is a warfare. We go forth, not against flesh and blood, but against principalities and powers. There is no discharge in this war. Wherefore put ye on the whole armor of God: the girdle of truth, the breastplate of righteousness, sandals of the preparation of the gospel, the helmet of salvation with its waving plume, in your right hand the sword of the Spirit, which is the word of God. Thus armed and panoplied,

> "Fight on, my soul, till death
> Shall bring thee to thy God.
> He'll take thee at thy parting breath
> Up to his blest abode."

Here is abundant stimulus — the banner and the bugle-blast, the hope of victory, and the crown of righteousness that fadeth not away.

The Christian life is also husbandry. Go forth, bearing the precious seed; sow beside all waters; scatter the seed-corn along through the furrows, though it seem like wasting your children's bread. Bury your life for Jesus' sake; for except a corn of wheat fall into the ground and die, it abideth alone; but if it die, it bringeth forth much fruit. Here again is inspiration. The sower sees with prophetic eye the waving harvest. He hears the groaning of the loaded wains on their way to the granaries and the song of the harvest-home. As it is written, "He that goeth forth and weepeth, bearing precious seed, shall doubtless come again with rejoicing, bringing his sheaves with him."

The service of Christ is also a strenuous game. We stand like the Olympic athletes, with our feet at the crimson line, stripped to the waist, every nerve and sinew tense, eyes fixed upon the distant goal. The galleries are filled with a great cloud of witnesses; wherefore let us run with steadfastness the race that is set before us. "Forgetting the things which are behind, and reaching forth unto the things which are before, let us press toward the mark for the prize of the high calling of God in Christ Jesus." Ah! here, too, is inspiration!

But what is there to quicken the pulse in this dull picture?—two patient, meek-eyed oxen, with their necks bowed to the burden, asking no question, making no suggestion, uncomplaining, unresisting, plodding on, plodding on.

The yoke means labor, to begin with. The Christian life is more than creed. It is more than a name on a church roster. It is more than emotion, hosannas, and hallelujahs. It is more than self-culture. It involves more or less of these, but something far beyond. Go, work! We sing, "The gospel ship is sailing, sailing, bound for Canaan's happy shore." But in fact this business is not a ship in which a man can pay his fare like Jonah, engage an outside stateroom, and so pass comfortably on to the better land; it is a trireme rather, with many banks of oars—an oar for every soul, and every soul bound to bend to his oar until the keel shall grate upon the sand of the Far Country.

A young man asked of Jesus, "Are there few that be saved?" He answered, "Strive to enter in; for many shall seek to enter in and shall not be able." The word "strive" is, literally, "*agonize*."

> "There's a work for me and a work for you,
> Something for each of us now to do."

The yoke means, also, self-abnegation. "If any man will come after me, let him deny himself." These patient oxen are not working for themselves. They have no purpose of their own; they only, always do their master's will.

The three steps to heaven are these: "out of self, unto Christ, into glory." But the beginning is out of self. The man who truly follows Christ puts self more and more into the background. Self-pleasing, self-emolument, self-salvation, self-culture, all these dwindle in view of the ever-increasing importance of caring for the interests of a perishing world and the glory of God. A better hymn than "When I can read my title clear," is "Throw out the life-line;" and better still, "All hail the power of Jesus' name!" We do not come up to the full measure of the stature of Christ until our lives are blended with his; not until we can speak as Luther did: "If any man come and knock at my breast and ask, 'Does Martin Luther live here?' I answer, 'Nay, not now; he did; but now Jesus Christ lives here.'"

The yoke, furthermore, means co-operation with Christ. This is indicated in the term cross-bearing. "If any man will come after me, let him deny himself, and take up his cross and follow me."

At this point let us correct a misapprehension. There are good people who speak of their sorrows and adversities as crosses. A bad temper, a hacking cough, a bereavement, a vicious appetite, a skeleton in the closet; these are referred to as crosses. Indeed, they are hard to bear, and there is a great reward for those who patiently endure "the whips and scorns of time, the slings and arrows of outrageous fortune." Here is the promise: "No affliction for the present seemeth joyous, but grievous; but in the end it worketh the peaceable fruit of righteousness to them that are exercised thereby." Nevertheless these are not crosses. The harrow is one thing, the cross another.

What is the cross? It gets its name and all its significance from the analogy of the cross of Jesus. And what was that? A voluntary work which he undertook for the salvation of men—a work involving pain, unceasing effort, self-sacrifice, even unto death. This was not thrust upon him; he had power to lay it down and power to take it up. He lifted his cross and carried it up the slopes of Calvary until his great heart brake under it. And this he did voluntarily, for the deliverance of the world from sin. The cross which he invites us to bear, is like his own; it means participation in the great work of delivering the world from its shame and horror of sin. "As the Father hath sent me into the world," he said, "so send I you." He came to answer the world's cry for help. He sends us also to answer it. No man has taken up his cross, therefore, in the true sense, until he has entered into fellowship with Jesus in his great work for the deliverance of the souls of men.

All this is suggested in the figure of the yoke. Does it seem beyond our strength? Let us turn then to the brighter side.

II. "*My yoke is easy.*" This is singular. It is a paradox. Yokes are not easy as a rule. Ask the slave in Pharaoh's brickyard, making bricks without straw under the lash of a hard task-master, whether he finds his yoke easy: and he will tell you that he wets his pillow with his tears. Ask the captive dragged at the chariot wheels of his conqueror, if he finds his yoke easy; and he will answer, "It is bitterer than death." Ask the sensualist who has pursued pleasure until pleasure has turned upon him with a whip of scorpions,—who has lived in self-gratification until the last Sodom-apple has changed to ashes on his lips,—whether his yoke is easy: and he will say as Lord Byron did,—poor Byron, who died of old age at thirty-six:—

> "My days are in the yellow leaf;
> The flowers and fruits of love are gone;
> The worm, the canker, and the grief
> Are mine alone!"

Now ask the old father sitting with his Bible on his knee, burdened with his years, and searching out with dim eyes the exceeding great and precious promises, how he has found Christ's burden; and he will tell you, that it has been light as the feathers on a bird's wing with which it mounts toward the skies. But why is this? What makes the Christian yoke easy, while all others are so heavy to be borne?

(1) *It is because this yoke is always for two.* It is not his will that any of his followers should bear it alone. Did He not say, "Lo, I am with you always, even unto the end of the world?" No friend is so near; He is nearer than seeing, nearer than touching. His help is more than sympathy; omnipotence is behind it.

Have you been making a brave effort to conquer a darling sin? Have you gone out full-armed with holy purpose to overthrow a habit that has gained dominion over you? and have you failed, failed again and again ignominiously? Ah, my friend, you left him out of the reckoning! Try it again, and try it with Jesus at your side; the Mighty One who never lost a battle, and who longs to fulfil to you his great promise, "the gates of hell shall not prevail against you." It is not you alone who are to get the better of your sins; it is Christ and you.

Have you a difficult duty to perform? Do you shrink from it as hard and forbidding? Remember that this yoke is for two, and when you go to meet this responsibility, say to yourself, "Not I, but Christ and I." We sing, "One more day's work for Jesus;" suppose we put it this way, "One more day's work *with* Jesus."

> O blessed work with Jesus,
> O rest at Jesus' feet;
> There toil seems pleasure,
> My wants are treasure,
> And pain with him is sweet,

Have you been offering a prayer for years, and mourning because there was no answer nor any that regarded,—a prayer perhaps for the conversion of a dear friend or the reclaiming of a wayward son? You have sprinkled the mercy-seat with your tears in vain, crying, "How long, O Lord, how long?" Alas for your intercessory success! you have made your prayer alone. Now kneel again at the mercy-seat and feel that close beside you is kneeling the One who ever liveth to make intercession for you, and say within your heart, "It is not I who make this prayer, but Christ and I."

We who are appointed as ambassadors to preach the gospel of salvation, ascend our pulpit stairs with trembling knees, saying, "Who is sufficient unto these things?" O brethren of the ministry, we forget. This is not our work; we are but underlings. We do not preach alone; he stands beside us in the sacred place. It is not I, but always Christ and I. "Lo I am with you," is his word. And ours should be, "I can do all things through Christ which strengtheneth me."

(2) *The yoke is also easy by reason of the* mens conscia recti; *that is, the sense of doing right.* In all the world there is nothing so uplifting as a good conscience. I know that it is right to love God. I know that it is right to surrender myself as a living sacrifice to the Lord Christ who gave himself for me. I know that it is right to spend and be spent in the behalf of my fellow-men. If a bad conscience makes cowards of us all, by the same token a good conscience nerves the heart and strengthens us like a girdle about our loins.

An old chronicler says of Saint Perpetua, that as she was brought from her dungeon and led under the great arch to the Arena, her inquisitor called her attention to the roar of the lions and said, "There is yet time to speak the word and live." She laid her hand upon her heart and answered, "I have that here which makes me fearless," and so passed on to death. As the wild beasts fell upon her, she lifted her eyes and hands to heaven and sang, "Glory to the Father and to the Son and to the Holy Ghost, as it was in the beginning, is now and ever shall be, world without end. Amen." A little later her mangled body was carried out on a bier; and the old bishop of the city laid his hand upon her blood-stained face, gently parted the clotted hair, and said, "I give thee joy, my daughter!" A strange word at such a moment. And yet why not? There is nothing better in heaven or on earth than the sense of right doing. There is nothing better to live by, nothing better to die by.

(3) And there is still another consideration which makes the *yoke easy and the burden light; that is, the great reward.* No man hath given up aught for Christ but that he shall receive in this present time an hundredfold and in the time to come life everlasting.

In this present time an hundredfold! Here is a rare investment in gold-bearing bonds. If there were no eternity, if there were no heaven, the service of Christ pays for itself here and now. We take of the grapes of Eshcol before we reach the Promised Land. There are moments when we enter the closet bowed down under great burdens and meet the Lord; and presently come forth with something glistening on our eyelashes and something throbbing fast in our veins, to tell of a joy the world cannot give, a joy which is found only in communion with God. These are earnests, foretastes, partial payments for our encouragement along the way. They are like the chaff which was thrown upon the Nile, to tell the starving people by the Delta, that there was plenty and to spare in Joseph's granaries higher up. They are momentary joys given to cheer us while we bear the heat and burden of the day.

But, as Bunyan says, "The milk and honey are beyond the wilderness." In the time to come life everlasting! Here we pause. It is not possible to tell the meaning of those words. "Eye hath not seen, ear hath not heard, neither hath it entered into the heart of man to conceive, the things which God hath prepared for those that love him."

How little will seem all the cares and burdens and cross-bearings of this present life when we are yonder. In the time of King Herod an indiscreet youth named Agrippa was fond of singing the praises of his friend Caligula who had a presumptive claim to the throne. For this he was cast into a dungeon and loaded with chains. One day there was a footfall in the corridor and a voice cried, "Caligula reigns! Long live Caligula!" The door was thrown open and Agrippa was led forth. Purple was exchanged for his rags, a tetrarchy for his narrow cell; his chains were weighed and their weight in gold was given him. O friends, the crowning day is coming when Christ shall triumph over all. Then what shall be the joy, the satisfaction, the honorable promotion, of those who have followed and faithfully served him?

Is there one among you who is cast down and discouraged? Has the way seemed rough, the burden heavy? Have you been thwarted, opposed and perhaps inclined to give up? Take heart, my friend, *Per crucem, ad lucem! Per aspera, ad astra!* By the rough road to the stars! I hear the songs of heaven coming this way. I see the light streaming through the gates. The odors of the King's garden flow toward us. O the hosannas and hallelujahs! The glory dazzles like a sun-burst. Life! Life! Eternal life!

"Toil on; in hope o'ercome
The steeps God set for thee;
For past the Alpine summits of great toil
Lieth thine Italy".

AN UNFINISHED LETTER.

"Having many things to write unto you, I would not write with paper and ink: but I trust to come unto you and speak face to face, that our joy may be full."—II. John 12.

In the year 68 the Emperor Nero died and the world breathed a sigh of relief. Prison doors were thrown open and the sound of breaking chains was heard throughout the Empire. An old man who had been for years an exile on the lonely island of Patmos, found his way to Asia Minor. It was the Apostle John, the sole survivor of the old guard. Whither should he go? He looked toward Capernaum; but his home there was desolate, his father Zebedee was dead, and James, his beloved brother, had been slain by Herod's sword. He looked toward Jerusalem; but the clouds which were to burst in the awful storm of Titus's conquest, were already gathering over that doomed city. Whither should he go? He betook himself to the fellowship of a little company of Christians in Ephesus, who worshipped under the shadow of the great temple of Diana, and there he passed the remainder of his days.

It is believed that John lived to be above one hundred years of age. In his decrepitude he was wont to be carried to the church in a litter; and there, lifting his trembling hands above the congregation, he would say: "Little children, love one another!" In his later years he made an itinerary of the churches of Asia. It would appear that during one of these journeys he had met the children of a long-time friend, and had found them living an earnest Christian life amid innumerable temptations. He could not forbear writing his congratulations to their mother, the widow Kyria. We have this letter in his Second Epistle, which is addressed, "To the Elect Lady."

It was not an easy matter for this old man to write. See him bending over the parchment. His eyes are dim, his hands tremulous. With much labor he traces the lines: "Grace be with you, mercy and peace, from God our Father and from the Lord Jesus Christ, the Son of the Father, in truth and love." Then follow his congratulations: "I rejoice greatly that I have found of thy children walking in truth." Then an exhortation as to mutual love. Then an earnest admonition as to false teachers: "For many deceivers are entered into the world, who confess not that Jesus Christ is come in the flesh. Whosoever abideth not in the doctrine of Christ, hath not God. If there come any unto you and bring not this doctrine, receive him not into your house, neither bid him God speed." At this point the letter breaks off abruptly. The old eyes were too dim, the fingers too stiff and tremulous. A brief postscript, and he will have done: "Having many things to write unto you, I would not write with paper and ink: but I trust to come unto you, and speak face to face, that our joy may be full."

How like life itself is this epistolary fragment! For what is life but a short letter with an eternal postscript? It is a dream, an eagle hastening to the prey, foam upon the waters, a swift ship, a cloud sweeping overhead, a tale that is told. "We need no reed," says Matthew Henry, "no pole, nor measuring line, wherewith to take the dimensions of our days; nor any skill in arithmetic wherewith to compute the number of them. No; we have the standard of them at our fingers' ends; it is but one handbreadth in all."

Is life worth living then? Not if its sum total is here and now. If death ends all, it were easy to account for the sixteen suicides recently reported in this city in a single day. Why should a man endure an insufferable burden of pain and trouble "when he himself might his quietus make with a bare bodkin?" The sooner it's over, the sooner to sleep.

> "Out, out, brief candle!
> Life's but a walking shadow."

But death does not end all. The brief period that we call life, is merely the preface of an endless serial. Indeed life does not begin until this period of preparation is over. Death is Commencement. We climb the steps of the great temple, bearing our burden with us, until worn and weary we reach the threshold; the door flies open, and a good angel, whom we have strangely called the King of Terrors, bids us enter and begin to live.

> "Life, we have been long together,
>   In pleasant and in stormy weather;
> 'Tis hard to part when friends are dear,
> Perhaps, 'twill cost a sigh, a tear.
> Then steal away; give little warning;
> Say not, 'Good night,' but in some brighter clime
> Give me, '*Good morning*'!"

We drop the stylus from our trembling fingers, fold up the parchment, go forth into the presence of the great verities, and see face to face forever.

So is it with all life's ambitions. No purpose is completed here. "All life's sweetest chapters end like the fourteenth of John, 'Arise, let us go hence'." All our purposes end in the middle of a sentence, like "Edwin Drood." It is safe to say that Methuselah, having lived nine hundred and sixty and nine years, called his sons about his death-bed and enjoined them to complete what he had left undone. The Lord Christ alone could say, "*Tetelestai!*" His life was rounded and complete.

There are many things, indeed, which cannot be written with pen and paper. When Dr. John Elias was asked to print his sermons, he answered, "Impossible; you cannot put fire into cold type." Our life here is—like letter-writing—a temporary expedient. Its noblest thoughts and purposes and aspirations await for their full expression the eternity when we shall stand face to face with truth and God.

I. *We find incompleteness in the pursuit of knowledge.* To the knowledge of visible things we apply the pretentious term Science, which is from *scire*, meaning "to know." But how little we really know! "The summit of wisdom," as Socrates said, "is to be aware of our ignorance." Or, as John Owen put it,

"All things I thought I knew; but now confess,
The more I know I know, I know the less."

Here is a pebble. We crush and analyze it. We determine its component parts. We discover that it is formed of certain materials and governed by certain forces acting according to fixed laws. But more than this we cannot write with pen and paper. There is more beyond, but the curtain falls on our bewilderment. And this is the Science of Geology.

Here is a blade of grass. I tear it apart, dissect and analyze. The color scheme and the pattern of the fabric are plain to see. But in my scrutiny I have come upon a strange thing which is called Life; and I can write no more; the curtain falls. And this is the Science of Biology.

I gaze upon the stars. "Look how the floor of heaven is thick inlaid with patines of bright gold." Here are ten thousand times ten thousand and thousands of thousands; and, as I gaze, still more come wheeling into place like ships to join an infinite armada. I turn upon them my scientific implements, make a spectral analysis, and measure the distance from planet to planet. Then my gaze wanders to the interstellar spaces, and I query, "What lies beyond?" But there is no answer, nor any that regardeth. My essay is broken in twain. And this is the Science of Astronomy.

I am standing at the manger and gazing into the face of the Child. I hear voices saying, "Here is God wrapped in swaddling bands," and, "Here Godhood and manhood are woven warp and woof into one Fabric." But what shall I write? "Great is the mystery of Godliness, God manifest in flesh; angels desire to look into it!" No more. Again the curtain falls. And this is the Science of Theology.

But is this all? Is knowledge then the touching of merely the outermost fringe of truth? Then were

Agnosticism the logical conclusion. But this is base and sordid and unworthy of us. As if we were to say, "I have caught a glimpse, and, lo! it was delusion." Nay; blessed be God, where eyesight fails, faith begins. "We know in part, but we shall know even as we are known." What is faith? "The substance of things hoped for, the evidence of things not seen." Our natural faculties cannot reach beyond the circumscription of our finger tips, but faith reaches out into the infinite. "Now we see through a glass darkly, but then face to face." The fragment of our knowledge ends thus: "To be continued in our next."

By faith we solve the mystery of the pebble, and behind the law catch sight of the Law-giver. By faith we lift the curtain that falls at the announcement of life, and stand face to face with the Life-Giver. By faith we gaze through the interstellar spaces and behold One seated on a throne, high and lifted up. By faith we hear from the lips of the Christ-child the message of the gospel, "God so loved the world that he gave his only begotten Son, that whosoever believeth in him should not perish, but have everlasting life." The best that scientists can do, is to write the unfinished letter; it is for faith to complete it.

II. *We observe a similar incompleteness in our efforts at character-building.* The most discouraging thing in the world is to try to be somebody, to come up to the full stature of a man as made in the likeness of God. We have ethical rules, noble aspirations, and a splendid Ideal. The elements of worth and true greatness are in every man. We have a conscience that determines betwixt the worse and better reason. We look into the face of the perfect One and long to be like him. But we are continually thwarted and disappointed. Sin strengthened by habit has an almost irresistible grip upon us. Heredity is against us; our forebears are dragging us down. Environment also is against us. So, alas! there is no difference; we all come short of the glory of God, and of the glory of manhood as God has revealed it.

If there is any who questions the truth of this generalization and is moved to say, "I, for one, am not so characterless as you would make me out," see how small a thing will put him down. If God were to come and say to you,—"Friend, I am disposed to be as lenient as possible in your case. I will not judge you by the sum total of your life; but tell me a single deed you have done which is so absolutely free from all taint of sinful motive or selfishness that you would be willing to adventure your eternal destiny upon it, and that shall be your criterion at the great day"; where would you lay your hand upon it?

But none who has caught the high spirit of Christianity will, for a moment, hesitate to admit his own unworthiness. The world criticises Christians; and there is abundant ground for it. No one knows better than ourselves the vast gulf between our character and our Ideal. We are our own severest critics. The good we would, we do not, and the evil we would not, that we do.

Was there ever a more earnest striver than the Apostle Paul? Yet how incomplete was his endeavor! Hear his confession: "Brethren, I count not myself to have apprehended, as though I had already attained, or were already perfect." The perfectionist is a mere masker, deceiving nobody, not even himself, least of all his God.

But shall we end the record here? Is there no postscript? Is there nothing to look forward to? The past is indeed not without its encouragement; for, despite the fact that the motions of sin are still in us, we must have grown by very virtue of our life. "I am not what I ought to be, I am not what I mean to be; but by the grace of God I am what I am." An eternity is before us. Sin loses its grip in the article of death. The chains shall be broken, and we shall rejoice in an infinite freedom of spiritual growth. "Now are we sons of God, and it doth not yet appear what we shall be; but when he shall appear, we shall be like him, for we shall see him as he is."

III. *And there is a like incompleteness in our work.* We set out to accomplish great things for God. We dream dreams and see visions, and they dissolve about us like castles in the air. We are cut off in the midst of our days, and the story ends with "Finis." But is this, again, the end? I do not think so little of life, and I have not so poor an opinion of the God who made it. There is something beyond. The loose threads of the unfinished fabric will be gathered up; the preparation of these years will all be utilized in the endless æons.

An English lad was moved by a noble ambition; he would prepare himself to do some great thing for God. He plodded through his text books, finished his theological course, and settled in his first parish at Anworth. There he declared the unsearchable riches of Christ with flaming lips. He looked for a harvest of souls, but it came not. He agonized in prayer, and still it came not. He wrote just before he died,—

> "O! if one soul from Anworth
> Meet me at God's right hand,
> My heaven will be two heavens
> In Immanuel's land."

So ended his life. The pen fell from his trembling fingers; but shall the biography of Rutherford end there? "One soul" did he long for? The harvest that he never saw, has grown luxuriant upon his grave. Thousands on thousands of souls rise up to call him blessed. From the high heaven, where he sees face to face and knows even as he is known, Rutherford sees of the travail of his soul and is satisfied.

The two most indispensable men of the Old Economy, as it would appear, were Moses and Elias. The former led the children of Israel out of their bondage through the wilderness to the border of the promised land. And just there, when it seemed as if himself alone could lead them in, he was called up into the mountain where he sang his death song:

"*O Lord, we spend our years as a tale that is told. The days of our years are threescore years and ten; and if by reason of strength they be fourscore years, yet is their strength labor and sorrow: for it is soon cut off, and we fly away. Let thy work appear unto thy servants and thy glory unto their children. And let the beauty of the Lord our God be upon us: and establish thou the work of our hands upon us: yea, the work of our hands establish thou it.*"

And Elias the great reformer wrought for the deliverance of Israel in a time of great spiritual need. He had brought the nation to the very verge of pure religion, when God sent the chariot of fire. As he went upward, the voice of lamentation was heard: "O my father, the horses of Israel and the chariots thereof!" Thus the work of these two mighty men seemed to be broken in the midst and to have reached an utter end.

But when a thousand years have passed, lo, here are Moses and Elias on the mount of transfiguration, and they speak with Jesus of the decease which he shall accomplish at Jerusalem! The continuity of their lives was not broken at all. In the interim they had kept abreast of the history of God's people and were in full sympathy with its magnificent denouement in the work of redemption. Thus in the fulness of time God did establish the work of their hands upon them.

What, now, are the practical lessons of our theme? First, do not forget or omit the postscript. He is a foolish man who leaves eternity out of the reckoning. It is the thought of eternity that makes life worth living. It is otherwise a thing of mere threads and thrums. It needs the infinite outlook to complete it. The world has known no greater artist than Raphael. What Madonnas he painted! what faces of Christ! And he died at thirty-seven. Has he ceased to paint, think you?

> "When earth's last picture is painted,
>   And the tubes are twisted and dried;
> When the oldest colors have faded,
>   And the youngest critics have died;
> We shall rest,—and O! we shall need it,—

> Lie down for a moment or two,*
> Till the Master of all good workmen
> Shall set us to work anew.
>
> "And those that were good, shall be happy;
> They shall sit in a golden chair;
> They shall splash at a ten-league canvas
> With brushes of comet's hair.
> They shall have real saints to draw from,
> Magdalene, Peter and Paul,
> They shall work for an age at a sitting,
> And never be tired at all.
>
> "And only the Master shall praise us,
> And only the Master shall blame;
> And no one shall work for money,
> And no one shall work for fame;
> But each for the joy of working,
> And each in his separate star,
> Shall draw the thing as he sees it
> For the God of things as they are."

And finally, live to-day. We must make our beginning here. As the tree falleth, so also shall it lie. Let us not waste our years in pursuits which would be out of place in the eternal life. Let us cease chasing thistle-down and playing with yellow dust; these are not worthy of immortal men. The present life is momentous, because, and only because, it looks on toward eternity. We must walk while it is day, for the night cometh. *Ab hoc momento pendet æternitas!* Our seventy years here and now are more important than seventy cycles cut out of eternity, because the making of all eternity is in them. Write your brief letter well, my friend; but always remember that there are things which cannot be written with ink and paper. Live to-day, if you would live forever.

---

* A liberty is here taken with Mr. Kipling's theology. He writes "for an æon or two"; but we shall not lie down for an æon or anything like it. The question of soul-sleeping was settled definitely and finally when Jesus said: "To-day shalt thou be with me in Paradise."

THE STEPS TO THE IVORY THRONE.

"And there were six steps to the throne with a footstool of gold."
II. CHRON. 9, 18.

The glory of Jewish history found its consummation in the reign of Solomon. The magnificence of his establishment centered in the House of the Forest of Lebanon, and the tower before it, on which were suspended a thousand golden shields like the necklace of coins adorning an oriental bride. The brightest point of splendor in this palace was the throne. It was of ivory overlaid with gold, and on either side were six golden lions, symbols of sovereign power. It was a great day in Israel when Solomon ascended the six steps from the golden footstool and took his place on that magnificent throne. No fabled grandeur of the kings of Samarcand was comparable with this. It found expression in the proverb, "Solomon in all his glory."

The rabbis in their traditions loved to dwell on the transcendent beauty of this ivory throne. The Arabian legends are mellifluous in praise of it. The sacred historian himself is moved to say, "There was not the like made in any kingdom." Nevertheless as Solomon was a living type of One to come, whose perfections should surpass his as the sun outshines a glowworm, so the ivory throne is a mere suggestion of one that borrows an unspeakable glory from the Christ who sits upon it, to wit, The Throne of True Manhood. The place of highest exaltation is by the side of Jesus in the estate of regenerated and sanctified character. To be a true man, loyal to truth, reverent toward duty, high-spirited and magnanimous, with "noble thoughts seated in a soul of honor," moved by great purposes and free from the corrupting power of sin—this is to be greater than Solomon in all his glory, this is indeed to sit on an Ivory Throne as younger brother of the Ideal Man.

I. As yet, however, under the dominion of sin, we stand but at *The Golden Footstool.* Here is the dignity of our fallen manhood; we are created in the image and after the likeness of God. In every element of our tripartite being we bear the tokens of our noble birth. Our body stands erect in an imperial attitude with face toward the skies; our minds can grasp the solemn truths of nature and the endless life; our spirits can think our Father's thoughts and bow the knee in worship before him. We have thus all the essential qualities of kingship except the crown. Something has happened. The blood royal surges through our veins, but the king's purple is stripped off. The crown prince stands at the Golden Footstool, clothed in unseemly rags, with an impotent reed in his hands.

> So fallen, so lost!
> The light withdrawn which once he wore!
> Of all the rare endowment, naught
>   Save power remains,
> A fallen angel's pride of thought,
>   Still strong in chains.

Of his lost heritage he has nothing left but memory and hope. He has within him, even at his worst, a reminiscence of something lost; the fluttering of helpless wings which Plato thought to be memorial of a pre-existent state. And his eyes are uplifted to the Ivory Throne. He knows that there are great possibilities within him. He hopes to regain his manhood. In his best moments he cries with Augustine, "Lord, thou hast created us for thyself, therefore our heart is restless within us, until it find its rest in thee."

II. And the way is provided for his restoration. There are *Six Steps leading from this Golden Footstool to the Ivory Throne.*

(1) *We must begin with an acknowledgment of sin.* It would be superserviceable for me to say to any man that he has sinned and come short of the glory of God, for all are conscious of it. There is not a pulse-beat, not a twinge of the nerves, not a mental process, which does not cry "Amen" to the words, "Thou art a sinner." We know and feel it. We cannot ignore or disguise it. It needs no Bible or preacher to declare it.

But there is a misapprehension here. We need a definition. What is sin? It is the fashion in many quarters to regard it as an unfortunate disease, for which we are to be rather pitied than blamed. A thief summoned before a criminal court is defended as a victim of kleptomania. An inebriate who has wittingly taken an enemy into his mouth to steal away his brains and forged upon himself the chains of habit, is defended on the plea of dipsomania. By the same token, if David were arraigned before one of our courts in the matter of Bathsheba, he would be called an erotomaniac; helpless, pitiable and inculpable, because the fever of illicit passion had taken possession of him. Not so, however, did he regard himself; for when conscience awoke, he staggered up to his chamber on the housetop, threw himself upon his knees in an agony of penitence, and acknowledged his personal responsibility in the cry, "O God, against thee, thee only, have I sinned, and done this evil in thy sight." Here then is the definition of sin: it is any want of conformity unto, or transgression of, God's holy law.

Have you, my friend, formed such a conception of sin? Does it stand forth in your conscience as an act or habit of rebellion against the divine authority? If not, you have not begun to tread the stairway leading to the restoration of manhood and the favor of God.

(2) *The next step upward is in an acknowledgement of death;* that is, of the consequence of sin. For death follows sin as effect follows cause.

But what is the death that follows sin? It is the antithesis of life: "This is life eternal, to know God." It is life to be in harmony with God's purposes, to be ever in filial relation and communion with him. And death is to be out of harmony with his purposes and to be exiled from him. This means an eternal dethronement; never to realize the possibilities of our nature; never to attain unto manhood which in its verity is peace with God. Exile from God! All hell, the gnawing worm, the unquenchable fire, is in the words, "Depart from me!"

Let it not be thought, however, that death is by an arbitrary edict; it is the inevitable result of the laws inherent in our nature. We are under the law of holiness, because we are made in the likeness of God. If a planet flies from its orbit, what shall save it from the wreck of matter and the crash of worlds? If a man transgress the law of his being, he fixes his destiny in alienation from God. His word, "The soul that sinneth, it shall die," is not an edict, but the statement of a fact which is interwoven with our being; that is, "Sin, when it is finished, bringeth forth death." His "Depart!" is but a forensic announcement of the just sentence of law.

Have you, my friend, formed this conception of sin? Do you realize that without holiness no man shall see God? Have you read clearly over the gateway of the celestial city, "There shall in no wise enter here anything that worketh abomination or maketh a lie?"

(3) *And then it is necessary that there should be an acknowledgment of impotency.* As long as a man thinks he can get himself out of this difficulty by main force, there is no hope for him. How shall he save himself from the record of the past? By penance? Nay; reason revolts at the thought of lashing one's body for the sins of his soul. By morality? It is more than we can do to keep up with our current liabilities. You cannot save your property from going under the hammer for delinquent taxes by paying the taxes for 1897. By reformation? Hell is paved with good resolutions. He who is satisfied to turn over a new leaf, is sure to find that the new leaf is much like the one before it. Do your best; yet the past unexpiated still confronts you.

The man who endeavors to save himself, is like a falcon brought from its nest in the fastnesses of the hills; hooded, blindfold, and bound with a golden chain to the huntsman's hand. It can seek no quarry except at its master's will. It has wings, and eyes to gaze undazzled at the sun; but when it ventures forth, its flight is ever arrested by the golden leash.

> "Rise, my soul, and stretch thy wings,
> Thy better portion trace."

Alas! we cannot, for we are held back by the leash. There is a "war in our members," so that "the good we would, we do not, and the evil we would not, that we do."

Have you discovered your inability? Are you weary of vain efforts at reformation? Are you moved to confess, "I cannot!" Then you are half way up.

(4) *And now to prayer.* The next step brings us to our knees. We look unto the hills from whence cometh our help. Why is it that a man, however impious, cries, "My God!" or, "God have mercy!" in moments of critical danger? It is because in our deepest souls we know that in the last emergency there is no hope except from God.

It is a false pride in self-reliance that will not let us bow the pregnant hinges of the knee. It was a sinner sinking in the quicksands of his guilt and calling on God for mercy, who sang the grateful song, "This poor man cried and the Lord heard and saved him out of all his troubles. The Lord is nigh unto them that are of a broken heart, and saveth such as be of a contrite spirit. O taste and see that the Lord is good: blessed is the man that trusteth in him."

Have you, my friend, taken your place by the side of the publican? Have you put away all self-righteousness, and, beating upon your breast, made this appeal, "God be merciful to me a sinner"? If so, help is near; you are not far from the kingdom of God.

(5) *The next step is acquiescence.* For God has a plan of salvation all his own. You must put away all prejudgments and let him have his way with you. It is not for a penitent sinner to say how God shall deliver him. You may imagine it is easy for God, now that you have made your prayer, to reach down his omnipotent arm, and without further ceremony lift you up; but that cannot be. It is impossible, by the laws of the Divine Being, that he should ignore your sin. He cannot restore you to his favor with your sins unexpiated and your iniquities still upon you. His truth forbids, his justice forbids, his holiness forbids.

A man in prison, worn with the burden of his chains and weary of the darkness, hears the footfall of the jailer and the clang of his keys; he cries, "O let me out! It is so easy a matter for you to turn the key; throw open this door and release me from these dreadful walls!" But the jailer answers, "I could not if I would, for there is a power behind this key, and an edict vaster than these walls, that forbids. Were I to release you, the law would still pursue you with a whip of scorpions, and justice, like the furies, would be on your track." In like manner I say, If God were to take you with your sins unshriven into his kingdom, the law unexpiated would confront you there and make a hell of heaven.

But God has an effective plan for your deliverance.

It is revealed in these words, "God so loved the world that he gave his only-begotten Son, that whosoever believeth in him should not perish, but have eternal life." He *so* loved the world and you—not in such a manner as to save you in disregard of truth and justice and holiness, for that were impossible—but so as to expiate your sins, fulfill the law, and satisfy justice in the vicarious death of his only-begotten and well beloved Son. Thus it is written, "Mercy and truth are met together; righteousness and peace have kissed each other." And thus the problem is solved, "How can God be just and also the justifier of the ungodly?" And the great question is answered, "How can a man be just with God?"

Do you acquiesce in this plan? Are you willing to be saved in this way? Then are you within a single step of the Ivory Throne.

(6) *The last step is faith.* For passive acquiescence is not enough. Here is a hand reached down, a hand with nail-prints in it. The ever-glorious Son of the Father, who is Elder Brother of us all, is thus eager to lift us up. Get hold of that hand, as you care for life, for your eternal destiny depends upon it!

No man will deny that the God who in his infinite wisdom has devised this plan of salvation, who has provided for our deliverance at so great cost and offered all without money and without price, had the right to affix a condition upon it. The sole condition is an appropriating faith. All that God asks, is that we shall be willing to receive his unspeakable gift and that we shall stretch forth our hand to grasp it.

III. *Thus have we climbed the steps to the Ivory Throne.* It is the throne of manhood,—restored manhood in

Christ. It is not the throne of divine sovereignty. When Salome asked of Jesus in behalf of her two sons that one of them should sit on his right hand and the other on his left in his kingdom, he answered, "It is not mine to give." But it is his to give a place to every one of his followers beside him on the throne which he occupies as the glorified Son of Man. Here we become partakers of the divine nature, attain unto the fulness of his stature, participate with him as joint heirs of the great inheritance and dwell in close and eternal relationship with him. Here we shall reach ultimately the summit of the possibilities of human character in the fulfillment of the promise, "Now are we the sons of God, and it doth not yet appear what we shall be; but we know that when he shall appear, we shall be like him, for we shall see him as he is."

The glory thus promised is for all who are willing to climb to it. The Christians of Laodicea were urged to aspire after it in these words, "To him that overcometh, will I give to sit together with me in my throne." He is the great Overcomer, who for the joy that was set before him endured the cross, despising the shame. As his disciples who overcome in his strength, we share in his glory—the glory of a victorious and resplendent manhood—and occupy the throne with him.

I appeal to all that is best and noblest in human nature; to the dreams and ambitions and aspirations that beckon us away from sin to eternal life. Let us realize the possibilities of our nature; we are in constant danger of allowing them to go by default through our folly and thoughtlessness. *Sursum corda!* Up with thy heart, O son of the living God. Thou wast made to live forever. Reject not the proffer of life. "He came unto his own, and his own received him not; but"—hearken to this gracious word—"to as many as received him, to them gave he power to become the sons of God."

SELAH.

The Jews were a musical people. In their temple at Jerusalem there was a choir of four thousand trained voices. The central division of this choir was led by Heman, the right by Asaph and the left by Jeduthun. These bands of singers led the service antiphonally from the great galleries, and the congregation made response like the sound of many waters. And this choir was supported by a vast orchestra of one hundred and twenty trumpets, with harps and psalteries and cymbals. It is hardly possible for us at this distance to realize the tremendous impressiveness of a devotional service conducted in this manner, on the occasion of the great annual festivals, when, literally, millions of people came up to Jerusalem to participate in the worship of God.

The Hymn-book used on such occasions was the Psalter. It is in five parts, compiled at different periods and bound together probably in Ezra's time. It contains a hundred and fifty sacred songs. Some of them are arranged in groups; as the Songs of Degrees, which were used by pilgrims journeying to the feasts; the Hallelujah Psalms, beginning with "Praise ye the Lord"; the Alphabetic Psalms, arranged in the order of the alphabet, that the children might the more easily commit them to memory. We learn from certain prefatory words that one-third of the entire collection was dedicated "To the chief musician"; the term "Nehiloth" means that the song was to be accompanied with wind instruments, and "Neginoth" by stringed instruments. "Higgaion" directs that it should be sung as a recitative; "Alamoth" by treble voices; "Sheminith" as a bass solo; "Mahalath" denotes a soft accompaniment upon the lute; and "Ma'aloth," in the Psalms of Degrees, directs that they should be sung as the procession mounted the temple steps. The titles of some of the favorite Psalms are also significant; as "The Golden Song"; "The Hind of the Mountain"; "The Lilies," and "The Dove Silent among Strangers." We are thus led to believe that the Psalter occupied a large and wealthy place in the Jewish heart.

In this Hymn-book we frequently come upon the word, "Selah." It occurs seventy-one times in the Psalms and thrice in the prophecy of Habakkuk. There is a wide difference of opinion as to its precise significance; but authorities are generally agreed that it was a musical term. In the Septuagint it is regarded as giving the key-note. The weight of scholarly opinion marks it as an intimation to the orchestra; a call for the blast of trumpets and the response of the stringed instruments, as if to say, "Here let all unite in making a joyful noise unto the Lord!"

Is there a lesson in "Selah" for us? It is written, "All Scripture is profitable for doctrine, for reproof, for correction, for instruction in righteousness." We may believe, therefore, that this oft-recurring word

is not without significance. Here is its meaning for us:—*Set your life to music!*
We are too dull, cold, stupid in our devotion. We are too numb, formal and passionless. Let us draw near to the altar with an outburst of melody.

> "Dear Lord, and shall we ever live
> At this poor dying rate ;
> Our love so faint, so cold, to thee,
> And thine to us so great?"

"Aye, it is easy enough to say, 'Up with your heart and your voices; let the trumpets blare and the harps make a joyous sound!' But circumstances alter cases. Some of us are too busy with matters of serious moment, and others have all the music crushed out of them by the burdens of life." But an examination of the Selahs shows that they cover all possible experiences. Pain and pleasure, midday and midnight, doubt and sorrow and the death shadow, all give place to the orchestral melody. The religion of the Bible is, under all circumstances, the religion of praise.

The time for harp and psaltery to be silent, if ever, is *in the dark experience of conviction of sin.* But hear what the psalmist says, "My bones wax old through my roaring all the day long; thy hand was heavy upon me. Selah!" Why? He proceeds, "I acknowledged my sin and thou forgavest it. Selah!" And again, "Thou art my hiding place ; thou shalt compass me about with songs of deliverance. Selah !"

The night of contrition is illuminated by many stars of promise. The man who feels his burden has reason to rejoice because the arm of the Almighty is made bare to lift it. The great sacrifice is accomplished and the fountain is opened for sin and for uncleanness. The Son of man has power on earth to forgive sins.

II. The psalmist finds occasion for praise, also, *in the bitter hour of temptation.* There are three Selahs in the forty-sixth Psalm: "God is our refuge and strength, a very present help in trouble. Therefore will not we fear, though the earth be removed, and the mountains be carried into the midst of the sea. The Lord of hosts is with us; the God of Jacob is our refuge. Selah!"

A man is at his best, indeed, when he is going out against the adversary. We wrestle not against flesh and blood, but against principalities and powers. Now lift the battle-hymn! What is so magnificent in human experience as the conquest of an evil habit? What joy is comparable with the joy of victory?

It is said that when Wellington was riding away from Waterloo, as he came into the open where the bullets were whistling about him, an aide said, "My lord, I pray you take heed, for your life is in danger here." He replied, "What matters it? We have won the victory! Life is of little consequence, now that the enemy flies."

Do you know, my friend, the delight of returning from moral conflict laden with spoils? If so, these words are not meaningless: "Count it all joy when ye fall into divers temptations, knowing this, that the trying of your faith worketh patience. Blessed is the man that endureth temptation, for when he is tried he shall receive the crown of life which the Lord hath promised to them that love him."

III. And again, David was moved to exultant praise *in his earnest quest of truth.* He knew his own ignorance, but he was no melancholy agnostic. He looked toward the heavens and saw them so vast and himself so little, that he wondered how the Lord could be mindful of him. Yet he rejoiced in what he knew and sang praises in the hope of knowing more. So it was Galileo's delight to watch the stars and count them with the naked eye; but the supreme moment of his life was reached when, with the aid of a lens, he discerned the mountains in the moon and Saturn's rings. There are moments in life when a new truth comes to us like a sunburst, and the harps and trumpets must help us lift the hymn.

In the village school at Stratford-on-Avon the form is shown whereon the lad Shakespeare sat when he conned his A, B, C. Let him not despise the day of small things, for the time will come when out of these rudiments he will splendidly enrich the world's literature. The soliloquy of Hamlet and all other productions of the great master are mere combinations of the alphabet with a glowing, exultant soul behind them. Let us not lament our intellectual shortcomings, since the little that we know is material for indefinite education, and all eternity is before us.

IV. So, also, *in the psalmist's work for God;* he had need for choir and orchestra to assist him in the joyous discharge of every duty. If he were watching his flocks on the hill sides at Bethlehem, or ministering at the altar in Jerusalem, or gathering material for the building of the temple, or marching forth against Canaanitish tribes he must still pause and cry,

"Selah!" as later the Covenanters marched and fought for freedom with the shout, "For Christ's Crown and Covenant!"

We have not enough of joyousness in our Christian work. We speak too much of duty and obligation, and think too little of the honor that is put upon us in being permitted to join hands, in the glorious work of the kingdom, with the only-begotten Son of God.

It is related of George Story of blessed memory, that, in the midst of a life devoted to sensual pleasure, he went up to the Doncaster races. He stood looking idly on while the balls flew up and down, and the horses, in clouds of dust, went speeding around the track, hearing the shouts from the betting stands and the acclamations of the multitude; then, as he closed his eyes for a moment, he heard a voice: "Is this, George Story, a proper life for a man made in the image of the eternal God? Is there nothing better for thee? Lo, here is a sickle at thy hand; go, thrust it in and reap for me." And there was born within him in that moment a great purpose, which by God's grace he was enabled to realize in a life of noble power and usefulness. All the pleasures of the past vanished like the lifting of mists before the rising sun. His years were passed in toil that was full of laughter and merrymaking; his supreme joy was to feel an utter weariness of a well-spent day.

V. *In affliction.* Over and over again the psalmist cries, "Selah!" when life's burdens are heavy upon him. Thus in his flight from Absalom, "Many there be that say unto me, 'Where is thy God?' Selah!"

At this point there is no difference. We are born to sorrow as the sparks fly upward. Pain, neglect, calumny, poverty, bereavement, persecution; these are in greater or less measure the portion of all. The only question is, How shall we bear them? Shall we sink down in discouragement and surrender to despair? Or, shall we praise God that our light afflictions, which are but for a moment, are working for us a far more exceeding and eternal weight of glory?

The only sacred writer, apart from the psalmist, who uses the term Selah is the prophet Habakkuk. And this is singular, for he lived in the reign of Manasseh, the darkest period of Jewish history. He was contemporary with Jeremiah the wailing prophet, who wished that his head were waters and his eyes a fountain of tears that he might weep day and night for the slain of his people. But the song of Habakkuk was pitched in a higher key. He also dwelt among the ruins that were left from the invasion of Nebuchadnezzar; he saw the desolation, but he saw also the bright light in the cloud. He believed in a good time coming. He foretold the ultimate destruction of Chaldæa. He closed his brief prophecy with a transporting song of exultation which he dedicated "To the chief singer on stringed instruments," to be sung on great occasions in the temple service:

"God came from Teman,
And the Holy One from Mount Paran. Selah!
His glory covered the heavens,
And the earth was full of his praise.
And his brightness was as the light;
He had rays coming forth from his hand.

> And there was the hiding of his power.
> He stood and measured the earth;
> And the eternal mountains were scattered,
> The everlasting hills did bow."

Thus looking far into the future, he perceived the Almighty coming to the relief of those who trusted in him. And with all his heart he believed in the better day. Here are his last words:

> "Although the fig-tree shall not blossom,
> Neither shall fruit be in the vines;
> The labor of the olive shall fail,
> And the fields shall yield no meat;
> The flock shall be cut off from the fold,
> And there shall be no herd in the stalls:
> Yet will I rejoice in the Lord,
> I will joy in the God of my salvation."

So we should set even our bitterest sorrows to music; for He giveth songs in the night. Our tribulation worketh hope and hope maketh not ashamed. The nightingale is said to sing most sweetly when a thorn presses against her breast. So may the Christian in adversity rejoice because of his great faith in God. Up with your hearts and voices, all ye that labor and are heavy laden! "I reckon that the sufferings of this present time are not worthy to be compared with the glory which shall be revealed in us."

VI. And the rejoicing of David was with him *to the very end*. A quaint father says, "God leaves the sugar ever in the bottom of our cup." One of the Psalms seems to have been composed for the special strength and comfort of those who approach the eternal world. "The Lord is my Shepherd; I shall not want. Yea, though I walk through the valley of the shadow of death, I will fear no evil: for thou art with me; thy rod and thy staff they comfort me." Let the orchestra play softly now. Pianissimo! A soul is going to its God.

> "While I draw this fleeting breath,
> When mine eyelids close in death,—"

now, Selah! Let harps and trumpets strike a higher note, for the sorrows of earth are vanishing and the lights of heaven grow bright;

> "When I soar to worlds unknown,
> And behold Thee on Thy throne;
> Rock of Ages cleft for me,
> Let me hide myself in Thee."

And then the endless glory. The winter is past, the rain is over and gone. Here is the great multitude upon the glassy sea with harps of gold. Here are the angels and archangels lifting the song, " Holy holy, holy, Lord God Almighty!" Shall we take part in the great rejoicing there? Let us then attune our hearts and voices to the thanksgivings of the earthly life. Set your life to music. Your grief for sin, your battle-pains, your eager search for truth, your sowing and reaping, your heartaches, your death-anguish; set them all to music, for in heaven we shall see how all these, by divine grace, were made to work together for our good.

> "I'll praise my Maker with my breath,
> And when my voice is lost in death
>   Praise shall employ my nobler powers;
> My days of praise shall ne'er be past,
> While life and thought and being last,
>   Or immortality endures."

ONE CHURCH.

"That they all may be one; as thou, Father, art in me, and I in thee, that they also may be one in us: that the world may believe that thou hast sent me."—John 17, 21.

The last interview of Jesus with his disciples in the upper room is invested with a peculiar solemnity. On that occasion he seemed to take them, more deeply than ever, into his confidence. He gave them a clear glimpse into heaven in the words, "In my Father's house are many mansions: if it were not so I would have told you. I go to prepare a place for you." He led them into the secret place of his pavilion in those parabolic words, "I am the vine, ye are the branches. Abide in me, and I in you." He brought them into the very innermost of spiritual mysteries when he gathered them about the sacramental table and instituted the memorial feast; for here is the key to that saying, "Except ye eat the flesh and drink the blood of the Son of Man, ye have no life in you." And then the sacerdotal prayer. There was never a prayer like this; and here is its refrain, "That they all may be one."

He was standing under the shadow of the cross when he made that prayer. He saw in the future a bereaved and lonely company; a flock without a shepherd, needing the support of mutual prayer and sympathy. He looked further and saw them bowing under the ax, torn by lions, bound to the stake, or fleeing to find shelter in dens and caves of the earth; and he knew that in those dreadful days they would need the courage of fellowship. Looking still further down the centuries, he saw them engaged in bitter controversies, wrangling in councils, parting asunder, marching against each other on embattled fields, and he saw the world looking on with a glad amazement and crying, "Aha! Aha!" Thus for his own glory, as for the welfare of his followers, he prayed, "O my Father, grant that they all may be one, that the world may know that thou hast sent me."

One thing is certain; it was the wish of the Master that his Church, the world over and through all the centuries, should be a congenial and harmonious fellowship. This is suggested in his words, "And there shall be one flock and one shepherd." It is set forth also under the figure of a happy household; as when Paul says, "I bow my knees unto the Father of our Lord Jesus Christ of whom the whole family in heaven and earth is named." The relation of believers to each other is elsewhere likened to a living organism of which Jesus is the head: "So we, being many, are one body in Christ, and every one members one of another;" and again, that we "may grow up into him in all things which is the head, even Christ, from whom the whole body fitly joined together and compacted by that which every joint supplieth, according to the effectual working in the measure of every part, maketh increase of the body unto the edifying of itself in love."

All true followers of Christ believe in Church Union. They certify to that fact in the historic confession, "I believe in the Holy Catholic Church," which is according to the same creed "the communion of saints." But a great deal that is said of Church Union is mere vapouring, inane and profitless. Let us reason together as to this matter and, if possible, arrive at a sensible view of it.

It is claimed that the Church is a divine ordinance. All God's works are characterized and controlled by fixed laws. If the Church is a divine work, it must conform to them. What are these laws?

I. *Unity.* Here is one of the mighty ordinances of the universe. It is observed in every department of the divine handiwork.

Let us begin at the bottom; that is, in the kingdom of inanimate matter. Here the unifying principle is the *Law of Form.* A grain of sand, a snowflake, a diamond, a mountain of granite are all alike under the domination of this law.

A step higher and we find ourselves in the vegetable kingdom. Here the unifying principle is *Life.* It is a great mystery. The biologist, whose name indicates a special acquaintance with living creatures, cannot even define it. He tears asunder a living thing in pursuit of the life principle; but it ever evades him. He can neither produce nor define it. Nevertheless in this kingdom it is the all-pervading fact. A grain of wheat, a rose-bud, a lofty pine are all brought into kinship and dominated by it.

A step higher and we enter the animal kingdom. We are here in the presence of a new principle, to-wit, *Instinct.* It is somewhat more than life and somewhat less than reason. All things within the boundaries of this realm are by it enabled to sustain themselves and secure their well-being. The sea-anemone, the nightingale, the Gordon setter are alike, though not equally, endowed with it.

The next and final step brings us into the presence of man. The kingdom here is the kingdom of God. The unifying principle is *Spirit.* The race is bound together by it. This is more than life, than instinct, than reason. It is a filial bond by which humanity is brought into communion with God. A man can pray. He can reason with his brother or his Father as to great verities. He exercises a sovereign will in moral acts. He is always conscious of a divine birth, of a fall from his high estate, of a possible reconciliation with God. In this he is infinitely removed from all the lower orders of life. It is as if sun, moon and stars bowed down before him. He alone is a being of two worlds: he is in this world yet not altogether of it; a pilgrim and a sojourner, looking for a better country, even an heavenly, and for a city which hath foundations, whose builder and maker is God.

II. *Diversity in unity.* We shall not find uniformity. This is contrary to the analogy of the divine work. The orbs of heaven are unified by a common law, all circulating about a single centre; yet divided into systems, each having its own centre and every orb its own orbit. And there is one glory of the sun, and another glory of the moon, and another glory of the stars.

So, if we begin again at the bottom of terrestrial things, we shall discover this diversity. No two snowflakes are identical in form; all are fabricated in the same loom; yet, if it were possible to gather all that shall fall in the storms of the coming winter, we should not find two of them precisely alike. The same is true in the higher kingdom of vegetable life. The leaves of the forest give token of a common law, yet no two in Vallombrosa are indistinguishable from each other. So on the butterfly's wing you will always find the marvelous fleck of color, yet there is an illimitable diversity. The same is true of men. We speak of "the human family" and thus show our belief in the unifying force, but the diversity is equally plain, for there are no precise duplicates among us.

This is a distinguishing characteristic of the divine work. Man aims at uniformity; God at diversity in unity. A manufacturer of cotton prints makes ten thousand dress patterns all alike; but see how God clothes the forest in this autumn time,—with what diversity of tapestry, what garlands and festoons of ever-varying leaf and vine. No matter where you find Turner's sunsets, you can recognize them; he mixes the same colors and with the same brush lays them on canvas. Now turn your eyes westward at the close of day and see God's sunsets! These are not the colors that you saw last night; here is a pattern that was never seen before. The masterpiece of the sculptor Powers was his Greek Slave; he made three copies or replicas, and, lo! they are facsimiles, line for line and curve for curve. God makes sixteen hundred millions of human beings to occupy the earth to-day and no two of them have faces just alike. Nevertheless, the life, the reason, the spiritual faculty, the unifying principle is in all. They think, but they do not think the same thoughts. They feel, but they do not have the same emotions. They reason, but they do not reason to the same conclusions. So everywhere there is diversity in unity.

III. "*Natural Selection;*" that is, segregation. All things in God's universe get together in coteries; they group themselves by sympathetic attraction.

This holds even at the bottom. Gold is found in veins, in pockets and in placers; it flocks by itself, seeks its own. In like manner trees and plants are indigenous to one clime or to another; they adjust themselves to their environment like families. In the animal kingdom we observe the separation of the denizens of air and earth and water; each group finds its own habitat; the menhaden go in schools, the waterfowl in flocks, the beasts of the forest in herds.

In pursuance of this law we should expect to find men falling into companies, nor are we disappointed. Here are Shem, Ham and Japheth going forth from Ararat to pursue their several ways. We may easily mark the divergent lines of their development. They form the three races of men; the three races which are distinguishable the whole world over. And each of these races in turn is divided into nations; nations that separate from each other, take up their several abodes and assume their distinct place in history. In the natural course of events each of these nations is subdivided into communities, and within any of these communities are found the various levels of society. Caste, however we may deplore it, is not peculiar to India. It is the inevitable result of the law of segregation, each seeking its kind. Coteries are formed by the attraction of mutual taste and temperaments.

Here is the "Submerged Tenth" and here is the "Upper Ten-thousand"; and those who are in the one would not be in the other. Here are political parties, also divided along the line of normal cleavage. Here are labor-guilds on the one hand and monopolistic trusts on the other. Here are secret societies of such a character as that those who are in would not be out, and those who are out would not be in. Here are clubs and the militia and associations of innumerable sorts, implying no necessary antagonism, but merely the coherence of sympathetic minds. This is natural selection. It may be regulated by considerations of justice and human rights; but to undertake to destroy it would be to do violence to the natural order of things.

IV. Now as to the application of these considerations to the problem of *Church Union*.

1. As to the law of *Unity*. The Church is bound together by one vital and formative fact; that is, a common faith in the Lord Jesus Christ. This is what we mean when we say, "I believe in the Holy Catholic Church, the Communion of Saints." It is made up of all, everywhere and throughout all ages, who are sincerely enlisted under the banner of the cross. This is the unifying principle; no diversity of names or minor considerations can disturb it. "Ye are builded together upon the foundation of the apostles and prophets, Jesus Christ himself being the chief corner stone." And "Other foundation can no man lay than that is laid, which is Jesus Christ."

2. The law of *Diversity* is as obvious among the great multitude of Christian believers as it is everywhere else in the universe of God. The eleven men

who went out of the upper chamber to become the nucleus of the Holy Catholic Church were as unlike as possible; John the mystic, Peter the zealot, Thomas the doubter and the others went their several ways. It was not long before they were multiplied into thousands, but each of these thousands was an independent thinker, having Christ at the centre of his heart but holding his own standpoint for the making of his creed.

There are now some hundreds of millions of Christians on earth; all are one in Christ, avowing their fellowship in the words, "One Lord, one faith, one baptism, one God and Father of us all." Yet these believers are at all points—the sole exception being the unifying principle of a common faith in Christ—diverse one from another. They do their own thinking in their own way; make their prayers according to their individual convictions; live in pursuance of the dictates of personal conscience; being as dissimilar in moral constitution as in feature. "They are distinct," we say, "as the billows, yet one as the sea." The sea rolls to and fro in perpetual restlessness, surging in foaming masses upon the shores of all islands and continents, into bays and deltas and estuaries everywhere, yet there is a power that holds it ever as one. The moon reaches down her white arms out of heaven and twice each day lifts and rolls this mighty, surging flood in the unresting movements of the tides. So does Christ pervade and dominate and sway the universal church. O glorious faith! O infinite power of the gracious Christ! In the sublimity of our human nature we are free to differ, but in the sympathy of an all-pervading faith we are one in Him!

3. Then as to *Natural Selection*. The segregation of believers was inevitable from the beginning. It was only a question of time when the church should divide into Greek and Roman. Do we say it was a frivolous thing to part asunder on the phrase *Filioque?* There may be room for a difference of opinion there, but the ground of separation lay further back; that is, in the difference of the Greek and the Roman temperament. And again, it was only a question of time when Protestantism should come forth out of the Roman fellowship. And for this again there was a reason: the birth of Protestantism was an expression of the renaissance of religious liberty.

It was furthermore inevitable that Protestantism should itself, in the course of time, be divided into denominations. Some men are so constituted that they cannot frame a system of belief without beginning at the sovereignty of God; these are Calvinists. And to complain against their segregation is to find fault with nature itself. There are others who in looking at doctrine, take their standpoint at the freedom of the human will; these are Arminians. Let them flock by themselves. There are some who are so constructed as to love the pomp and circumstance of a liturgical service. We may not be able to sympathize with these; but let us not object to their fraternization because we are not formed that way. This segregation indeed is as it should be. While human nature is as it is, it is difficult to conceive of any other order of things; it is simply the carrying out of certain laws which are interwoven in the constitution of the race. It is useless to oppose it. A oneness brought about by mechanical pressure must be artificial at the best and merely superficial. An illustration may be found in the worst periods of papal history, where we see either spiritual deadness on the one hand, or on the other hand repressed, seething discontent like inner fires seeking vent at every joint and fissure. It is impossible to contend against the natural order of things.

Now as to practical considerations. What are our duties as individual Christians in these premises? Or, what can we do to aid and further the fulfilment of our Lord's prayer that his disciples the world over may be one?

First: *We may cease clamoring for uniformity.* There is nothing in this cry. The thing is impossible of accomplishment and undesirable any way. The most teasing, irritating, trouble-fomenting people are those who, in the interest of what they call Church Union, are ever and anon rising to say, "There is dissension; and, brethren, you are all wrong; and you will never be right until you take down your neighborly fences and cease from differences of opinion in the fellowship of Christ." The influence of such people is wholly divisive and disintegrating. The trouble is all in their mind's eye. The differences of opinion are natural and inevitable. The divisions are such as grow out of the constitution of the race and the order of things.

Second: *Let us cease claiming for our own denomination any exclusive title to the franchise of the Church of God.* There is room here for an application of the axiom, "The whole is larger than any of its parts."

He may be a true Christian at heart, but is a narrow-minded bigot, who joins in the cry of any coterie of believers, "The temple of the Lord are we." For is it not written, "The body is not one member, but many. And if they were all one member, where were the body?" And again, "There are diversities of operations, but it is the same God which worketh all in all." To claim the divine blessing and exclusive ecclesiastical function for my limited circle, is to put on airs which the Lord rebukes, the church contemns, and the world laughs at. This is the leaven of the scribes and Pharisees; and "except your righteousness exceed the righteousness of the scribes and Pharisees, ye shall in no case enter into the kingdom of heaven."

Third: *Let us enlarge our hearts in a magnanimous charity toward all who love our Lord Jesus Christ.* "The real cure for disunion," says Joseph Parker, "is not in the abolition of sects, but in the abolition of sectarianism." Let us believe in the sincerity of those who, calling themselves after the name of our Master, differ from us in minor things. Pray for all who are of the household of faith. Pray for Greeks, Romanists and Protestants. Pray for the sister denominations. Men do not quarrel when on their knees. We are brethren, and the injunction which the patriarch gave to his sons departing for Egypt, is wise counsel for us: "See that ye fall not out by the way."

And finally: *Let us emphasize our common faith in Christ.* Back to Christ! My friend, trundle your own opinions out of the way at the approach of his chariot. Let us make much of his life, much of his glorious teachings, much of his redemptive work on

Calvary, much of his resurrection from the dead, much of his intercession at the throne of heavenly grace, much of his great commission. The Church can well afford to differ in all things else whatsoever, if only it will agree to advance in all its multitudinous divisions as one great army to the conquest of the world for him. "Go ye into all the world and evangelize." Oh, for the day when we shall all be too busy, too joyously busy in fulfilling that great commission, to carp and criticise and make arrogant claims! The world awaits the awaking of the Church.

On the night before the battle of Trafalgar, the admiral, Lord Nelson, summoned his lieutenants Collingwood and Rotherham, between whom there was a quarrel of long standing. From the deck of the flag-ship he pointed out the enemy's fleet. "Tomorrow," he said, "I and you must go out to meet them. Shake hands for England's sake. Shake hands and make up!" The world awaits the united onward movement of the Church for evangelization. A hundred years of foreign missions have passed, and Armageddon draws near. The Prince upon his white horse, with his white battalions, on the borders of the heavens, rides this way. The trumpet sounds the reveille to Greek and Romanist and Protestant,—to all bodies of believers whatsoever, to arise and go forth in the Master's name. All other considerations dwindle into nothing now. Shake hands and make up, for the Master's sake! is the word. Go ye, go ye unto the uttermost parts of the earth. Go ye forth as one great mobilized army. Go ye out under the banner of the Lion of the tribe of Judah. "All power is given unto me in heaven and on earth; go ye, therefore, and preach the gospel; and, lo, I am with you alway, even unto the end of the world." To hear his voice, and with one impulse rise and obey, will be to accomplish a glorious fulfilment of his prayer "that they all may be one, that the world may know, O Father, that thou hast sent me, and hast loved them even as thou hast loved me."

THE LOGIA.

"We ought to remember the words of the Lord Jesus, how he said—."—Acts 20, 35.

The thinking world is just now criticising and discussing an old papyrus scroll known as the "Logia," or "Sayings of Jesus." It was found last winter with a multitude of other ancient manuscripts, of more or less value, in the ruins of Oxyrhynchus in lower Egypt. It is a mere fragment consisting of seven disconnected sentences, as follows:

"1.———*and see how to draw out the mote that is in thy brother's eye.*

"2. *Jesus saith, If ye do not fast toward the world, ye will not find the kingdom of God; and if ye do not celebrate the Sabbath aright, ye will not see the Father.*

"3. *Jesus saith, I entered into the midst of the world, and in the flesh I appeared unto them ; and I found them all drunken, and none did I find thirsty among them ; and my soul laboreth for the children of men, for they are blind in their hearts and they do not see their poverty.*

"4. *Jesus saith, Wherever they may be, there they are not without God ; and just as one is alone, thus I am with him. Lift the stone and there thou will find me; cleave the wood, and I am there.*

"5. *Jesus saith, A prophet is not welcome in his own city, nor does a physician effect cures among those who know him.*

"6. *Jesus saith, A city that is built and established on the top of a high hill can neither fall nor be hidden.*

"7. *Jesus saith, Hear this*——"

As to the genuineness of these "Sayings of Jesus" there may be a wide difference of opinion, but it will be generally agreed that they contribute little if anything to our possession of spiritual truth. The first, third, fifth and sixth of these sentences are mere repetitions of Scripture. The second is ascetic, the fourth is mystical and the seventh is valueless, being abruptly broken off. The general verdict upon the Logia is, that what is true in them is not new, and what is new is not true.

The question naturally arises, How are these and similar pseudo-Scriptures to be accounted for? Our Lord during his ministry was universally regarded as an extraordinary teacher of great spiritual truths. He laid a fearless hand on problems which affrighted and bewildered the accredited theologians of his time. He taught "as one having authority, and not as the scribes." His name and doctrine were discussed in all quarters. The common people heard him gladly. The rulers hated and conspired against him. In one judgment all were agreed: "Never man spake like this man." His death, instead of suppressing the general interest, increased it. The air, in the early flush of the Christian Era, was full of rumors concerning him. There were legends and traditions innumerable passing from mouth to mouth. It was clear that if posterity was to have the full benefit of his wonderful teachings, there must be a rigid sifting and an authoritative canon.

To this end "holy men" were divinely appointed

to prepare the New Testament. These men were chosen from among the disciples; it being pre-requisite that they should have been eye-witnesses of the ministry of Jesus. They wrote "as they were moved by the Holy Ghost." No doubt they made use of current manuscripts; but whether as authors, "redactors," or immediate recipients of revelation, they wrought under the direct control and supervision of the Spirit. When they had finished the volume, it was sealed with a seal of divine authority and the word "Finis" closed it.

But very many legends and untrustworthy traditions were left over; many of these have survived to this day. It would be strange were it otherwise. There are more than fifty apocryphal gospels. One of our local newspapers recently printed what purported to be the "Report of Pontius Pilate to the Roman Emperor respecting the Trial, Conviction and Execution of Jesus of Nazareth." This is simply one of the immense multitude of extra-canonical and frequently spurious traditions. The fragment now under consideration is another. The temple of the New Testament canon was built by inspired writers and finished to the laying of the top stone of the corner. All within that temple is divine; all without that temple may be of archæological interest, but the divine seal is not upon it.

But why this general and consuming interest with respect to a mere fragment of papyrus—a tattered leaf, tantalizingly short, and containing nothing new or of surpassing value? Why should the world of scholars and thinking people be so exercised about it? The incident has an important bearing on the two vital problems of to-day, to wit: *The Bible as the Written*, and *Christ as the Incarnate Word of God.*

1. *Its bearing on the Biblical Controversy.* This is preëminently the controversy of our time. For years we have been witnessing a most insidious and persistent assault on the trustworthiness of Holy Writ. It was inevitable that, amid the furious winds of such a tempest, there should be in many quarters a loss of confidence in the truth of Scripture. "Continual dropping wears away a stone." A man who had listened for years, even with the most unbiased mind, to persistent and malignant scandals uttered against the integrity of his own mother, could scarcely enter her presence without looking askance at her. We welcome, therefore, whatever shall restore our impaired confidence in the authenticity and absolute veracity of the Word.

The Evangelist John closes his gospel with these singular words: "And there are also many other things which Jesus did, the which, if they should be written every one, I suppose that even the world itself could not contain the books which should be written." This is generally regarded as an hyperbole; an oriental way of saying, Of all teachers, he was the greatest, and of all teaching his was the most prolific and universal. But there is a sense in which the statement of the evangelist may be regarded as literally true. There is indeed an element of infinitude in the doctrine of Jesus. His lifetime is from everlasting to everlasting, and wisdom has eternally dropped from his lips, as light emanates from the sun. It is but an infinitesimal part of this wisdom which is contained in Holy Writ. The Scriptures are not intended to be an encyclopedia, but a compendium of truth for the uses of human life. There are many truths outside, there are many Logia which may indeed be veritable echoes of Jesus' voice, but the temple is finished, and it affords no room for the rejected débris which lies around it. Here is the important matter: *The Book is sufficient; and, because sufficient, it is complete and closed forever.*

1. *It is sufficient for salvation.* The red thoroughfare of blood runs all through its inspired pages. The way from sin to pardon is clearly marked out. This is a faithful saying and worthy of all acceptation, that Christ Jesus came into the world to save sinners. "The blood of Jesus Christ cleanseth us from all sin;" and, "without the shedding of blood there is no remission" for sin. "He that believeth on the Son hath everlasting life;" and, "There is none other name under heaven given among men whereby we must be saved." Here is enough. What more shall be added?

We are told of a sinful man who, having gone to his own place to endure the pains of everlasting shame and remorse, entreated that a drop of water might be brought to cool his parched lips. It was refused, because whatsoever a man soweth that shall he also reap, and in the place where the tree falleth there it shall be. He then asked that a messenger might be sent from heaven, to admonish his five brethren who were still on earth, lest they should come into the same condemnation. This also was refused in the words, "If they believe not Moses and the prophets"—that is the Scriptures—"neither would they believe though one rose from the dead.'

That is to say, the Scriptures are clear, complete and sufficient as to the plan of salvation. No Logia can add to their force. If, despite their plain warnings and invitations, men are still determined to run upon the bosses of God's shield, they could not be prevented even though a troop of angels were to come with new Sayings of Jesus to entice them.

2. *The Scriptures as we have them are sufficient for the building of character.* The proof is in their influence on men and nations. A Christian is defined to be "the best type of man." And the best type of nation is the one that finds its constitution in the Scriptures. Were you a shipwrecked mariner and asked to determine whether you would drift upon the mercies of a Moslem, Buddhist or Christian community, you would not take a moment to decide. God's Book makes men. It is a chart whereon the course of right conduct is clearly marked. Seafaring men make frequent visits to our marine office to report new reefs or derelicts. But in the Scriptures every hidden rock and every floating hulk are indicated. It is impossible to suggest any valuable addendum to its ethical code. It touches every point in the circumference of human life.

3. *The Scriptures furnish an entire equipment for every good work.* Everything here is needful; nothing is superfluous. "All Scripture is profitable for doctrine, for reproof, for correction, for instruction in righteousness, that the man of God may be perfect, thoroughly furnished unto every good work."

To the minds of thoughtful people such considerations as these must serve to deepen confidence in the old-fashioned Book. To say that we love our Bibles is not enough. We may love them and still regard them with misgivings. It was a sorrowful day for Nero when he lost confidence in his tutor, Seneca. He had learned in his boyhood to love the old philosopher and for a time he dutifully followed his teachings. His love did not falter; he brought his teacher back from exile and clothed him with honor at the imperial court. But there were those among his associates who laughed at Seneca's melancholy face and pointed their fingers at his scholar's robe. Nero still for many a long year cherished the old man as his friend, and gave him a place at his own table, but no longer heeded his instructions. It is to be feared that some regard their Bibles in the same way. They love them still, but the air has been so full of adverse criticism, that there has been a waning of confidence. Nevertheless the Book remains as ever, an infallible rule of faith and practice, sufficient and complete for all human uses. "The heavens being on fire shall be dissolved and the elements shall melt with fervent heat," but "The word of our God shall stand forever;" "the mouth of the Lord hath spoken it."

II. *Let us now consider the bearing of the Logia on the problem of Christ.* He was an incomparable teacher. "The words that I speak unto you," he said, "they are spirit and they are life." And again, "Heaven and earth shall pass away, but my words shall not pass away."

Why this general interest in the finding of new sayings of Jesus, a few inconsequential words that have escaped the rasure of time and fluttered down to us? Not critics only nor antiquarians, but the people everywhere, are exercised about them. Not long ago a new poem of Milton's was found among the old manuscripts of the British Museum. It was no trifling event, the discovery of a hitherto unknown production by the author of "Paradise Lost." Nevertheless it was only a nine-days' wonder and many of you doubtless have not even heard of it. But the mere suggestion that we have come upon an incoherent echo of the voice of Jesus of Nazareth is a very different thing. The world takes note of it.

Who was this Jesus, this incomparable Teacher? There he stands at the remote distance of nineteen hundred years, demanding an answer of every thoughtful man. He was no scholar, no philosopher, was indeed quite unfamiliar with the teaching of the schools. He was a man of the people; a carpenter, his hands callous with toil. *Ecce Homo!* He rode into Jerusalem, those going before and those following after crying, "Hosanna! Hosanna!" and the people standing in their doorways asked, as the world has been asking ever since, "Who is this?"

But Jesus is more than a figure of the remote past. He has come down through history, making his mark on all the centuries, with an ever-increasing retinue of followers to this day. It was in vain that they crucified him. The centurion, on the evening of the great tragedy, went back to Pilate and reported, "He is dead. I stood by with my quaternions after he had been nailed upon the cross, and, when the three hours of his mortal anguish were over, I caused a soldier to thrust a spear into his side and there came forth blood and water. My mission is accomplished; the Nazarene is dead." A messenger went up to the Hall Gazith and made a similar report to the Sanhedrin: "I stood with the multitude under his cross. I saw the strange noonday darkness gather about him, and, when it lifted, I heard him cry with a loud voice, '*Tetelestai!*' 'It is finished!' Then as I came away I turned and saw his form dark against the sky. The Nazarene is dead; we shall hear no more of him."

But this was not enough. His words still lived, and because of their power it was as if his spectre walked the earth. To put an end to his doctrines, the sword was unsheathed and the fagots were lit. There were bonfires of men; the smell of hissing flesh was in the air and martyrs died with the Logia on their lips. There were bonfires of Bibles; the air was filled with the smoke of crackling parchment, but the word was not destroyed. *Nec tamen consumebatur!* Verily, his words are spirit and life.

The sayings of Jesus have been the most potent factor in the history of the Christian Era. Weighty words! He uttered the Golden Rule which is, by common consent, the great unifying force among men and nations. He spoke the parable of the Good Samaritan: "A certain man went down from Jerusalem to Jericho and coming upon one who had been waylaid and robbed and left for dead, he bound up his wounds and cared for him." In this simple story lies the solution of all problems of sociology. It is the inspiration of all benevolence and kindliness. He said, as he gathered his friends around the sacramental table, "Do this in remembrance of me", and at that word the Church came into being—a great living organism through which his Spirit is working with ever-growing power for the deliverance of the world from sin. He said, "Render unto Cæsar the things that are Cæsar's"; the fundamental maxim of wise politics and sound government, which found an echo in Paul's sermon on Mars' Hill, later still in Magna Charta, and last of all in our Declaration of Independence. All the institutions of civil and ecclesiastical freedom rest upon it. He said, "Go ye into all the world and evangelize," and at that word eleven men set out to the conquest of the world. Their numbers were multiplied, until to-day there are hundreds of millions living and preaching the Evangel, by which they shall presently usher in the Golden Age. Aye, his words are spirit and they are life.

He alone of the great teachers survives. Where are Plato, Seneca, Epictetus, Socrates, Sakya-muni? These "built their nests in the temple of fame as swallows in the spouts," and the first shower washed them away. But a strange interest in the teachings of the Nazarene prevails everywhere and increasingly among the children of men. "Are the people fools?" as the Sanhedrin said of those that hung upon his lips. Is the world all wrong that it should attach more importance to a mere questionable fragment of his sayings than to the teachings of the sages? Who was this Jesus that all eyes should thus continually be turned upon him?

But he comes nearer still. The problem is of vital personal interest. He stands face to face with you and me, asking, "Who say ye that I am?" The personal factor will not be eliminated. If the gospel is true, our answer to his question must determine our eternal destiny. His words, weighty in themselves, are reënforced by his personal presence. When Lycurgus had made his memorable Code, he disappeared from Sparta, alleging that his presence would prevent the due enforcement of his laws. But Jesus is ever present with his word. "Lo, I am with you alway, even unto the end." To receive his sayings is not enough; he asks that he himself may be received into our hearts as Prophet, Priest and King. The secret of eternal life is not merely to accept his doctrine as true, but himself as the veritable Word of God.

EVERYBODY'S PREACHER.

"And all bare him witness, and wondered at the gracious words which proceeded out of his mouth."—Luke 4, 22.

The people of Nazareth had assembled in unusual numbers at the synagogue, for it was rumored that their townsman Jesus was to preach the sermon of the day. He had been making an itinerary among the villages of Galilee and the fame of his miracles and discourses was spread abroad. The people of his native town were most eager to hear him. The ruler of the synagogue opened the service with prayer and then called on two of the elders to read from the sacred scriptures. At this point it was permitted to invite any visitor, whose orthodoxy was unchallenged, to expound the lesson. This courtesy being extended to Jesus, he advanced to the bema. The scroll was placed in his hands; he unrolled it and read from the sixty-first chapter of Isaiah the lesson of the day: "*The Spirit of the Lord God is upon me, because he hath anointed me to preach the gospel to the poor; he hath sent me to heal the broken-hearted, to preach deliverance to the captives and recovering of sight to the blind, to set at liberty them that are bruised, to preach the acceptable year of the Lord.*" The eyes of all in the synagogue were now fastened upon him. "This day," said he, "is this Scripture fulfilled in your ears." The discourse which followed was in demonstration of his own Messiahship. "And all bare him witness, and wondered at the gracious words which proceeded out of his mouth."

Let us emphasize this "all", inasmuch as our purpose is to set forth the adaptation of Christ's teaching to the needs of all sorts and conditions of men.

It would be interesting to analyze our Lord's discourses from a homiletic standpoint. It could easily be made to appear that he possessed all the elements of true eloquence; such as simplicity, directness, picturesqueness, logical coherence, warmth, earnestness and convincing power. But the quality which made him Everybody's Preacher was distinctly and exclusively his own. In the synagogue that day there were priests, rabbis, doctors of divinity, farmers, vine-dressers, handicraftsmen; and all alike were spell-bound by his gracious words. You have, perhaps, seen a portrait wrought by a great master, with eyes that had the singular quality of gazing at you wherever you went. A like characteristic we observe in the teaching of Jesus. Coleridge said: "It finds me." Indeed, it searches for and finds all men. Jesus was able to address himself to the wants of the multitude all and singular, for "he knew what was in man."

He had something to say to the poor. And the poor of his time were poor indeed. We make a distinction between "God's poor" and the "devil's poor." We take a sympathetic interest in the relief of such as are thrifty and industrious but unfortunate. Our Lord, however, had a place in his heart for the ne'er-do-weels; for such as are wandering our streets to-night thriftless, penniless and friendless. There are women whose faces are sodden with drink, drawing thin shawls around their shivering shoulders. There are men with sunken cheeks and watery eyes, shuffling along with hands stretched out for alms. Who cares for them? O, it is pitiful; near a whole city full, friends they have none. They live forlorn, die unlamented and are buried without ceremony in the potter's field. Who cares? He cares! The heart of Jesus is warm with pity toward them; his gospel makes room for them; he hears their helpless moan, their bitter cry. Once when he was asked for his Messianic credentials, he replied: "The blind receive their sight, the lame walk, the lepers are cleansed, the deaf hear, the dead are raised and the poor have the gospel preached to them." God be praised! The meanest beggar in the world has one true friend, who tells him that it is never too late to mend, that the past may be retrieved, that penitence wins pardon and that a man who turns from his evil ways, though poor as poverty, may be incalculably rich toward God.

And Jesus had a message for the rich. The rich in those days were very rich, for the wealth of the world was concentrated in the hands of a few. But our Lord did not denounce them indiscriminately. He respected the rights of property. He recognized the fact that a man may have abundant possessions and yet be righteous. But he was no sycophant. When he sat at the tables of the wealthy, his table-talk was full of plain truths. He warned them against avarice: "It is easier," said he, "for a camel to pass through a needle's eye," than for a man whose heart is set upon riches to enter the kingdom of God. He told them it was better to part with all their earthly possessions than to lose life, character, and endless happiness: "Go sell all that thou hast and give to the poor," he said to one whose wealth was his hindrance, "and come, follow me." He stated plainly that there were rich men in hell and poor men in heaven. He showed how a man might be very respectable, clothing himself in purple and fine linen and faring sumptuously every day, and still be guilty of unconscionable folly. He spake this parable unto them: "The ground of a certain rich man brought forth plentifully; and he thought within himself, What shall I do, because I have no room where to bestow my fruits? And he said, This will I do: I will pull down my barns and build greater; and there will I bestow all my fruits and my goods. And I will say to my soul, Soul, thou hast much goods laid up for many years; take thine ease, eat, drink, and be merry. But God said unto him, Thou fool, this night thy soul shall be required of thee: then whose shall those things be? So is he that layeth up treasure for himself and is not rich toward God."

He had much to say to workingmen. He was himself a member of the Third Estate. He knew what it was to shove the plane and drive the saw, to grow weary and wipe the perspiration from his brow. One word of his, "The laborer is worthy of his hire," has in it the possible solution of all controversies between capital and labor. He sympathized with honest toil; he knew the fret and worry and fatigue of bread-and-butter work; and he knew the proneness of the toiling class to lose themselves in the sordid routine of common tasks. He stands at the door of every workshop saying, "O men of labor, let your souls rise above the hand-to-mouth struggle! Be in your labor, yet not of it. Be not unmindful of higher service; give room to nobler aspiration." He stands in the midst of the common people as he stood among them on the slopes of Olivet and urges the lesson of the life of trust: "Take no anxious thought for your life, what ye shall eat or what ye shall drink; neither for the body, what ye shall put on. For the life is more than meat and the body than raiment. Behold the fowls of the air: they sow not, neither do they reap, nor gather into barns; yet your heavenly Father feedeth them. Are ye not much better than they? And consider the lilies of the field, how they grow; they toil not, they spin not; and yet I say unto you, that Solomon in all his glory was not arrayed like one of these. If God so clothe the grass of the field, shall he not much more clothe you, O ye of little faith? Take, therefore, no thought for the morrow. But seek ye first the kingdom of God and his righteousness and all these things shall be added unto you."

He had a message for the wise. Sharp was his rebuke to those who were wise in their own conceit. Some of the Doctors of Divinity in those days were deeply concerned in such questions as, "How many steps are there in a Sabbath day's journey?" They were sophists, splitters of hairs. "Woe unto you, blind leaders of the blind," he cried; "ye have taken away the key of knowledge! Ye stand in the doorway of the kingdom of heaven, refusing to pass in yourselves and blocking the way of honester people who fain would enter in." But others of these Doctors were not "sophoi," but "philosophoi," that is, honest seekers after truth; and he gave them great truths to ponder on. To one such who visited him under cover of the night, he announced the great doctrine of Regeneration, evoking the response, "How can these things be?" Whereupon he followed it with a greater doctrine, "God so loved the world, that He gave his only-begotten Son, that whosoever believeth in him should not perish, but have everlasting life." If Nicodemus was in quest of sublimities and profundities, here indeed was something to think of. When that eminent Rabbi left the home of Jesus, bewildered and wondering, the great ocean of unfathomable truth was rolling before him.

He had a message also for the simple. He took a child upon his knee and said, "Except ye become as little children in your attitude toward truth, ye shall in no wise enter the kingdom of God." On another occasion he lifted his eyes to heaven and said, "I thank thee, O Father, that thou hast concealed these things from the wise and prudent and hast revealed them unto babes." The truths which were announced by this great Teacher were indeed so profound that the wise may ponder on them forever, and yet so simple that the wayfaring man, though a fool, need not err in this heavenly thoroughfare.

He preached God,—the profoundest of truths; yet the most unwise and unlettered can say, "Abba Father." He preached sin,—an awful fact, a theme of protracted theological controversy, yet present to the personal conscience of the humblest. For who does not know that he has sinned and come short of the glory of God? He preached salvation,—a matter of long dispute in the schools of philosophy—yet in such terms that no man can excuse himself for not apprehending it. "As Moses lifted up the serpent in the wilderness," said he, "even so must the Son of Man be lifted up" in the anguish of vicarious death, "that whosoever believeth in him may have everlasting life." Look and live! There is life for a look at the crucified One. Love and faith are the two arms with which a child embraces its mother. Love and faith are within the comprehension of all. Love and faith are the two prerequisites to pardon and the endless life.

So the doctrines that Jesus preached are indeed an ocean on the shore of which the sages stand dreaming dreams and seeing visions and losing themselves in contemplation of its depths; but little children play along the beach, laughing and making merry, and the great ocean murmurs about them and laves their feet.

He had a message for doubters too. He lived in an age of doubt. The Jews were weary of an empty liturgical service, and the gods of the Pantheon had lost their hold on the minds of the people. There were agnostics who said like Pliny the elder, "There is only one thing certain, namely, that there is nothing certain." There were others who, with a desperate abandon, lent themselves to an utter denial of all truth. Such was Pilate, who, with a curling of the lip, asked of Jesus, "What is truth?" The great Master cast no pearls before him; he answered not a word. But there were others still who, having lost their bearings, longed to know. One such went wandering in the darkness, after the crucifixion of Jesus, like a blind man groping along the wall. Poor Thomas! His best Friend was dead, his fondest hopes were crushed. He had heard in a roundabout way of the resurrection of Jesus, but he was incredulous; it was indeed too good to believe. For all such doubters, grieving by reason of their unbelief and eager to learn, the Master has infinite sympathy and consideration: "Then saith he to Thomas, Reach hither thy finger and behold my hands, and reach hither thy hand and thrust it into my side; and be not faithless, but believing. And Thomas answered and said unto him, My Lord and my God!" O doubting friend, reach forth and lay thy hand upon his wounds. Touch Jesus! To know him, to commune with him, is to believe. All doubt vanishes when the light of his countenance shines upon us.

And he had much to say to believers. What a high ideal of character he sets before them! "Be ye perfect; be ye holy, for God is holy." And what a searching word as to their influence! "Ye are the salt of the earth; but if the salt have lost its savor, wherewith shall it be salted? it is thenceforth good for nothing but to be cast out and trodden under foot of men. Ye are the light of the world; let your light so shine before men that they may see your good works and glorify God." And what frequent and urgent exhortation to usefulness! "Say not, It is yet four months and then cometh the harvest. Lift up your eyes and see that the fields are white already unto the harvest. Thrust in your sickles and reap!" The barren fig-tree, the parable of the talents, the stumbling-block and the millstone, the great commission, all these are for believers. His standard of Christian living is very high: "If any man will come after me, let him deny himself, and take up his cross and follow me."

And most searching of all was his message to hypocrites. This comes to all who are living under a mask. He saw them ostentatiously flinging their golden offerings into the trumpet-shaped mouths of Corban; and when a poor widow came by, modestly dropping in two farthings, he said, "Behold, she hath given more than they all." He saw them wearing long robes, with broad phylacteries, and frontlets between their eyes, standing on the corner of the streets and making long prayers in order to be seen and heard of men; whereupon he said, "Two men went up to the temple to pray; the one a Pharisee and the other a publican. And the Pharisee prayed thus with himself, God, I thank thee that I am not as other men are. But the publican stood afar off, not daring to lift up so much as his eyes unto heaven, but beating on his breast and crying, God be merciful to me a sinner. I say unto you, This man went down to his house justified rather than the other." His message to all pretenders is this: Be what you seem; be honest as the light! God sees you through and through; all things are naked and open before him. Off with your masks, off with your disguises! "Woe unto you scribes and Pharisees, hypocrites; ye are as whited sepulchres, fair without, but within full of dead men's bones and all uncleanness." And to the people he said, "Except your righteousness shall exceed the righteousness of the scribes and Pharisees, ye shall in no wise enter the kingdom of God."

But sweetest, tenderest and most helpful was his word to the sorrowing. "Blessed are ye that mourn, for ye shall be comforted." In those days when the dream of immortality had grown thin and tenuous and the bereaved were almost without hope, he stood beside the open grave saying, "I am the resurrection and the life. He that believeth in me, though he were dead, yet shall he live. And he that liveth and believeth in me shall never die." He bade them lift up their eyes from the darkness of the grave to the open heavens: "In my Father's house are many mansions; if it were not so, I would have told you. I go to prepare a place for you." There is to be a glorious reunion of saints in the better life. The parting here is not "Farewell," but "*Auf wiedersehen.*" Death does not end all.

Most of all, he spake to sinners. He came to deliver them from the shame and penalty of their sins. The reproach of his enemies was, "He is the friend of publicans and sinners." His defense was, "I am come to seek and to save the lost." He was not ashamed to converse with the adulterous woman of Samaria by the well of Sychar at high noon, though he knew that the finger of every passer-by would be pointed at him. He perceived that her sin-stricken heart was longing for pardon and restoration to purity, and he put the cup of living water to her thirsty lips. His whole ministry was passed in seeking the lost. The love of the great Father has never been so wonderfully set forth as in his three great parables: a woman with a lighted candle seeks anxiously a lost coin; a shepherd with lantern in hand goes out on the dark mountains after the lost sheep; a father looks longingly toward the hills over which his wayward son went long ago to waste his substance in riotous living, and when he sees him returning, in rags and tatters, he goes forth to meet him while he is yet a great way off, and falls upon his neck and kisses him. This is the message of Jesus to sinners: The only-begotten Son of God has come forth to seek them. His last miracle as he hung upon the cross in anguish was to save a malefactor who, grieving over a misspent life, was dying by his side: "To-day thou shalt be with me in paradise." So he proves himself willing to save, eager to save, able to save, even unto the uttermost. He is indeed the friend of sinners. He hath power on earth to forgive sin.

Finally he had a message for hearers; for such as have long listened to the truth, yet not heeded it. You, perhaps, have been familiar with the gospel since the day when, at your mother's knee, you heard the old, old story. You have listened in the sanctuary again and again to appeals and exhortations. You have read your Bibles over and over and seen the bloodstained face of the Redeemer on every page and heard his voice saying, "Come unto me and I will give you rest." To you and all others whose ears have been dulled and whose hearts have been hardened by long hearing, he addresses this faithful admonition: "*Whosoever heareth these sayings of mine and doeth them, I will liken him unto a wise man which built his house upon a rock; and the rain descended and the floods came, and the winds blew and beat upon that house; and it fell not: for it was built upon a rock. And every one that heareth these sayings of mine and doeth them not, shall be likened unto a foolish man, who built his house upon the sand: and the rain descended, and the floods came, and the winds blew and beat upon that house; and it fell: and great was the fall of it.*"

He that hath ears to hear, let him hear.

WHAT THE LAW COULD NOT DO.

"What the law could not do in that it was weak through the flesh."—Rom. 8, 3.

A great problem is before the mind of Paul; to wit, "Who shall deliver me from the body of this death?" As for himself, he had practically solved that problem in coming to Christ; but there were multitudes of others who were still in despair under the bondage of the law. He wastes no breath in convincing them of sin or of sure retribution; he assumes the "certain fearful looking for of judgment." His own conception of guilt is that of a corpse bound to a culprit's neck. This was the most dreadful form of punishment known in ancient times.

> "The living and the dead, at his command,
> Were coupled face to face and hand to hand,
> 'Till, choked with stench, in loathed embraces tied,
> The lingering wretches pined away and died."

The true character of sin—its shame, its bondage, its terrific possibilities—are present at one time or another to the consciousness of every man. But how to be delivered? There's the question. "O wretched man that I am! who shall deliver me from the body of this death?"

To this problem there are two possible solutions, and only two: one says, "Keep the law and live by it"; the other says, "Believe in the Lord Jesus Christ and thou shalt be saved." There is no other alternative. A man is either in bondage under the law, or else he is under grace, abiding in the glorious liberty of the children of God.

A lot of rough fellows were giving their testimony in the Seaman's Bethel a few evenings ago, when one arose and said, "I have no need of Christ or his gospel. I am a moral man and try to do right as near as possible. That's enough for me. I am willing to take my chances with the rest of you at the judgment bar of God." No doubt there are many who, although they may not express themselves so frankly, are of like mind and living in the same way.

To such persons the apostle addresses his argument as to the futility of hoping for salvation under law. He was entitled to speak on this subject; for he had earned the degree of Doctor of Laws in the University of Jerusalem, as a pupil of the great Gamaliel, who was called "The Flower of the Law." He speaks of himself as having been a Pharisee of the straitest sect. His business as a rabbi was to expound the law, and the purpose of his life had been to observe the law, in its most minute particulars, in the hope of thus attaining to the endless life. He had measured his prayers and counted them, as a nun tells the beads of her rosary. He had paid tithes, fasted oft, done penance and addressed himself to good works with the utmost scrupulosity. But one day on the high road to Damascus his eyes were opened; he saw that his merit-making was labor lost; a great light shone into his soul and a voice said, "I am Jesus!" From that moment he was no more a legalist, but a believer in grace. He trusted in Christ for salvation. Grace became his sign-manual. His usual greeting was, "Grace be unto you."

His Epistle to the Romans is distinctively addressed to legalists. In it the apostle undertakes to put the law on a right footing. His proposition is, "By the deeds of the law shall no flesh be justified," and his *Quod erat demonstrandum* is the mighty truth which was sung by Wesley,

"I'm a poor sinner and nothing at all,
But Jesus Christ is my all in all."

The apostle here vindicates the law as efficient for its proper uses. "The law is good," he says; and again, "The law is spiritual;" and again, "The law is holy and the commandment is holy and just and good." But there are certain things which the law cannot do. It has its proper functions; but too much must not be required of it. Water quenches thirst but cannot satisfy hunger. A millstone is a good thing in its place, but we shall probably agree that a millstone is not a good thing to be tied about a man's neck when he is learning to swim. To everything its proper uses.

Certain things the law can and does accomplish:—

I. *The law expresses the mind of God.* It is written: "No man hath seen God at any time." If you wish to form a just conception of some one you have never seen, you make inquiry as to his voice, his features, his moral and mental characteristics. We proceed in like manner in "finding out God." There are voices in nature and in providence to help us; but nowhere shall we get so clear a delineation of the divine character as at Sinai. The precepts and principles here enunciated give a clear outline of his nature and attributes; they speak of his justice, his righteousness, his truth. And the one clear, composite impression which we receive from the Decalogue is that the Lord is a holy God.

II. *The law declares the whole duty of man.* As we are made after God's image, our highest attainment is Godliness; that is, Godlikeness. The precepts that set forth the divine character furnish by the same token the perfect rule of human behavior. "Be ye holy, saith the Lord, for I am holy."

It is a noteworthy fact that the Ten Commandments are universally recognized as a perfect code. Men scoff at Christ, at the gospel, at the inerrant Scriptures; but there is a general consensus as to the faultless character of the Decalogue. What a Paradise our world would be if only men everywhere would obey it!

III. *The law draws up an indictment against all who violate it.* It shows a man his natural face as in a glass. He who comes to the flaming mountain with a mind free from prejudice, is certain to be filled with fear and trembling; "for by the law is the knowledge of sin."

A young man was lately arrested and tried for forgery. He made an earnest plea in his own behalf, alleging his former good character. The court was disposed to deal leniently with him. The officer who made the arrest said, "Your Honor, if you will wait a moment, I think I can convince you of the true character of this man." He went to the Rogue's Gallery and came back presently with a picture of a youth wearing a striped jacket and with his hair cropped short. It was this same innocent-looking prisoner at the bar. All men are put to shame in like manner by the testimony of the moral law. It takes a "snap-shot" at every one of us a hundred times a day, and always with the same result; it catches us invariably in the overt act of sin.

IV. *The law pronounces sentence upon us.* "The soul that sinneth, it shall die." We are said to be "condemned already." In this matter the law works automatically. To be sure, by reason of his justice, God must ratify its action; but if it were conceivable that God should cease to be while the law continued, the result would be precisely the same. For sin and penalty are yoked together as cause and effect.

How can we be so stolid and unconcerned in the face of such tremendous truths? Do we call them in question? Or, can we evade their logical conclusions? So did Belshazzar feel secure in his festal hall. He knew that a hostile army surrounded his city; but had he not laid in provision for twenty years? On with the feast! All over the walls were cuneiform inscriptions to his glory. His wives and concubines were about him and a thousand of his lords. "Bring the sacred vessels that my royal father took from the Jewish Temple!" It was done. The revelers drank deep from the sacramental cups. But on a sudden the king's face was blanched with terror and his knees smote together. Yonder on the wall were spectral fingers writing. Bring the seers, the astrologers, and let them interpret! MENE, MENE, TEKEL; "Thou art weighed in the balances and art found wanting." And, UPHARSIN! What means Upharsin? "Thy kingdom is divided and given away!"

This is the message of the law to every man: "Weighed and found wanting," and "Thy kingdom is rent from thee." Shall the matter end here? Shall the law take its course? Shall the sentence be executed? "He that doeth the law shall live by it, and he that disobeyeth shall die by it."

We have seen what the law can do and does. Let us turn now to the other side and inquire what the law cannot do.

First, it cannot compel obedience. It has to deal with men who are possessed of independent wills. Had men been created otherwise than with moral freedom, they would have been no more capable of positive character than stocks or stones or graven images or hitching-posts. But moral freedom involves the power to do right or wrong at pleasure. The law says, "Thou shalt"; a man can answer, "I will not." And the awful calamity is that we all by nature are disposed to antagonize the law. This is not the time for a discussion on depravity; let it suffice to call attention to the universal fact. We would rather break than keep the law. Did you ever see a sign, "No Trespassing," without feeling inclined on the instant to climb the fence and cross that particular field?

It is not the law's fault that it cannot enforce itself. The words of the apostle are, "What the law could not do in that it was weak through the flesh," that is, by reason of our infirmity. As I passed along Nassau Street yesterday in dreamy mood, I heard a voice say, "Please help me over." A blind man stood helpless on the corner, waiting for some one of the thronging multitude to lead him over the crossing. I took his arm; and as we passed on, I observed that his eyes were wide open and uplifted. The sun shone brightly; the light had all its usual potency; but, alas! it was weak through his flesh. Had I led that man to the best of our opticians and said, "Give him spectacles," he would have replied, "My services are of no value in this case; I can do nothing for him." So is it with the law. It is intrinsically mighty, but utterly disabled in the case of a wilful man.

Secondly, *it cannot ignore sin.* Here again it works automatically, as if it were a machine made of levers and wheels. It has no heart to pity, otherwise it would not be law. It is all eyes. It must take cognizance of every sin.

And here is a startling fact—you may resent it, but the logic is beyond all peradventure—"Whosoever shall keep the whole law, and yet offend in one point, he is guilty of all." There is a manifest reason for this. A chain is measured by the strength of its weakest link. A ship held by an iron cable is, if one link be broken, at the mercy of the storm. In order to break the electric connection between America and the British Isles, it is not necessary to destroy the whole submarine cable; cut out one inch and you break the circuit. If you would wreck a train on the New York Central, do not take the trouble to tear up the track clear from New York to Albany; dig under a single rail at Garrison's and the thing is done. So is it with the strength of the moral law as a saving power. "He that keepeth it shall live by it"; but a single sin breaks the charm. It makes a man a sinner, arrays him against the law, and brings him under the penalty: "The soul that sinneth it shall die."

Thirdly, *the law cannot absolve from sin.* It cannot pardon. Hence the proverb, "Relentless as law." It cannot make allowances or receive excuses. It is vain for us to stand at Sinai and say, "I did not think," or, "I did not intend," or, "I will never do it again." The law turns neither to the right hand nor to the left, but moves straight on.

It was a true word that Anne of Austria said to Richelieu: "My Lord Cardinal, there is one fact which you seem to have entirely forgotten: the law of Jehovah is a sure paymaster; it may not be at the end of every day or month, but I charge you, my Lord, to remember this, the law sooner or later is a sure paymaster!"

Fourthly, *therefore the law cannot save.* The one thing which we require of it is absolutely impossible. It can justify no flesh. It is written, "We are all concluded under sin." The word "concluded" here means literally "shut up." We are all in prison condemned and awaiting the execution of our sentence. The law can do many things for us in this emergency: it can bring us food and water, nosegays and books to read; it can promise us a decent burial; it can buy us a shroud, a black cap and a beautiful silken rope for our neck; it can promise a eulogy and a Latin epitaph; it can do everything but the one thing needful,—it cannot open the doors, it cannot let us out into freedom and light. At this point, if we are reasonable men, we cry for a kind of help which the law cannot give us.

And yet the law is not impotent at this juncture.

In mentioning what it could do, I designedly omitted one thing; namely, "*The law is a schoolmaster to lead us to Christ.*" It cannot save, but it can point us to the Saviour. It cannot save, but it can terrify us with its lightnings and thunders until we flee from the flaming mountain to the mountain that is stained with blood. Here the Merciful One hangs upon the cross, the Mighty to Save.

> "O safe and happy shelter,
> O refuge tried and sweet;
> O trysting-place where Heaven's love
> And Heaven's justice meet!
>
> There lies beneath its shadow,
> But on the further side,
> The darkness of an awful grave
> That gapes both deep and wide.
>
> And there between us stands the Cross,
> Two arms outstretch to save,
> Like a watchman set to guard the way
> From that eternal grave."

"*For what the law could not do in that it was weak through the flesh, God sending his own Son in the likeness of sinful flesh, and for sin, condemned sin in the flesh; that the righteousness of the law might be fulfilled in us.*" He bore our sins in his own body on the tree. He that believeth in the Lord Jesus Christ shall be saved. The blood of Jesus Christ cleanseth us from all sin.

You must take your choice, my friend. You must! You must live either under the law or under grace. You must go on in a hopeless endeavor to work your way to everlasting life, or you must trust in Jesus and let him save you. Does your pride stand in the way? An infidel once said, "I tell you frankly, I am not willing to be saved *gratis.*" But grace is gratuity. The unspeakable gift of God is without money and without price. "Only believe." If you are ever saved, you must be saved that way.

As Napoleon rode through the Rue de Rivoli, returning from the front with his victorious army, a young girl ran out of the crowd and threw herself before his horse's feet. "Mercy, sire!" she cried. "What will you, my daughter?" he said kindly. "O sire! mercy for my father; he is the officer whom you have sentenced to death for treason." The face of Napoleon hardened. "Your father shall have justice," he replied. At that saying, her fervor increased: "O sire, not justice, but mercy! Justice means death! Mercy! mercy, sire!" And this, friends, is the only plea that a sinner can offer before God. Justice means death. Law means shame and despair forever. Let us beat upon our breasts and make our plea, "God be merciful to me a sinner!" And he who is able to save even unto the uttermost will hear and answer us.

"I THIRST."

(*A Sacramental Meditation*)

"After this Jesus, knowing that all things were now accomplished, that the Scripture might be fulfilled, saith, I thirst."—John 19, 28.

This is the shortest of the "Seven Sayings on the Cross." It is as brief and simple as the wail of a little child. The chronicler makes no comment, attempts no explanation. This is characteristic of the Holy Scriptures. Had our sensational journals been an institution of that time, there would have been a very different report of this singular event. What head lines! What prolixity and particularity! What surmises and suggestions and hypotheses! What harrowing delineation of the death anguish; the blanching face, the fever-bursting eyes, the parched lips! But there is nothing of this in the sacred narrative. "After this Jesus saith, I thirst."

Yet the person and work of Christ are comprehensively set forth in this pathetic cry.

I. It represents him as *the perfect Son of God*. We also are called sons of God, but in a lesser and lower sense. He is the divine, the coequal, the eternal, the only-begotten and well-beloved Son.

At his baptism, "He went up straightway out of the water; and, lo, the heavens were opened unto him, and he saw the Spirit of God descending like a dove and lighting upon him: and, lo, a voice from heaven, saying, This is my beloved Son, in whom I am well pleased." No such word was ever spoken of a mere man. No such distinguishing praise was ever addressed to any creature whose breath is in his nostrils. Why was the Father so well pleased with Jesus? Not only because of that peculiar filial relation which he sustained to the Father in the eternal generation, but because he alone lived up to the full measure of the divine plan. All his earthly life was fulfilment; it had been predicted in its minutest particulars. The Old Testament is full of the prophetic forecast; his birth, the time and place of it, his humble environment, his ministry, the manner of his death, the parting of his raiment, the piercing of his side, his resurrection from the dead, his ascension. All these may be read in the glowing hierogram which runs through revelation like a golden thread. And the life of Jesus, like an indenture, fitted at every point and in every way into this eternal plan.

Here is the significance of these words, "That the Scripture might be fulfilled." It had been written a thousand years before in the sixty-ninth Psalm: "In my thirst they gave me vinegar to drink." Even in this particular he must meet the prophetic manifest; wherefore, he cried, "I thirst!"

All lives are divinely marked out. God has great purposes concerning each of us. And the best human life is that which measures itself by the eternal purpose. But, alas! we all come short. The best of God's children is a disappointment to him. It is written of the human race, whom God had intended to be a holy, harmless and undefiled people, that when they had corrupted their way upon the earth and filled it with violence, "it repented Jehovah that he had made man on the earth, and it grieved him at his heart." Who shall adequately depict the parental sorrow and disappointment which is suggested in those words? And of all the descendants of Adam there has never been one who has come up to the high level of the Father's purpose concerning him; not one who can say, "My Father, I am what thou intendedst me to be"; not one who can say, "I have finished the work thou gavest me to do." But this should be our supreme ambition; as it is written, "Work out your own salvation." Not salvation in its narrow sense, to wit, a mere deliverance from eternal fire, but that larger salvation which takes in all manhood and character, all influence and usefulness. Hew to the line, my brother. Work out your own salvation to the very uttermost. Work it *out!* Come up to the full measure of the divine plan. "Work out your salvation with fear and trembling, for it is God that worketh in you."

II. In the cry, "I thirst!" we note also the setting forth of Jesus as *the perfect Son of Man.* It is "the cry of the human." In our contemplation of Jesus we must never lose sight of his perfect humanity. No heresy is more disastrous to our faith than that of the Docetists, who held that Jesus was not a veritable man, but God dwelling in a semblance of mortal flesh; that his body was a phantom; that the reality was God.

It is written, "Forasmuch then as the children are partakers of flesh and blood, he also himself likewise took part of the same." And again, "In all things it behoved him to be made like unto his brethren." And again, "We have not an high priest which cannot be touched with the feeling of our infirmities, but was in all points tempted (that is, tried) like as we are, yet without sin."

But if Jesus is to enter wholly into the fellowship of humanity, he must not be free from the experience of pain; for this, as Dryden says, "is the porcelain clay of human kind." It is a singular fact, that up to this point in his passion our Lord had given no token of physical pain. For twenty hours he had been enduring shame and buffeting with a patience that seems superhuman; he had been mocked and scourged and spit upon; he had been nailed to the cross, and for three mortal hours had hung between heaven and earth; yet not a murmur, nor a cry of pain escaped him. Was he then above human experience? Would he die like a Stoic, or like an Indian tied to the stake "who dies and makes no sign"? Had he no nerves? Was he superior to pain?

No; this bitter cry discovers his full humanity. He dies like other men. At night when the battle is over, the dying who lie scattered over the field forget their bleeding wounds in the anguish of mortal thirst, and on every side they feebly cry, "Water! Water!" Ah, Jesus understands that. At this moment some one somewhere is dying, and close by stands a friend ministering to the last desire, wetting the fevered lips. Christ knows that anguish, for he also at the last moment cried, "I thirst."

Why did he not call to the rescue his illimitable power in this moment of pain? Why was it necessary that he should thirst? Was it not he who had smitten the rocks among the mountains, that all the springs might gush forth? Were not all the brooks that went murmuring through the meadows under his control? Rivers were rolling to the sea; clouds full of water were floating overhead; legions of unseen angels were round about his cross, ready to minister to him; yet in this supreme moment of anguish there was not a drop for his thirsty lips. He must keep his Godhood in reserve, that he may enter into the full sorrows of humanity. Aye, he can be touched with a feeling of our infirmities. He was "in all points" such as we are. He was very man of very man.

III. Still further, he here shows himself to be *the perfect Mediator between God and man*. It must never be forgotten that the pain of Jesus was vicarious pain. On the cross he exchanged places with us: "He was wounded for our transgressions, he was bruised for our iniquities, and by his stripes we are healed." "He bare our sins in his own body on the tree."

The cry, "I thirst!" was expressive of physical pain, but of something deeper also. Our Lord was entering into a region of sorrow, shame and remorse for sin. He so far identified himself with us that, as he penetrated the dark region of the atonement, he lost self-consciousness more and more. It is the cry of souls under the lash of sin's whip of scorpions which he utters here; for he descended into hell for us.

The word that expresses Gehenna better than any other is "thirst." This was in the mind of the Greeks when, in their mythology, they doomed Tantalus, the son of Jupiter, for the murder of Pelops, to stand breast deep in water, which ever receded as he bent toward it with burning lips. There is a like conception in our Lord's parable of Dives, who in the region of despair prayed that one might be sent to dip the tip of his fingers in water and cool his tongue; "for," he said, "I am tormented in this flame." The thirst here is not physical thirst any more than the flame is material fire; but it expresses an awful, unsatisfied longing and hopeless regret. If our Lord in vicarious anguish is to take upon himself our penalty to the very uttermost, he must know this experience. The burden of the world's sin was upon him. He forgot himself. He exchanged places with those who were doomed to pass under the dark portals of eternal death. His thirst was the thirst of the perishing children of men.

Is there one who says, "I do not believe in hell." Where have you been, my friend? You surely have not read the newspapers. O the endless chronicles of woe! The want and squalor, the surrender to bestial vices, the crime, the hopeless remorse! O the long procession to death! We say that heaven begins here and now. And why not hell, also? The cry of Jesus, "I thirst!" is the cry of the sinning, suffering, despairing multitude. He must enter into this profound depth of sorrow if he would relieve it. Thus in his last anguish he touches with one hand the world that he came to save, and with the other the infinite God who alone can save it. And therein he becomes a perfect mediator, the only mediator between God and man.

So he reveals himself in this utterance in the entirety of his nature and personality as perfect Son of God, perfect Son of Man, and perfect Mediator. And here is manifest the whole *rationale* of redemption.

In this triple character he meets the spiritual want of the whole world "groaning and travailing in pain together until now"; for thus he is able "to save them to the uttermost that come unto God by him."

All this must make a tremendous appeal to thoughtful men who have not yet accepted Christ as their Saviour. For he bears our mortal thirst, that he may put the cup of living water to our lips. To the woman of Samaria he said, "If thou knewest who it is that saith unto thee, Give me to drink, thou wouldst have asked of him and he would have given thee living water." In his passion of death he offers the gift of life. O, if thou knewest, thou wouldst ask him. For whosoever drinketh of the water that he will give, shall never thirst; but the water that Christ giveth, shall be in him a well of water springing up into everlasting life.

I remember hearing, when I was a boy, the great orator, John B. Gough, pronounce an apostrophe to a cup of water held in his hand. He spoke of it in words of rare eloquence; as "gushing from the heart of the mountains, dropping from the clouds of heaven, laughing, and full of life." But there is something sweeter and more refreshing than that. I hear the murmur of a river that flows from beneath the throne of God and of the Lamb; a pure river of water of life, clear as crystal; on either side of it are living trees which bear twelve manner of fruits, and their leaves are for the healing of the nations. Ho, every one that thirsteth, come ye to the waters! Whosoever is athirst, let him stoop down and drink and live forever!

But the profoundest appeal of this death cry is to

those who follow Christ. "If thou knewest who it is that saith unto thee, Give me to drink"—what then, beloved? Ah, surely you would give him to drink! By all your love, by all your devotion, by all your vows of loyalty, you would instantly give him to drink. And this you can do by putting the cup of cold water to the thirsty lips of his little ones.

It is pleasant to know that there was one at Calvary that day who was moved by this appeal. It is written, "Straightway one of them ran and took a sponge and filled it with vinegar and put it on a reed and gave him to drink,"—probably one of the soldiers, hardened to deeds of cruelty in long Roman campaigns. His comrades mocked him, saying, "Let be; let us see whether Elias will come to save him." But he disregarded them; for his heart was touched. It shall be remembered as a memorial of him forever, that he heeded the dying Jesus' mortal cry, "I thirst!"

The world is perishing for want of the water of life. The cry of Jesus is the cry of the slums, of the lapsed masses, of the friendless and despairing, of thieves and murderers, of the pagan multitudes, of those who dwell in the regions of darkness and of the shadow of death, of the poor and unbefriended and unholy everywhere. Would you give Jesus to drink? Then put the cup of water to their lips. For it has pleased Jesus to identify himself with the needy everywhere. "I was an hungered," he says, "and ye gave me meat; I was thirsty and ye gave me to drink; I was a stranger and ye took me in, naked and ye clothed me, sick and ye visited me, in prison and ye came unto me."

This is practical Christianity. To weep at Calvary is no evidence of devotion to Jesus. He cries, "I thirst"; and he plainly tells us how we may satisfy his thirst. We are to give to the people—the suffering multitudes for whom he died—the cup of cold water in his name. They are perishing—in our streets, on our frontiers, in pagan lands, everywhere—for want of it. They drink at earthly fountains only to thirst again and stagger on in their great need. Run with the Holy Grail—the name of Jesus graven deep upon it—and give them to drink. They are anhungered and naked, they are sick and in prison; their pain is the pain of Jesus. It is he who, with their hoarse voices and fevered lips calls for the satisfying draught—and calls to thee.

> "There is a doorway in a narrow street,
>   And close beside that door a broken stair,
> And then a low, dark room.
>   The room is bare;
> But in a corner lies
> A worn-out form upon a hard straw-bed,
> No pillow underneath his aching head:
> A face grown wan with suffering, and a hand
> Scarce strong enough to reach the small, dry crust
> That lies upon the chair.
> 'Go in,' the Master says, 'for I am there!
>   I have been waiting wearily in that cold room,
> Waiting long, lonely hours,
>   Waiting for thee to come.'"

This is the message: If thou lovest Christ, take Christ to the people. He alone can quench the deep thirst of the undying soul. Give them to drink in the name of him who burned with their fever on the cross. Give ye them to drink! And remember the word of the Lord Jesus, how he said, "Inasmuch as ye have done it unto one of the least of these, ye have done it unto me."

KNEELING AT OPEN WINDOWS.

"Now when Daniel knew that the writing was signed, he went into his house; and his windows being open in his chamber toward Jerusalem, he kneeled upon his knees three times a day, and prayed, and gave thanks before his God, as he did aforetime."—Daniel 6, 10.

At this time Daniel was eighty-one years old. He had distinguished himself as a statesman and diplomat. He was the Bismarck of Babylon, with a long record of public usefulness unstained by rumor of malfeasance or betrayal of trust.

His story reads like a romance. He had been brought as a captive from Jerusalem at the age of twelve. On account of his comeliness and intellectual promise he had been selected, with other captive youths of noble lineage, to receive an education in Babylonish lore. He was assigned to the royal bounty at the king's table. A difficulty here confronted him. The meat that was spread upon the table, had previously been offered on the altars of pagan gods. It is written, "He purposed in his heart that he would not defile himself with the king's meat." The alternative, which he chose, was a simple diet of pulse and water. He was the stuff that heroes are made of. The boy is father of the man.

Time passed. Step by step he rose to successive positions of honor and responsibility until, the Medo-

Persian empire being divided into one hundred and twenty satrapies, he was made one of a triumvirate to rule over them. But his success and faithfulness had provoked the hostility of his pagan confrères; envy ever "hates the excellence it cannot reach." In matters of public trust they could find no occasion against him; he was vulnerable only at one point, that is, his religion. He was a Jew, a nonconformist. For more than fourscore years, he had been loyal to his ancestral faith. And just there the trap was laid for him.

The conspirators knew the weakness of their king. They said to him, " King Darius, live forever ! We have consulted together and recommend an ordinance, that whosoever for thirty days shall ask a petition of any god or man, save of thee, O king, shall be cast into the den of lions." It was, in fact, a proposition to deify the king. He was overcome by their flattery. The proclamation was drawn up, and the royal seal was affixed, making it "a law of the Medes and Persians which altereth not."

No prayer for thirty days. What a disconsolate period ! The temples of Bel, Nebo and Merodach forsaken. Household images put away. No sacrificial fires on the altars. No ceremonial processions through the streets. The sorrowing must not plead for comfort. Nay, the children must not even cry for bread. But when Darius drove out in his chariot of state, all Babylon must prostrate itself before him as before a very god.

And if any refused ? The den of lions ! The ferocious beasts, kept for the grim amusement of a semi-barbaric court, pacing up and down, famished, with eyes aflame, await their prey. Death for a supplication! Who dares brave it?

The people are under espionage. Spies are sent out for trangressors. "If ye find any, bring them hither; and, above all, watch the house of Daniel the Jew." They had not long to wait. Aha! Yonder he kneels at his window, in plain view. Daniel is in the meshes, caught at last.

This is the figure which we are to contemplate:

I. *A man on his knees.* It is our noblest posture. The first of the Christian emperors, when asked in what attitude he should be portrayed, said, "Paint me on my knees, for I have attained to eminence in that way." If it be true that we are God's offspring, it follows that we are never so loyal to our birth and the noble laws of our being, as when in close and friendly communion with God.

My friend, have you prayed to-day? Is it possible that you have lived on God's bounty, breathing his air, eating his food, rejoicing in his sunshine, and have not had the grace to acknowledge it? A dog will lick the hand of the master who feeds him. It is the suggestion of common courtesy that, confessing ourselves to be dependent on God's bounty, we should say, "I thank Thee."

Let it be observed that Daniel was accustomed to pray. "He knelt down and prayed and gave thanks, *as he did aforetime.*" He was wont to make his supplication; had an appointed place and had stated times, thrice each day. It is a matter of great importance to form a habit of prayer. The word "habit" is significant; it comes from *habeo*, meaning "to hold" or "to fit." The word is used to indicate either a way of living or a suit of clothes, and indeed the two are much alike. A coat adjusts itself in creases and wrinkles to its wearer. As time passes, we say, "It fits, it sits well, it grows easy." And thus it is with any moral wont; in time it adjusts itself, grows easy, becomes a matter of course.

All men pray in moments of emergency. In the face of sudden danger they cry out instinctively to God. I have seen many die, but never one who did not feel the necessity of prayer in that "hour that tries the soul." But he who has formed the habit meets all emergencies with ready ease. He prays "as aforetime." Nothing takes him unawares. The onslaught of the adversary finds him with his armor on. When he reaches the valley of the shadow, he leans on his accustomed staff.

> Prayer is the Christian's vital breath,
> The Christian's native air;
> His watchword at the gates of death,
> He enters heaven with prayer.

II. *The windows of Daniel's chamber were open.* We are not told why; perhaps only that the cool west wind might blow in.

It is not said that Daniel opened them on this occasion; but, "his windows being open, he knelt down, and prayed, and gave thanks before his God." The true worshiper does not make a spectacle of his piety. Our Lord has something to say upon this point: "And when thou prayest, thou shalt not be as the hypocrites are, for they love to pray standing in the synagogues and in the corners of the streets, that they may be seen of men." And he speaks with grave displeasure of a certain Pharisee who, planting himself in a conspicuous place, prayed thus with himself, "God, I thank thee that I am not as other men are."

But observe: the windows of Daniel's chamber being already open, he did not shut them. We may imagine that on entering the room and finding the windows thrown back, he reasoned thus: "What shall I do? Here is the spot where I have been accustomed to kneel before God. But spies are probably at this moment observing me. Why should I kneel? Will it not answer every purpose if I make my supplication in the privacy of my own breast? Yet that would blur the record of my former life. Suppose, then, I close the lattice. Why not? If I am enclosed in the toils of my adversaries now, my usefulness will end. Shall I close the windows then? Nay; by all that is true, noble and manly, I cannot! What is there in my religion to be ashamed of; or whom shall I fear? Have I not the sure promise of God? Nay; I'll be no coward. I'll pray as I have done aforetime, and trust in my God." And down he dropped upon his knees.

III. *It is said that his windows were open toward Jerusalem.* Why toward Jerusalem? Was it because the home of his boyhood was there? An old lady said to me yesterday, that she had just returned from a visit to New Haven; there she sought the old homestead, to find not a vestige left except a venerable elm that had stood before her father's door. "I would have kissed it," she said, "but for the passers-by. As it was, I stood and affectionately stroked the bark of the old tree." It may be that Daniel too had often looked away through those open windows, in fond remembrance of the scenes of his former life.

But there was something more. It was ordained that the Jews scattered abroad in their captivity should worship with their faces toward the Holy City. There was a profound reason for this; the "Hope of Israel" centered there. The rites and ceremonies of their religious economy, all pointing toward the Messiah, were observed there. It was on the heights of Mount Moriah that Abraham had lifted the sacrificial knife above his son, "his only son whom he loved"—a passion-play, a foregleam of Calvary. It was on those same heights, at the threshing floor of Araunah, that the destroying angel of the pestilence had stayed his hand in answer to the intercessory prayer of David,—another foregleam, a silhouette of the great deliverance, a prophecy of the cross. And there Solomon had reared the temple, the "House Magnifical." But what was that temple without its altar? And what was the altar without the sacrifice? And what was the sacrifice without the blood? Thus all things in the worship at Jerusalem were significant of Christ.

We also pray with our windows open toward Jerusalum; but it is the Jerusalem above, where Christ sitteth in light and glory unapproachable, evermore making intercession for us. The shadows of the old dispensation have vanished before the sun. Judaism as an ethnic religion has been merged in Christianity as the universal faith. Our Lord said to the woman of Samaria, "Believe me, the hour cometh when neither in this mountain, nor yet at Jerusalem, shall ye worship the Father; but the true worshipers shall worship the Father in spirit and in truth." That hour came when, hanging on his cross, he cried, "It is finished!" It was probably at that instant that the priest engaged in lighting the evening lamps in the temple, saw the veil before the Holy of Holies rent, as by an unseen hand, from top to bottom, signifying that henceforth the mysteries of the faith, merged in the glory of Christ, were open to all the children of men.

The power of prayer is in this shibboleth, "For Jesus' sake." Our windows thus are open toward the throne of the heavenly grace where our Lord ever maketh intercession for us.

I do not mean to say that when Daniel turned his face toward Jerusalem he fully understood all this; but he lived up to the measure of his prophetic light. He must have known that there was no more virtue in the west than in any other point of the compass, for God is everywhere. But in turning his face thither, he did homage to a great truth, which was in dim outline before him. We who stand on the hither side of the cross, are in the glory of the gospel day. We trust in the power of our Saviour's blood. We expect to be answered for his sake. Wherefore, our eyes are ever toward him.

IV. *Now as to the sequel.* The guards are walking to and fro before the lions' den. Daniel is within. They had expected to hear the roar of the famished beasts, the tearing of flesh and crunching of bones; but there is a strange silence. They wonder, confer, draw the great stone aside to see. The beasts are huddled yonder in a corner, as if cowed and fearful! Daniel kneels with his face uplifted. What is there between him and them?

In the meantime the king had retired to his bed-chamber; but he could not sleep. "His sleep went from him." He tossed to and fro uneasily; he was "sore displeased with himself"; for he loved his faithful chancellor whom he had committed to the lions. Look on that picture and then on this! While Daniel kneels calmly in the face of danger, his king is tortured by an evil conscience. At the first glimmer of the dawn he rises and betakes himself to the den of lions. The silence is ominous. In a lamentable voice he cries, "O Daniel! Has the God, whom thou dost worship, been able to deliver thee?" And a voice from within answers, "O king, live forever! My God hath sent his angel to shut the mouth of the lions, that they might not hurt me." Roll back the stone; let this man out. Vindicated? Nay, more; tried as fine gold is tried in the furnace. A sevenfold better man than when he went in. And another royal decree is issued, "Let all men in my dominion tremble before Daniel's God."

What is the lesson? *It pays to stand for principle.* In the long run it is bad policy to sacrifice principle to policy. We weaken and die of compromise. One of the significant dates in American history is March 7th, 1850. On that day a great statesman, namesake of Daniel, shamed the record of a long lifetime of public usefulness. He had been identified with the cause of freedom and humanity. He had stood side by side with Henry Clay in many a bold crusade for human rights. In his memorable reply to Hayne he had given the best exposition of constitutional government that has ever been heard in our legislative halls. But on March 7th, 1850, alarmed by threats of civil war, he bowed like a doughface to kiss the feet of the oppressor. His fall was lamented by Whittier in a poem called, "Ichabod," in which Daniel Webster was likened to Noah, drunken and uncovered in his tent:—

>"So fallen! So lost! The light withdrawn
>   Which once he wore;
>The glory from his gray hairs gone
>   Forevermore.
>Then pay the homage of old days
>   To his dead fame;
>Walk backward with averted gaze,
>   And hide the shame."

The men whom we delight to honor in the record of the past, are those who have been willing to stand for the truth against the world; who have faced the scourge, confiscation, exile and death, for principle; who in moments of danger have been ready to say, "Here I stand, I cannot otherwise. God help me!"

Let us bring this story up to date. The modern Daniel is the Daniel we have to do with. The merchant who reads this stirring tale of heroism has no lack of opportunity to emulate it; in his commercial life he meets the question again and again, "Shall I be governed by considerations of policy or of principle?"

The young woman in social life must determine, over and over, whether she will be true to her vows of Christian faithfulness, or yield to the allurements of frivolity and worldliness.

The young man in the life of the busy city is ever tempted to cowardly surrender; yonder is the wineglass, yonder a hand beckoning from the doorway of her whose feet take hold on hell.

Are your windows open toward Jerusalem ? Kneel down, no matter who beholds, and make your prayer. Let your light so shine that men may see your good works and glorify God. Speak up, man; no mouthing or mumbling, in God's name ! Be true to your faith; true to your convictions; true to the teaching of Scripture; true to your conscience; true to Christ who bought you with his precious blood. Quit yourself like a man, and the God of Daniel will never leave you nor forsake you.

"IN THE DAYS OF HEROD THE KING."

A CHRISTMAS SERMON.

"Now when Jesus was born in Bethlehem of Judea in the days of Herod the king."- Matt. 2, 1.

This petty ruler was called "The Great." He was the founder of the Herodian family. He had risen from an humble Idumean origin by successive steps of promotion to be governor, tetrarch, provincial king. But what's in a name? The spectre with the scythe and hour-glass breathes, and, lo, all titles vanish like the fabric of a dream.

He was a clever politician, knowing how to adjust himself to the ups and downs of circumstance. He was true successively to Pompey, Cæsar and Cassius. In his religion also he was a time-server and sycophant. He courted popularity but made himself universally unpopular. He rebuilt the Jewish temple, and placed the golden eagle of Rome above its entrance; and the Jews hated him. He built a temple on Mount Gerizim for the Samaritans; and the Samaritans despised him. He built a temple at Cæsarea for the pagan gods, and was repaid by plots and conspiracies. His life was in constant danger: He found it necessary to surround himself with a circle of foreign mercenaries and his capital with a chain of fortified towns.

His personal character was an open scandal. His tyranny in public administration was only equalled by his private vices. He had ten wives; he murdered one of them and three sons. The Emperor Augustus is credited with this epigram, "It were better to be one of Herod's swine, than one of his children."

He reigned thirty-seven years. Despite his vices he had many of the qualities that go to make a successful ruler. He combined with an iron will a courageous spirit and great shrewdness. He had much to do with the triumphant campaigns of Rome which resulted in the subjugation of the world. He was a famous architect, delighting in magnificent temples and palaces; but of these not one stone is left upon another. *Afflavit Deus!* The implacable logic of events has left this man no monument.

He died as the fool dieth; his soul shaken with remorse, his frame consumed with fever, his joints racked and rent asunder by gangrene. He was buried with ostentatious display somewhere under the palms of Jericho, and no man knoweth of his grave.

His greatness was superficial and transient. His only place in history and his only title to immortality are due to his casual contact with a certain Peasant Child.

I. "*The days of Herod the king.*" The phrase is more than a notation of time. An age or generation is a composite photograph of the individuals who compose it. If you strike the average of men and events at the beginning of the Christian Era, you will get Herod the king. He stands for an epoch, for an order of things.

1. *His days were days of peace.* For the third time

in the history of the Roman Empire the great gates of the temple of Janus were closed. But, alas! it was the peace of a base and utter stagnation. All nations of the earth had been made to pass under the yoke of imperial Rome.

The Jews, after a long and stubborn defense of their autonomy, had been obliged to yield; the sceptre had passed from Judah and the lawgiver from between his feet. The mission of this people had indeed been fully accomplished. They had been "chosen" to cherish the true religion and hand down its oracles to succeeding ages. They supposed that their religion was an exclusive prerogative; but in their final dispersion they carried monotheism among the nations everywhere, and so bore their part in the preparation for the coming of Christ.

The Greeks had been engaged for centuries in the perfecting of a language for the uses of art, science and philosophy. It is difficult to see how the new religion could have found an adequate expression in any other. The Greeks meant their language for the use of Plato and Demosthenes; but in its elaboration they were unwittingly doing their part toward the formulation of the Gospel of Christ.

The Romans had now gathered these and other nations under their imperial sway. They had extended their lines of influence over the entire civilized world. They had built roads and cast up highways for their armies. They had made thoroughfares for their commerce over all the seas. They built those splendid highways, as they supposed, for the march of Cæsar's cohorts: in truth they were destined for the heralds of the evangel.

The triple preparation was now accomplished. God had subsidized the three great nations for the fulfilment of his purpose. The world had become acquainted with monotheism; a language had been framed for the best utterance of religious thought; the roads were ready for the heralds. The all-prevailing peace was a token of the fulness of the time.

2. *The days of Herod were days of darkness.* It had been written in prophecy, "The sun shall be turned into darkness before that great and notable day of the Lord." And again, "For, behold, darkness shall cover the earth and gross darkness the people." And again, "The sun and moon shall be dark, and the stars shall withdraw their shining."

The night had closed in. The gods of the pantheons had fallen from their pedestals. The lights of the golden candlestick were extinguished in the temple. Darkness of sin, darkness of ignorance, darkness of despair. A darkness like that of Egypt, which could be felt; so chill, so thick, that artificial lights went out. It was darkness like the falling of a funeral pall. It was a night full of ghosts and spectres and base superstitions—a night of fear and trembling and crying, "Would God it were day!"

Truth had fallen in the streets and Righteousness could not enter. The pagan priests looked into each other's faces and smiled at their mutual deceits. The two extremes of credulous superstition and blank unbelief held sway. When Pilate sneered with curling lip and lifted eyebrows, "What is truth?" he did but voice the spirit of his age.

And when truth has vanished, virtue dies. There was wickedness in high places and in low places.

Drunkenness and licentiousness walked hand in hand. The sanctions of morality were gone, and with them went humanity. Life was of little value. Wealth and power were in the hands of the few. There were kings and potentates and great landlords; but as for the people they were mere oxen, beasts of burden. Woman was at her worst. Wrong and selfishness ruled with a high hand. "The world before Christ," says Luthardt, "was a world without love." Matthew Arnold portrays the moral decadence of the time in truthful words:—

> "On that hard Pagan world disgust
>   And secret loathing fell;
> Deep weariness and sated lust
>   Made human life a hell.
> In his cool hall, with haggard eyes,
>   The noble Roman lay;
> He drove abroad in furious guise
>   Along the Appian Way;
> He made a feast, drank fierce and fast,
>   And crowned his hair with flowers—
> No easier nor no quicker past
>   The impracticable hours."

3. *But the days of Herod were days of expectancy.* It had been prophesied, "The people that sit in darkness shall see a great light." The last of the old prophetic line, standing and waving his torch in the early twilight of this Egyptian night, had cried "The Sun of Righteousness shall arise with healing in his wings." It is a true saying, "Man's extremity is God's opportunity." It is true also that the darkest hour is just before the dawn. The Messianic hope was abroad. Devout Jews like Simeon and Anna were waiting for the manifestation of the Hope of

Israel. Devout pagans like the Magi were watching the stars. Devout Greeks were speaking of the coming of Dikaios, the Just One. Virgil was writing his Ninth Eclogue. There were voices asking, " Watchman, what of the night ?" and through the darkness one great answering voice, from Seir, " The morning cometh!"

God struck the hour. Two figures came face to face; Herod the Great and the Peasant Child. And a conflict then began which shall not cease until the coming of the Golden Age. Judged from the standpoint of human considerations, it must be an unequal contest. For Herod has on his side all power, all patronage, armies and fleets, the authority of imperial Rome. And the Child? He seems as helpless as any babe that ever lay in a mother's arms.

The first move is the slaughter of the innocents. Herod and this Child have crossed each other's paths. and the Child must die. We hear above all frightened cries and frenzied shrieks, the voice of Rachel weeping for her children and refusing to be comforted. The flash of the swords of Herod's soldiery opens an interminable record of strife and persecution.

Let us pass from that dismal scene in Bethlehem down the centuries, amid the confused noise of battle, by the light of bonfires and auto-da-fés, to better days than those of Herod; to wit:

II. *The days of the militant Church.* We are able from this standpoint to determine the results of the conflict thus far. It was Herod's intent, in the slaughter of the innocents, to nip the Messianic promise in the bud. But there was one Peasant Child in Bethlehem whom all earth's armies could not slay.

He had come to accomplish a mighty work, and was immortal until that work was done. In vain do the kings of the earth set themselves in array against him. He that sitteth in the heavens shall laugh; the Lord shall have them in derision! And now that nineteen hundred years have passed, it is evident that all the malignity of the Herodian influence has been as futile as the brandishing of a wooden sword. Call the roll: "Herod the king!" There is no voice nor answer, nor any that regardeth; in all the world there is none so poor to do him reverence. Now call, "Jesus the Christ!" and, lo! four hundred millions rise up to call him blessed.

There are three forces existent, universal and magnificently potent, which attest the progress of the great conflict.

1. *The Bible.* This is the book of the Peasant Child. Take Him out and nothing remains of it. The Word Written shares the glory and the destiny of the Word Incarnate. The Herodian influence has ever been against it. Do you ask, "Why do men hate this Book?" Tell me, why did Herod hate the Child of Bethlehem? What has this book done? Good and only good all the days of its life. Yet foes without and skeptics within have combined to destroy it. But all in vain. Bonfires cannot burn it. Hostile criticism recoils upon itself. The Word of the Lord endureth forever; the mouth of the Lord hath spoken it. This Bible is the book of the ages. It is not catalogued with other books: their editions are of thousands; its editions are of millions. It is the Book, by itself, solitary and alone, guarded through the ages under the ægis of God.

2. *The Church.* This is the great organism through which the Spirit of Christ is manifest and potent for the salvation of the world. The Herodian spirit has ever opposed it. In the catacombs, among the mountains of the Vaudois, on the plains of Armenia, everywhere the slaughter of the innocents has gone on unceasingly; but the blood of the martyrs has been the seed of the Church.

> Unshaken as the eternal hills,
> Immovable she stands;
> A mountain that shall fill the earth,
> An house not made with hands.

3. *The living and dominant Christ.* He is the colossal figure of these days. His promise is fulfilled, Lo, I am with you alway, even unto the end of the present order of things.

It was the custom of Ralph Waldo Emerson to speak of the Bible patronizingly, as one of many noble books, and of Christ as one of earth's noblest men. On one occasion, lecturing in Kingston, Ontario, he mentioned in succession a company of historic teachers, such as Plato and Epictetus, Confucius and Sakya Muni, and was proceeding, "I say then that the world reverences and will ever reverence Jesus and his peers"—when a voice from the further gallery cried, "He has no peers! My Master has no peers!" All eyes were turned that way. It was the voice of a young pastor named Ormiston, who later became minister of this Collegiate Church. He afterwards remarked that he was quite unconscious of what he was saying, being carried away by an uncontrollable indignation. But never was a truer word; "He has no peers! Our Master has no peers!"

Other great men come and go, but Jesus abides forever. Others play their part in history and vanish; but he becomes more and more the central figure of the advancing centuries and the living promise of the Millennium. He was reckoned at the beginning as a root out of a dry ground, in whom there was no comeliness that men should desire him; he has become, in the logic of events, the chiefest among ten thousand, the one altogether lovely. His name is above every name that is named in heaven or on earth.

But the end is not yet. The conflict goes on. The world is not saved. The Herodians are still arrayed against the followers of Christ. Nevertheless we are assured of the outcome. Let us pass on through an indefinite vista of the future and come to the end of human history, to wit:

III. *The days of the Son of Man.* For he shall reign from the river unto the ends of the earth. The time is coming when no man shall need to say, "Know thou the Lord." For every man shall know him from the least to the greatest, and every knee shall bow before him.

We judge from the analogy of the divine methods, that Christ's triumph could be by no sudden displacement of adverse power. His days do not come with a sunburst, but like every dawn, the sun shining brighter and brighter unto the perfect day. This supreme harvest comes not like manna, but like the ripening of all fruitful fields,—first the blade, then the ear, then the full corn in the ear.

But the royal banners onward go. Two swords meet in the conflict; that of Herod drips with blood; the other is the sword of the Spirit which is the word of God. And he has said, "My word shall not return unto me void, but shall accomplish that which I please and prosper in the thing whereto I sent it."

Meanwhile the word for every Christian is, Lend a hand! Fall in and lend a hand! Ours is the privilege of service by words in due season and by the power of a holy life. The logic of history is hope; the logic of prophecy is faith.

> "For, lo, the days are hastening on
> By prophet bards foretold,
> Which through the ever-circling years
> Bring in the Age of Gold."

At the close of our Civil War, when Admiral Dupont was laboriously explaining why he had failed to get into Charleston harbor with his fleet of ironclads, he was interrupted by Farragut, who said, "But there is one reason which you have not given." "And what is that?" "You did not believe you could do it!"

It cheers the heart and nerves the arm to feel assured that we who are enlisted with the Christ are bound to win. You may read the final triumph in the sure word of prophecy, you may see it in passing events as they are recorded in the daily press, you may hear it loud and clear in the chiming of the Christmas bells. Hearken how they say as they swing, "For unto us a child is born, unto us a son is given: and the government shall be upon his shoulder: and his name shall be called Wonderful, Counsellor, The mighty God, The everlasting Father, the Prince of Peace!"

The story of Herod shows the doom of the Herodian influence. All opposition to the Peasant Child must go for naught. Not more vain were it for a scarabæus to plant itself against the progress of the armies of the Pharaohs, not more vain for a glow-worm to oppose the light of noonday, than for men whose breath is in their nostrils to oppose the triumphal progress of the Son of God. Lift up your eyes and see; all these gather themselves and come unto him; the rams of Nebaioth, the dromedaries of Midian, the ships of Tarshish! The kings of the earth bring the glory and honor of the nations unto him. Fall in and lend a hand! The red cross banner is advancing to the remotest corners of the earth. The Peasant Child has on his vesture and on his thigh a name written, King of Kings and Lord of Lords. His kingdom is an everlasting kingdom, and his dominion is forever and ever. The days of Herod are gone; the days of the stern conflict are passing; we hail the days of the Son of Man. The Christmas lights, the chiming of the Christmas bells, the laughter of the children in our homes, all hope and gladness are a prophecy of the Golden Age.

THE PASSOVER PILGRIMS.

A NEW-YEAR SERMON.

"And thus shall ye eat it; with your loins girded, your shoes on your feet, and your staff in your hand."—Exod. 12, 11.

At midnight on the 14th of Nisan, the children of Israel were assembled in their homes, awaiting the signal to march forth. They looked back over a dreary stretch of four hundred years of bitter bondage in Egypt. They had built Pithom and Raamses and, perhaps, the Pyramids. They had served under hard taskmasters with bastinado in hand. But the days of their slavery were over.

An unknown future was before them. They were going forth to toils and dangers that they knew not. It was a herculean enterprise, this émeute of two million slaves. There is no corresponding event in history. It suggests a marvelous faith and courage on the part of these people. The thought of the divine intervention must have stimulated and sustained them.

A man had been divinely sent from Midian to undertake for them. In the name of Jehovah he said, at the threshold of the palace, "Let my people go!" Then in quick succession came the river plagues, the insect plagues, the blight and murrain and darkness.

The last was to throw open the stubborn gates of Egypt,—this was the death of the firstborn. The people were assembled now, awe-struck and fearful, awaiting the midnight cry.

We are at the border of the years. Sins, sorrows, disappointments and failures are behind us. We reach forth unto the things that are before. The future beckons. Are we ready?

I. *The Passover.* The Israelites began their journey at the sacrificial altar. The Lord had commanded them to slay for each household a lamb, a firstling of the flock, without spot or blemish. Its blood was to be sprinkled upon the side posts and lintel of the door. "For," said the Lord, "I will pass through Egypt this night and smite the firstborn: and the blood shall be to you for a token upon the houses where ye are; and when I see the blood, I will pass over you." The blood having thus been sprinkled upon the doors, the flesh of the sacrifice was spread upon the table and all partook of it. The ceremonial of that eventful night is immensely significant. The lamb symbolized the "Lamb slain from the foundation of the world"; as it is written, "Christ our passover is sacrificed for us."

In the sprinkling of the blood there is a clear reference to the redeeming power of the cross. The law declares, "The soul that sinneth, it shall die." The life is in the blood. "Without the shedding of blood there is no remission." The blood cleanseth. "Come now, saith the Lord, though your sins be as scarlet, they shall be as white as snow; though they be red like crimson, they shall be as wool." If we are to enter upon the future as Passover Pilgrims, here is the right beginning : To apprehend by faith the power of the blood.

The New Year Eve is observed throughout China in a general payment of debts. There is not an almond-eyed pagan on our little Doyer Street who would not consider himself disgraced if he could not enter the new year with a clean balance sheet. We stand as debtors before the law; duty is only another word for debt. Sin brings us into hopeless arrears. What shall we do? Pass on into the future with an uncanceled score resting on us as an intolerable burden? That is unnecessary: for the sufferings of Jesus are a ransom. Its benefits are appropriated by faith. "Jesus paid it all, all the debt I owe." The blood washes out the old reckoning, so that we pass into the future glad-hearted and hopeful, and ready, by God's grace, to meet whatever may confront us.

There is a deep significance also in the eating of the flesh. It shadows forth our vital appropriation of Christ himself. We partake of him as our soul's food, his life becoming assimilated with our life. We enter into fellowship with him in service, cross-bearing, self-denial; and if we thus suffer with him, we shall also reign together. He identified himself with us in the great sacrifice of Calvary; we must needs identify ourselves with him in the experiences of the Christian life. So it is written, " Except ye eat the flesh and drink the blood of the Son of Man, ye have no life in you."

The second book of the Pilgrim's Progress opens with a picture of a desolate home. Here sits Christiana, sore-hearted and melancholy, her children gathered about her. A year ago her husband fled from the City of Destruction with his fingers in his ears, crying, "Life! Life! Eternal Life!" She refused to go; but now she wails, "Woe worth the day!" She would fain set forth, if she dared. "I also will be a pilgrim!" she cries; but fears and forebodings restrain her. There is a knock at the door. A messenger appears, saying, "Peace be to this house. The Merciful One has sent me to say that he is ready to forgive." He places in her hands a letter, written in characters of gold and exhaling the rarest fragrance. It is an announcement of pardon, and an assurance of divine guidance to the gates of the Celestial City. Then Christiana said, "Come, my children, let us pack up and be gone!" She placed the letter in her bosom, and ever and anon, along the way, she took it out and read it. She learned it by heart, she taught it to her children. It was one of the songs of their pilgrimage, and at the last it was her passport at the shining gate.

Our safety on the journey and our ultimate arrival are assured by accepting this proffered care and guidance of the Merciful One. The blood sprinkled on our hearts gives us the peace of pardon; and a vital apprehension of Christ as Saviour and Friend so links our destiny to his, that, as Rowland Hill used to say, "He can't go to heaven, and leave us behind."

II. *The Panoply.* It was not enough, however, that the children of Israel should partake of the Passover; they were commanded to harness themselves for the journey.

In Paul's letter to the Ephesians, conceiving the Christian life to be a stern campaign, he prescribes a soldier's panoply: "Wherefore take unto you the whole armor of God, that ye may be able to withstand in the evil day, and, having done all, to stand. Stand therefore, having your loins girt about with truth, and having on the breastplate of righteousness, and your feet shod with the preparation of the gospel of peace; above all, taking the shield of faith wherewith ye shall be able to quench all the fiery darts of the evil one. And take the helmet of salvation, and the sword of the Spirit, which is the word of God."

Our present thought, however, is not that of warfare, but of journeying. We are pilgrims and sojourners, looking for a better country and a city which hath foundations, whose builder and maker is God. We require, therefore, a pilgrim's equipment; to wit, girdle, sandals and staff.

1. *The Girdle;* that is, *resolution.* I do not say resolutions. The beginning of the year is marked by a multiplicity of these. It is a true saying that hell is paved with them. Not because they are severally unwise, but because, like a bundle of fagots, they are sure to be torn asunder, ere the year is closed, and scattered broken along the way.

You have been saying, "I will break off this or that evil habit;" or, "I will cut loose from certain pernicious associations;" or, "I will devote myself more scrupulously to business;" or, "I will do good as I have opportunity unto all men;" or, "I will be faithful in the discharge of my ecclesiastical duties." So far, so good. But there is one resolution that covers all, namely, "I will be true to my covenant with Christ." To say this in all sincerity is to tighten one's girdle for the whole year. All things are possible, with God's grace, to the man of noble purpose. There is no better watchword than that of the old Saxon knight, "Will, God and I can!"

2. *The sandals.* To be without the sandals means weariness and blistered feet, for we are to traverse desert sands. The shoes for our feet are *the Bible and Prayer.* Let not the dust accumulate on your Bible, my friend; let not the grass grow in the pathway to your trysting-place, if you would live an earnest, Christian life.

Do you believe in the Bible? Are you sure? These are days when a man needs to question his soul in these premises. The air is full of pedantic assumptions and ill-grounded reflections as to the veracity of the Book. It is quite the fashion among a certain class of callow thinkers to assume that the destructive critics have carried their point. You will scarcely find a group of young people anywhere in which there are not some vociferous deniers of inspiration. It takes courage under such circumstances to say frankly, "I believe in the historic view of the inerrancy of Holy Writ." A great majority of God's people the world over are of that mind; but why do they not say so?

The Bible must be the man of our counsel for the coming year. We shall make no mistake if we live by its precepts, profit by its admonitions and find our chiefest joy in its exceeding great and precious promises. It will provide us with food for our spiritual hunger, medicine for sickness and ammunition for every battle.

Then, pray without ceasing. Be instant in prayer. Begin the day with it; close the day with it; let all the intervening hours be full of it. The great steamers that carry on our international commerce cannot stop at every port along the way; it is sufficient to lay to and send in the jolly-boat. So while engaged in our common pursuits, if we may not turn aside in every emergency to seek the trysting-place or fall upon our knees, we can always send up an ejaculatory petition to the throne of the heavenly grace. In any case, neglect not "the gift of the knees"; for

> "Prayer is the Christian's vital breath,
> The Christian's native air;
> His watchword at the gates of death,
> He enters Heaven with prayer."

3. *The Staff;* that is, *Faith.* For whereon shall the Passover Pilgrim lean if not upon his faith in God?

The Israelites were told at the outset that God would go before them in a pillar of cloud by day and of fire by night. But they must needs believe for a while without seeing. When they set out from Raamses and the other Egyptian cities there was no directing cloud above them. A brief journey of possibly twenty-five miles brought them to Etham on the edge of the desert, and there behold! the cloud appeared.

No doubt there were some there who regarded it as nothing out of the common. "It looks like any cloud," they said; "have you seen a face, or has a voice proceeded from it?" And when the sun went down and the cloud was tinged with fiery splendor they said, "Is it not like other clouds on which the glory of a brilliant sunset lingers? How do you know Jehovah is there?" And how, indeed, could they know? Only by faith.

And as time passed their faith was strengthened; for to him that hath shall be given. The cloud was over them by day, a pavilion from the scorching sun. It went before them on the march, an unerring guide along the appointed way. And when the enemy pursued, it went behind the pilgrim host and was as the blackness of darkness to their foes.

It is only by faith that we apprehend the great verities of the spiritual life. Faith is the substance of things hoped for, the evidence of things not seen. We live by faith, we walk by faith; this is the victory that overcometh the world, even our faith.

It is precisely at this point that believers are asked to meet the severest assault of the adversary in our time. A wave of infidelity is sweeping over the world and making itself felt even in some of our Theological Seminaries and Churches, which puts forth as its bold pronunciamento a denial of the supernatural. Call it Rationalism, Agnosticism, Transcendentalism, or whatever you will; the underlying thought is invariably a denial of the supernatural. The proposal is to account for everything on natural grounds, and incidentally to reject all that cannot be tested by the physical senses.

It aims a poisoned shaft at our faith in God. It asserts the Godhood of law, force, the impersonal essence, a thing without eyes to see, a heart to pity or hands to help. And indeed if faith be rejected and the testimony of the senses be regarded as the court of last appeal, there can be no personal God.

It denies in like manner the nobility of man. It

traces his ancestry to an anthropoid ape, basing the argument on a hypothesis inferred from a facial angle. It reduces brain to phosphorus and conscience to friction. It makes immortality a dream, leaving man to die like the beasts that perish; for, if the testimony of faith be denied, there is absolutely nothing to be said against the assertion that death ends all.

It denies the divineness of Christ. We have recently heard a call from one of our Theological Seminaries for a "restatement of Christology." An effort is made to explain away the supernatural in the holy nativity. The miracles of Christ are referred to optical illusion. The divine quality in the blood-atonement is treated as a fable. The resurrection of Jesus from the dead is an invention or an afterthought of his disciples. Thus is Christ derided in his own house. Those who call themselves after his name have crowned him with thorns, clothed him with ribald purple, placed an impotent reed in his hands, and kissed their hands before him, crying, "Hail, King of the Jews!"

This is the tendency of our time. The safeguard is faith. To say that we are only able to believe what lies within the circumscription of the physical senses, is to take our place among the lower orders. All around and above us there is a world of invisible verities. Our glory is to escape from the bondage of the senses, to dream dreams and see visions. The strength of our Christian character is measured by the power and constancy of our faith. It is the domination of the invisible in common life that measures our subjugation to the authority of Christ.

Let us therefore be great believers. Let us cut

loose from the sordid and sensual, and reach after the things which are unseen and eternal. We are too much disposed to ask, "How little can I believe and be saved?" As beings of two worlds, we should bring faith not to its minimum, but to its maximum. *Credo* is a great word. How much can I apprehend of the great body of truth? How sincerely can I say, "I believe"? How far can I ascend out of the mists of the lower valleys of sordid and selfish living into the higher atmosphere of faith in the invisible and of confidence in the infinite God?

The year is before us. Are we ready? Have we sprinkled the blood and partaken of the flesh of the Paschal Lamb. Are our loins girt with resolution? Have we taken the Bible and prayer as our "pilgrim shoon"? Is the strong staff in our hand? Then let Sir Walter Raleigh greet us quaintly with a parting word:

> " Give me my scallop-shell of quiet,
>   My staff of faith to lean upon;
>   My scrip of joy, immortal diet;
>   My bottle of salvation;
>   My gown of glory, hope's true gauge,
>   And thus I take my pilgrimage!"

EUODIA AND SYNTYCHE.

"I beseech Euodia and beseech Syntyche that they be of one mind in the Lord." Phil. 4 : 2.

The Epistles are of great value, not only for their formulation of our Lord's teachings ; but for the light they throw upon the early life of the church. We learn from them that the primitive Christians were a singularly earnest, affectionate and simple folk. We catch, in the passage before us, a glimpse of their mutual relations. It is a dual biography in a nutshell; "I beseech Euodia, and beseech Syntyche, that they be of one mind in the Lord." These persons are nowhere else referred to. The outline is faint enough; yet on thoughtful consideration it reveals not a few interesting facts.

I.—*The persons here mentioned were women.* They were members of the Philippian Church, which is often spoken of as a "Woman's Church." A peculiar interest attaches to its origin. Paul, while tarrying at Troas, on the border of the Ægean Sea, saw in a vision a man clad in Macedonian garb stretching out his hands and saying, "Come over and help us!" The apostle was not disobedient unto the vision, but immediately took ship for Europe and turned his steps forthwith to the Macedonian city of Philippi. On the morning of the Sabbath, he set out to find the man of his vision. By the river-side, in a place where prayer was wont to be made, he found a company of women assembled, and to them he preached the unsearchable riches of Christ. The heart of Lydia the purple-seller was open to receive the truth. Thus the man of Paul's vision proved to be a woman; and this was the beginning of the Philippian Church.

It is frequently said by way of criticism that two-thirds of the members of the entire Christian Church are of the gentler sex. The statement is true, and is to be partly accounted for, perhaps, by the fact that women, on account of their peculiar life and occupation, have time to reflect upon the great problems of eternity. God pity the men, ever in the madding crowd, absorbed in secular affairs, who find so little leisure to consider the welfare of their immortal souls! But shall the fact referred to be regarded as a reflection on the character of the church? Before we leap to that conclusion, let us yoke with it another fact, to wit: Seven-eighths of the inmates of our prisons and penitentiaries are men. A fair deduction from both these premises can place no discredit upon the church for her preponderance of female membership. Indeed it speaks eloquently for her thoughtfulness and purity of character.

II.—We are given to understand that *Euodia and Syntyche were good women.* There is much in a name. Euodia means "fragrance;" Syntyche means "happiness." We are informed that they were "laborers in the gospel." It is probable that they were deaconesses. In those days it was a fine custom to appoint women for the special care of the poor. In our foreign missionary work we have found it necessary to revive that custom, in some measure, for zenana visitation. The homes of the Orient are open only to women visitors; and the gospel can never be made effective until it reaches these penetralia; for home is the centre of social and civil life.

We have a further intimation as to the character of Euodia and Syntyche in the statement that their names were written "in the book of life." This means more than good and regular standing in the Philippian Church; it leaves no question as to their sincere and vital fellowship with Christ.

III.—*These good women were not of one mind.* It would appear that their disagreement was generally known and deplored in the Philippian Church.

No doubt it was a great occasion among the Christians of this Macedonian city when Paul's letter was publicly read. It had been rumored among the people that such a letter had been received from the beloved founder of the church, who was at that time a prisoner in Rome. And there was great anticipation. At the appointed hour on the Lord's Day all were present to hear it. A deep silence rested on the congregation as the reading proceeded; but there was a rustle and a turning of faces at these words: "*I beseech Euodia and beseech Syntyche, that they be of the same mind in the Lord.*" The two women, who probably sat as far apart as possible on that occasion, must have heard with tingling ears. It was fortunate for them that their flushed cheeks were hidden by their veils. But still more distressed and mortified would they have been, had they known that their names were to be handed down to posterity only in connection with their unfortunate estrangement.

IV.— *The quarrel was about a trifle.* We infer

this from the fact that Paul asked for no investigation of their case. He did not advise that they be summoned before the official board. Indeed the whole affair would appear to have been much ado about nothing. It may have originated in a bit of gossip, a flash of temper, or an inadvertent word.

Is it not true that most disagreements have a slight origin? The Koran says that the first quarrel was between Adam and Eve soon after leaving Paradise, and began on this wise: Eve had somehow come into possession of a rude mirror; she looked and saw therein a woman who smiled at her in a supercilious manner, as if to say, "You think yourself fair; but look on me. Ah, wait until Adam sees me!" And Eve, meeting her spouse, forthwith took him to task for it.

We should find it difficult to account for most of our likes and dislikes. And as for our bitter disagreements, it would be quite impossible to justify them. The best that can be said is,

"I do not like thee, Dr. Fell,
The reason why I cannot tell."

V.—*It would appear that both women were to blame.* This may be inferred from their having an equal interest in the message: "I beseech Euodia and beseech Syntyche." Had it been otherwise there might have been some uncertainty as to which should make the first advances. Being equally concerned in the disagreement, they should emulate each other in making peace.

It takes two to make a quarrel. You must have flint and steel or you will get no spark. There is usually a quick temper on either side; the potency of fire in both steel and flint. And by the same token there should be no recrimination, but a mutual interest in reparation and peace. As a rule the less blameworthy of the parties may be known by his greater readiness to make the *amende honorable*.

VI.—*The results of this quarrel were far-reaching.* It has come down through nineteen hundred years. It casts a serious reflection on the character of the two women. It was a scandal in the Philippian Church and still remains as a reproach to it. "How far that little candle throws his beams!"

The Thirty Years' War, with its terrific bloodshed and desolation, began in a frivolous disagreement at table. A marriage had been arranged between the houses of Neuburg and Brandenburg. At the splendid espousal feast, the elector of Brandenburg threw a glass of wine into the face of his intended son-in-law. The youth went away in high dudgeon, and offered his hand to the Princess of Bavaria. In pursuance of that union, an alliance was formed with the royal house of Spain, and presently Neuburg and his army marched forth to engage in the long and bloody war. Nor is this a singular instance. The great events of history usually turn on small pivots; and not infrequently the destiny of kingdoms is determined by the agreements or disagreements of humble men.

VII.—*We do not know that Euodia and Syntyche were ever reconciled on earth.* It goes without saying that they are friends now; for is it not written, "Their names are in the book of life"? During all these centuries they have been in the Father's house, where there are no quarrels, but all see face to face and eye to eye.

The Scriptural mode of adjusting a disagreement is very clear. "If thy brother trespass against thee, go and tell him his fault between thee and him alone." Tell *him*. Tell him *between thee and him alone*. The trouble is that under such circumstances we are likely to tell everybody else rather than the one who has offended against us. The chasm is widened by thus blazoning the fault abroad. No whispering then behind your brother! There is a whole panorama of meanness in the word "backbiting."

And again it is written, "If thou bring thy gift to the altar, and there rememberest that thy brother hath aught against thee, leave there thy gift before the altar, and go thy way; first be reconciled to thy brother, and then come and offer thy gift." If this were transcribed into our vernacular, it would read like this: "If you come to the sanctuary to worship God and discover in your heart any hatred or resentment; or if you are aware that any of the brethren has had occasion to regard you in an unfriendly way, be assured that your devotions will give no sweet savor before your Father in heaven until you have set yourself right with your fellow man."

On one occasion Peter came to Jesus saying: "Lord, how oft shall my brother sin against me, and I forgive him? till seven times?" It was a question of fine casuistry. The Rabbi Ben-Sira had said, "If thou hast a grudge against thy brother, forgive him twice before thou cherish it." No doubt Peter thought he was going far beyond such Jewish narrowness in suggesting "seven times." It probably did not occur to him that the placing of any limit whatever on the magnanimity of Christian character gives it a rank foreign savor of narrowness and externalism. And Jesus answered, "I say not unto thee, Until seven times; but, Until seventy times seven." That is, the world of mercy knows no horizons. There should be no more limit to our mutual forbearance than there is to the grace of God.

The women who were parties to this Philippian quarrel are generic types. And the practical application is plain. I would not have it suspected that the occasion of the present discourse is any quarrel in the Collegiate Church; for it is a pleasure to say that in the years of my ministry I have never known a personal disagreement among you. However, it is greatly to be doubted if there is one here who has viewed this ancient quarrel as a mere "looker on in Venice." Have you no grudges, no hatreds nor jealousies? Is your heart all sweetness and light? Are you kindly affectioned toward all? Oh, let us open our souls to the influence of the heavenly Dove to-day!

But this is not so easy as might appear. The patching up of a disagreement is not a matter for mere resolution. There must be personal explanation, concession, perhaps an apology. There is nothing harder than to say, "I beg your pardon;" but a man is at his best when he says it. This is what Milton calls "the lowly loftiness of mind which is exalted by its own humiliation." A knight's tombstone in England bears this inscription:

> "Here lies a soldier whom all must applaud,
> Who fought many battles at home and abroad;
> But the hottest engagement he ever was in,
> Was the conquest of self in the battle with sin."

It would be difficult to find a man of sweeter spirit than John Wesley, if we may credit his biographers. And yet there was an occasion on which Joseph Bradford got the better of him. He had asked Bradford, his familiar friend, to carry a letter to the post. The reply was, "After service." "Nay, now." "I will not, until I have heard thy discourse." "Then our friendship ceases." "Very well, so be it." Wesley preached, and Bradford listened; the benediction was pronounced; and both went home to toss upon uneasy beds. The next morning Bradford said, "John, must we part?" "It is for thee to say." "Wilt ask my pardon?" "Nay, never! never!" "Then I will ask thine; John, forgive me!" The ice was broken, and they were friends faithful until death.

We who profess to follow the Lord Jesus Christ, cannot afford to endanger our inward peace, jeopardize our reputation and bring reproach on the goodly fellowship by falling out along the way. Oh, for the spirit of Nehemiah and those who labored together with him! We, too, are temple-builders. Our work is too important, our life is too brief, for criminations and recriminations, for the bickerings of the sordid, selfish life. Let this be our word to the demons of enmity who thrust out the lip and point the finger at us from the plain of Ono, "I am doing a great work, so that I cannot come down!"

Let it be remembered that we journey always on the narrow borders of the eternal world. If there are bitternesses to be healed or differences to compose, let us not wait until the shadows enfold us. I know of no more pathetic tale than that of the chronic quarrel of Commodores Barron and Decatur. They were both able officers who had served the United States faithfully. But year by year they nursed a petty disagreement until it found its dreadful consummation in the duello. They met on the field, breathing out mutual hatred; and at the first report, both fell. Side by side they lay dying. "Let us make friends," said Barron, "ere we meet before the throne of God." "I never have been your enemy," replied Decatur, breathing heavily, "and freely forgive you my death." "Would to God that you had said as much yesterday. God bless thee, Decatur!" "God bless thee, my friend!"

> Of all sad words of tongue or pen,
> The saddest are these, It might have been.

I beseech you, brethren, by the cross of Jesus Christ that ye love one another with pure hearts fervently. I beseech you by the Golden Rule that ye expect no more of kindliness from your fellows than you willingly accord to them. I beseech you by the hope of heaven that ye entreat one another as children of the Father, for so it is written: "Ye be brethren; see that ye fall not out along the way"— "Be ye kindly affectioned one toward another; in honor preferring one another; forgiving one another as God for Christ's sake hath forgiven you."

THE IMMEASURABLE GOD.

"Canst thou by searching find out God? canst thou find out the Almighty unto perfection? It is high as heaven; what canst thou do? deeper than hell; what canst thou know? The measure thereof is longer than the earth, and broader than the sea."—Job 11, 7-9.

In all satirical literature there is nothing so fine as that paragraph in Isaiah's prophecy which pictures before us a carpenter measuring a god. He has brought a cedar log from the forest, of straight grain, knotless and of sound heart, "that will not rot." He stretches out his rule and marks it with a line, and makes it "according to the beauty of a man." He surveys it with speculation in his eyes; for this god must not be over-tall to pass under the lintel, nor over-broad to be carried between the sideposts. He projects the figure with compass and chalk-line; and, finding the log too long, cuts it in two. Then he hews it with an adze, and fashions it with a chisel. But, anon, the pangs of hunger are upon him; he gathers up the chips, kindles them, and therewith bakes his food. He stands before the fire, rubbing his hands and saying, "Aha! I am warm." And having satisfied his hunger, he turns toward the half-carven image, the residue of the cedar log, and cries, "Deliver me, for thou art my god!"

Let us attempt the impossible—the measurement of God. But not in this workshop; the walls are too close, the air is too stifling. Let us go forth into the illimitable open, under the lofty canopy; for our God is a great God above all gods.

I. *As to his stature.* How great is He? Let us call Solomon to our help. In his prayer at the dedication of the temple he gave us this measurement: "Will God indeed dwell on the earth? Behold, the heaven and the heaven of heavens cannot contain him." (I Kings, 8, 27.)

Men have builded a niche for Jupiter, a pedestal for Thor, a shrine for Buddha. But God stretcheth out the heavens as a curtain, and he covereth himself with light as with a garment. Heaven is his throne, the earth is his footstool. The tapestries of his chamber are the glories of dawn and sunset. The walls of his temple recede infinitely as we gaze upon them. He dwelleth in light and glory unapproachable and amid voices of adoration that are as the sound of many waters and mighty thunderings.

> "The Lord our God is full of might;
> The winds obey his will.
> He speaks, and, in the heavenly height,
> The rolling sun stands still.
> His voice sublime is heard afar,
> In distant fields it dies;
> He yokes the whirlwind to his car
> And sweeps the howling skies."

The word that expresses the greatness of his personality is *omnipresence*. "Whither shall I go from thy Spirit? or whither shall I flee from thy presence? If I ascend up into heaven, thou art there: If I make my bed in hell, behold, thou art there. If I take the wings of the morning, and dwell in the uttermost parts of the sea; even there shall thy hand lead me, and thy right hand shall hold me. If I say, 'Surely the darkness shall cover me; even the night shall be light about me.' Yea, the darkness hideth not from thee : but the night shineth as the day: the darkness and the light are both alike to thee."

II. *As to his lifetime.* Let us call Moses to aid us: "Lord, thou hast been our dwelling place in all generations. Before the mountains were brought forth, or ever thou hadst formed the earth and the world, even from everlasting to everlasting, thou art God." (Ps. 90, 1, 2.) Again we are in the region of great dimensions. From everlasting to everlasting ! He is the sempiternal One.

"The days of our years are threescore years and ten; and if by reason of strength they be fourscore years, yet is their strength labor and sorrow; for it is soon cut off and we fly away." "The days of the years of Methuselah were nine hundred and sixty and nine years — and he died." And the gods of our handiwork are more ephemeral than we. The carven wood falls asunder of dry rot, and the graven statue crumbles into dust. But Jehovah is from everlasting to everlasting. Centuries come and go, but he abideth. Chaos and cosmos, principalities and powers; Egypt, Babylon, Rome; Cæsar, Alexander, Napoleon,—thrones, dynasties, great powers,—all are as spectres passing in a dream. "The cloud-capped towers, the gorgeous palaces, the solemn temples, the great globe itself, yea, all which it inherit, shall dissolve; and, like this insubstantial pageant faded, leave not a rack behind." But God is the same, yesterday, to-day and forever. He was before the beginning; and he shall be after the end.

The word which expresses his lifetime is *Eternity*. His being transcends time. No pendulum swings— no hour hand moves along the dial. To him there is no yesterday, to-day, or to-morrow; there is no succession of events. His life is *Punctum stans;* the everlasting now.

> Eternity with all its years
> Stands present to thy view:
> To thee there's nothing old appears,
> Great God, there's nothing new.

III. *As to the measure of his mind.* Here let us summon Isaiah to assist us: "My thoughts are not your thoughts, neither are your ways my ways, saith the Lord; for as the heavens are higher than the earth, so are my ways higher than your ways and my thoughts higher than your thoughts." (Isa. 55, 8, 9.) Here again we are in the region of great dimensions. How high are the heavens above the earth? Our largest visible neighbor is the sun; it is ninety-five millions of miles away. The Empire State Express would require a millennium to carry us there; and once at our destination we should see a shining orb so far distant that a cannon ball flying with the rapidity of light would require some hundreds of thousands of years to reach it. But this would only mark the nearer verge of the infinite concave of the heavens. And herein we find some slight expression of the infinitude of the mind of God.

The measure of mind is thought. How little are our thoughts! *Parturiunt montes; nascetur ridiculus mus.* We reach our intellectual best and highest when, as Keppler says, "we are thinking God's thoughts after him." There are three of his thoughts by which we may measure his mind:

1. *His thought of the world.* He has declared his purpose to save it. A lesser one would have cast it away, in its rebellion, as a father disowns a wayward and incorrigible son. History is the demonstration of his great purpose. To us events are threads and thrums, so that, confused and bewildered, we wonder what the outcome will be. The problem is full of minor problems and equations, all working toward an ultimate *quod erat demonstrandum.* The key is Redemption. The Flood, the Confusion of Tongues, the Jewish Dispersion, the Cross, the Great Commission, Magna Charta, the Reformation, Waterloo, the rise and fall of kingdoms and dynasties, are minor equations. One great thought runs through them all, glorious, eternal, proceeding with calm continuity toward the great consummation, the Golden Age.

2. *Another of God's thoughts is concerning man.* We have but a poor opinion of ourselves. In one of our favorite hymns we confess ourselves to be "worms of the dust." Those who move in scientific circles, while criticising this contemptuous expression, straightway proceed to prove themselves mere earthworms; born of bathybius; coming up to their present estate through a procession of bestial ancestors by the operation of such inevitable laws as natural selection and survival of the fittest; their brain mere phosphorus; their reflections and moral convictions the result of atomic friction; creatures of circumstance, bound for oblivion and a dusty grave.

But God thinks better things of us. We are his children, made in his likeness and after his image, his breath in our nostrils, inheriting a glorious birthright, capable of magnificent accomplishments, with sublime possibilities before us, our destination eternal life. Again the key is Calvary. We live like denizens of the earth; but the divine purpose in Christ Jesus is to make us forever "kings and priests unto God."

3. *And then, the great thought of man's relation to the world.* God might, perhaps, have lifted the earth back into its moral orbit by main strength. Or he might, in a great sunburst, have flooded it with light. But he said, "I will use men for its deliverance." We are his appointed agents in this blessed work. We strive together, in a goodly fellowship, by his appointment and under the power of his Spirit, for the accomplishment of his purpose in the restitution of all things. "Go ye, evangelize!" Sinners are to save a sinful world. It is a great business to which we are called, and well calculated to stimulate all our noble energies and to develop to the uttermost all the possibilities within us.

At this moment we are witnessing the effort of the Great Powers to dismember China. The "war lord" and his imperial rivals, with their brutal colonial policies, are hovering like highway robbers on the borders of the Celestial Empire, each intent upon securing a portion of its territory, with no more show of right than can be discovered in "the good old plan, that he may take who has the power, and he may keep who can." And God permits it. Do we wonder why? "The kings of the earth do set themselves, and the rulers take counsel together, saying,

Let us break his bands asunder and cast away his cords from us. He that sitteth in the heavens shall laugh; the Lord shall have them in derision." Who knows but that in the divine purpose the servants of God, working together in that great living organism which we call the Church, shall yet pursue the imperial robbers as they make off with this stolen territory and, after the calm methods of a blessed evangelization, seize the plunder and bring it, a "Celestial Empire" indeed, to be laid triumphantly at the Redeemer's feet?

IV. *As to the conscience of God.* Why not? It is true that metaphysicians, philosophers and theologians have made a strange omission here. Does not the moral faculty mark the highest dignity of man? Are we not made after the divine likeness? The moral sense is an inner vision by which we discern "between the worse and better reason," and an index finger which always points us toward the right. God himself is the source and center of moral distinctions. It is proper then to speak of his conscience, although we may be unable to measure it.

Let David help us at this juncture: "Thy righteousness, O Lord, is like the great mountains; thy judgments are a great deep." (Psa. 36, 6.) And Paul also: "O the depth of the riches both of the wisdom and knowledge of God! how unsearchable are his judgments, and his ways past finding out!" (Rom. 11, 33.) Our conscience is like a rusted needle on the pivot of a mariner's compass; it sticks and creaks and trembles, in its effort to point northward. But God's righteousness is like the great mountains which are unmoved by the winds and tempests that sweep over them. It is like the mighty deep which keeps an unruffled calm beneath the storms that superficially trouble it. His court is a court of equity; he issues no misjudgments. "Shall not the Judge of all the earth do right?" The scepter of the Lord is a right scepter; his ways are right; his judgments are right; his statutes are right forever and ever.

The word which expresses the divine conscience is *Holiness.* All heaven rings with the angelic tribute, "Holy, holy, holy! Lord God Almighty!" And the word which marks the highest attainment of human character is, Godliness; that is, God-likeness. To keep our moral decisions in line with the divine will, to determine all questions in casuistry by Revelation, to bring our conscience into such harmony with the divine conscience that our wills shall never cross his will,—this is to grow unto the full stature of a man.

V. *As to the heart of God.* Here again the measurement is infinite. "As far as the east is from the west, so far hath he removed our transgressions from us." (Ps. 103, 12.) How far is the east from the west? Turn the prow of your vessel toward the setting sun, sail on forever and you shall never reach it.

> "For the love of God is broader
> Than the measure of man's mind;
> And the heart of the Eternal
> Is most wonderfully kind."

It was the desire of David that his heart might be enlarged. But under the dominion of sin our capabilities are so limited that no man's heart is ever so great that his narrow breast cannot hold it. "Magnanimity" is a splendid word; but how trivial when compared with the love of the Infinite. This expresses itself in three progressive and cumulative words:

The first is *Pity*. "Like as a father pitieth his children, so the Lord pitieth them that fear him." At once we recall the picture of David staggering up the winding stairway to his chamber on the house top, crying, "O Absalom, my son, my son! Would God I had died for thee!" But pity of itself is helpless. Absalom was beyond the reach of his father's love.

The second is *Mercy*. It is more than pity, for it has an eager hand. The picture that comes to us is that of the good Samaritan gazing with compassionate eyes on the wounded stranger, crossing over, and ministering to his need. But there is a point at which mercy is unavailing. The wounds of the waylaid traveler may be beyond all service of wine and oil.

The third is *Grace*. It is more than pity with tearful eye; more than mercy with outstretched hand; it is an "arm made bare"—an omnipotent arm, bared for a mighty task. God's love finds its supreme expression in his grace as manifest on Calvary. It is his power to save. Here is the solution of the problem, "How can God be just and yet the justifier of the ungodly?" and of that other, "How shall a man be just with God?"

To measure the heart of the Infinite, we must get the dimensions of the cross. We call it the "accursed tree." Rather, it is the tree of life; its roots deep as hell, its crown in heaven, its branches, laden with the fruits of life, reaching out to the uttermost parts of the earth. On the cross the only-begotten Son of

God tasted death for every man. From the cross he offers redemption to the uttermost, not to respectable sinners only, but to thieves, harlots and reprobates. By the cross he saves utterly; nailing our indictment there, blotting out our sin, sinking it into the depths of an unfathomable sea, washing us, though stained as scarlet and crimson, until we are whiter than snow. This is the measure: "God so loved the world that he gave his only-begotten Son to suffer and die for it." That "so" is spelled with two letters, but it is vast enough to girdle the sin-stricken world and bind it back to God.

I said at the outset we were to address ourselves to an impossible task. All the dimensions by which we have sought to measure God have been infinite. His person is so vast that the heaven and the heaven of heavens cannot contain it. His lifetime is so long that it stretches from everlasting to everlasting. His mind is so great that his thoughts are high above ours as the heavens are above the earth. His conscience is like the high mountains and the mighty deep. And his heart finds expression in the removal of our sins as far as the east is from the west. Verily, our God is a great God above all gods. No golden band can compass his brow, no girdle bind his loins, no measuring line be laid upon him.

Our last word is a word of prayer. In Paul's letter to his Ephesian friends he desired them to form a just conception of the majesty of the God of Salvation as contrasted with that "Great Diana" under the walls of whose temple they dwelt. "For this cause," he says, "I bow my knees unto the Father of our Lord Jesus Christ, of whom the whole family in heaven and earth is named, that he would grant you, according to the riches of his glory, to be strengthened with might by his Spirit in the inner man; that Christ may dwell in your hearts by faith; that ye, being rooted and grounded in love, may be able to comprehend with all saints, what is the breadth, and length, and depth, and height; and to know the love of Christ, which passeth knowledge, that ye might be filled with all the fulness of God."

In this prayer he seems to be standing in a temple, vast and magnificent, whose walls forever recede as he gazes; above, below, on either hand stretching away illimitably. In view of this contemplation, how other gods dwindle and shrivel into naught. One alone remaineth; infinite, eternal, unchangeable. Canst thou by searching find Him out unto perfection? The measure thereof is longer than the earth, and broader than the sea. He is a great God above all gods!

HOW THE WORLDS WERE FRAMED.

"By faith we understand that the worlds have been framed by the word of God."—Heb. 11, 3.

The question of Origins is of universal interest. The child's bewildered eyes are asking, "Whence came I, and these things about me?" And it is a problem for the wisest minds, as well. Napoleon on the deck of a frigate on the Mediterranean, overhearing his marshals deny the personal God, pauses to point to the stars and ask, "But, gentlemen, whence came these?"

How shall we solve the query? By sight? Impossible. The facts lie beyond human cognizance. "Gird up now thy loins like a man," says God, out of the whirlwind; "for I will require of thee, and answer thou me, Where wast thou when I laid the foundations of the earth?"

Or shall we rest on hearsay? There is no lack of legends and traditions. Of making cosmogonies there is no end. The wise men of the past have wearied themselves in vain speculations; they have little to offer us.

Let us inquire of the Greeks. Their philosophers should be able to help in this investigation if there is any appreciable value in mere human wisdom. The starting point in their cosmogony, as elucidated by Thales, is water. In process of time it is wrought upon by an all-pervading energy, as the body is animated by the soul. Out of this energy proceed, in some inscrutable manner, all existing things. But there is no solution of the mystery here. The Gordian knot is cut; but we are left still to ask, "Whence the primal element and the pervading essence?"

Let us turn, then, to the Babylonians. The starting point in their natural philosophy is darkness. Out of the darkness proceeds a race of monsters. The mighty Belus slays a giantess; of half her body he makes the heavens, of the other half the earth; and, mixing her blood with the dust, he produces man.

What have the Hindus to say? They, too, begin with darkness. In the darkness is a golden egg; the egg breaks, and Brahma issues forth. He turns and makes of half the shell the heavens, of the other half the earth. Out of his own body proceed the various castes of men.

The Scandinavians place the Origin of all things in a profound chasm, wherein a conflict is going on between Fire and Ice. Out of this conflict emerges a race of giants. Ymyr, mightiest among them, is slain: his flesh produces the earth; his bones, the mountains; his hair, the forests; his blood, the seas and rivers; his skull, the dome of heaven; and from his eyebrows is made a wall around the earth to prevent its inhabitants from falling off.

And last, we inquire of the Egyptians. Their starting-point is a promiscuous pulp, from which the elements separate of their own accord. The mass takes fire, and the upper portion warms the lower into life. From beneath creep forth the reptiles, and out of the rising smoke the winged creatures of the air. The ooze of the river-bed—not unlike the evolutionist's *bathybius*—furnishes the material for man.

Such are the results of the efforts of human wisdom to produce a rational cosmology. We shall probably agree that little or no information is to be derived from this source. We turn, therefore, from speculation to science. Our century has been marked by a continuous effort on the part of scientists to produce a rational theory of the universe; this effort being complicated, in some quarters, by an avowed purpose to eliminate God. The results are not encouraging. The reason is plain: the scientific method is induction; it deals with facts and inferences. In this province there can be no hypothesis, for *scire* is "to know." The facts which stand as premises must be visible and tangible. The argument is that of cause and effect. But an origin is an entity without a visible cause; it is not to be accounted for by any operation of natural laws. The pure scientist has thus a necessary limitation, and frankly admits it. Science has its magnificent functions, but it cannot speak of origins with authority. It leaves unanswered the great primal question, ' Whence came I, and these things about me ? "

So there is nothing left but Revelation. Faith begins where science ends. It rests on divine authority. We turn, therefore, to the Mosaic account of the Creation. "By faith we understand that the worlds have been framed by the word of God."

But where did Moses get his information? To say that his record is a patchwork of current legends and traditions, is but to put the difficulty further back. The truth in cosmology, wherever found, must be by a direct revelation from God. But how? The word "revelation," or *unveiling*, describes the probable method. One may not speak dogmatically here; but there is force in the suggestion of Hugh Miller, that Moses received the divine communication in a series of panoramic visions. This is, indeed, after the analogy of the usual divine method. The seer, wrapped in an ecstatic trance, beholds a moving procession of events, broken by intervals of darkness, which are naturally characterized as night. Let us put ourselves in the dreamer's place and see what passed before him.

On the first canvas is a portrayal of chaos; a molten ball enveloped in igneous vapors. There is a conflict between the inward fires and the cooling winds from the illimitable fields of space. The outer surface of the earth is congealed again and again, only to be ruptured by the inward heat and thrown up into vast ridges of granite, "like ice-floes in a polar sea." The rising vapors are condensed in torrents of rain that pour down on the earth's surface, to be thrown back like water striking a white-hot cylinder. It is a hopeless battle. The fires are worsted; the earth gradually cools. A film forms over the molten sea; the primeval forms of continents appear. At length the rains find a lodgment and the rivers race toward the lower levels forming the primal seas. All is darkness and turmoil; reverberating artillery of the heavens, with fierce flashes of electric fire; black night and confusion worse confounded. Then a voice, "Let there be light!" And light is born; not in an instant, for this is cosmic light. A glimmer here and there reveals the unspeakable disorder of the frightful gloom; the glow brightens more and more, as light glimmers through a London fog.— The scene shifts. There is an interval of silence and darkness. "The evening and the morning were the first day."

In the second scene the clouds have lifted. The upper and the lower firmament are parted asunder; the outlines of continents and seas become plainly visible. The great canopy has been lifted overhead, and between that and the earth beneath sweep tempests of corrosive gases. Of this period alone it is not written. "And the Lord said, It is very good." As yet the atmosphere can sustain no form of organic being. The world is getting ready for life.—The curtain falls. The evening and the morning were the second day.

The third vision is of a great steaming greenhouse. From the sluggish waters springs a luxuriant vegetation. This is the age of bulbous plants, of sigillaria, and lycopodia, of ferns springing aloft, like towering pines, growing in incredible luxuriance, rapidly decaying, and falling upon one another until the steaming earth seems like a vast tamarack swamp. It is the carboniferous age. Forces are being bottled up for coming time.—The eyes of the dreamer close. The evening and the morning were the third day.

On the fourth canvas are seen glimmering points of light in the firmament above. Thus far there has been only cosmic light. The sun, moon and stars now appear in distinct outline; with them come the divisions of time. The pendulum begins to swing. The preparation goes on for summer and winter and seed-time and harvest. The world is getting ready for history.—The scene shifts. The evening and the morning were the fourth day.

The fifth vision brings in the lower orders of animal life. The egg-bearers appear; reptiles and fishes and birds. Here are creatures with eye-sockets a foot in diameter. Here are birds that leave mighty footprints on the soft formative rocks; lizards thirty feet long are crawling in the slime.—And the evening and the morning were the fifth day.

The sixth shows the mammals or higher forms of life. The earth is teeming with them,—beasts of the field and forest, of great rhinoceri and mastodons. There are ivory mines in Siberia which have been worked for a century and are still unexhausted.—And on this canvas, last of all, supreme and pre-eminent, appears man, having dominion over all living things, erect and sovereign, with face uplifted toward heaven and God; as it is written, "And God created man in his own image, in the image of God created he him."—And the evening and the morning were the sixth day.

Then the Sabbath. God has entered into his rest. "In six days the Lord created the heavens and the earth, and rested the seventh day." He left this period of rest as a heritage to those whom he had created after his own likeness and for his own glory. Wherefore, it is written, "the Lord blessed the Sabbath day and hallowed it."

How imposing this record as compared with the

puerile and grotesque cosmogonies of the false religions! What simplicity! What reasonableness! What an absolute tone of certainty! It makes no appeal to those who reject the supernatural; but it rests as the ultimate and authoritative record for all those who believe in the unseen and eternal. By faith, and by faith alone, we understand that the worlds have been framed by the word of God.

Our attention is called in this account to three stupendous facts; they are set forth in the words with which the Scripture opens, *B'reshith*, *Elohim*, *Bara;* that is, "In the beginning" "God" "Created."

1. *A beginning.* There is no beginning in any other cosmology; there is always something inscrutable beyond. For this reason there is a disposition among those who reject the Scriptural record to follow Plato in affirming the eternity of matter. This, however, is but an ignominious surrender of the problem. In the Scriptures we are carried back beyond man, organic life, cosmos, chaos, matter, nebula, into silence and solitude. And here we face the Great Original.

2. *God.* Back of the framing of the worlds, we confront him, "Source of all being, throned afar." We have not reached a blank domain of vacuity or nothingness. We stand in the doorway of the King's audience-chamber, saying, "Before the mountains were brought forth, or ever thou hadst formed the earth and the world, even from everlasting to everlasting, thou art God!" And from within there comes an answering voice, "I AM THAT I AM."

3. *Creation.* The word *Bara* suggests the making of something out of nothing. Do you say, "Impos-

sible!" Do you quote the venerable maxim, *Ex nihilo nihil fit*? But how do we know? All that we mean when we say that out of nothing nothing comes, is that we never saw it. In the nature of the case there can be no analogy. But let us not undertake to measure God by the rules of human life and action. All things are possible with God and nothing is too hard for him. We are like schoolboys in the playground, at recess, talking sagely about the infinite and indeterminable in loud, swelling words; the master comes, and what a scampering now! Thus God appears, when we in our proud wisdom have said our utmost, and speaks: "Ye do err, not knowing the power of God."

We observe also in the Mosaic record of creation *three points of striking coincidence* with the announcements of true science. And indeed there can be no real discrepancy. The same God who wrote the Scriptures has left himself on record in the stone book of nature. They must agree, for they bear the same imprimatur.

1. *The creative day.* "In six days the Lord made the heavens and the earth." But there are objectors who say: All research goes to prove that the periods of creation were of interminable length. The chalk cliffs, for example, are a product of animal life, being composed of the shells of minute submarine creatures. It is calculated that it would require a hundred years to produce a layer of a single foot; yet there are chalk cliffs on the coast of England a thousand feet deep, and beneath those cliffs are granite formations whose construction must have required some millions or perhaps billions of years. How

then could the world have been framed in six solar days ?—But who said it was ? Certainly not Scripture. Such an assertion is in direct contravention of the record. The Scriptures are not to be held responsible for the statements of foolish expositors. The word used to indicate the creative day is *Yom*. The same is also used in Gen. ii, 4, to denote the entire creative week. It is used in Leviticus xxv, 29, to indicate the year of jubilee. It is used in Jeremiah xlvi, 21, with reference to the long campaign of Pharaoh-Necho. It is used again in Ezekiel iii, 3, of the millennium; that is, the thousand years of the earthly reign of Christ. In Psalm ii, 7, it is made to cover all eternity. In these and other similar uses of the word we are given to understand that it means an indefinite period. We are not to think of God as a day laborer toiling between sunrise and sunset, and resting through the night. He makes no haste. He works through the illimitable ages by the calm processes of law. The eternal years are his.

2. *The order of the creative days.* Here again is a marvelous coincidence. The fossils and footprints in the layers of the primeval rocks are precisely in the Mosaic order. This is their succession: chaos, with the beginning of cosmic light; the dividing of the firmaments; the appearing of vegetable life in the palæozoic or carboniferous age; sun, moon and stars; the lower orders of life in the mesozoic age; the mammalia in the kainozoic age, with man as masterpiece and sovereign of all. We have spoken of this as a coincidence; is it not more? How shall we account for the fact that Moses, at that early period and with his narrow opportunities of learning,

should have thus anticipated the results of nineteenth century science?

3. *The creative act.* Here faith assists and supplements science. For there are certain questions at which science halts bewildered as on the verge of impassable gulfs; as here,—"Whence came matter?" Not a particle is man-made. We stand upon a ball of matter eight thousand miles in diameter, and no scientist has ever yet been able to produce an atom. And again, as to the beginning of life. Air and earth and water are teeming with it; yet no scientist can originate a bioplasmic cell, or animate a dead fly. Further still, as to the beginning of spirit, the divine part of man. A sculptor can make a statue, but can he give it a throbbing heart responsive to holy appeal, or cause it to articulate, "Our Father"? And then, as to the universal evidences of design, the adjustment of all things to their uses. To say that these are the result of law is no answer; for law is but blind energy if there be no Law-giver behind it.

The choice is obviously between chance and God. Did the present order of things come by fortuitous circumstance or did it proceed from a creative and controlling Mind? Let us see: There are sixty-one letters in our text. Suppose we take sixty-one leaden type, shake them together and cast them forth. Now calculate by the law of permutations and combinations how long it would require to produce by this method the words, "By faith we understand that the worlds were framed by the word of God." And how much more hopeless the problem becomes if we use as many letters as there are in the entire Scriptures. The period from the first glimmer of cosmic light to this moment, nay the vast æons of eternity itself, cannot be shown to be long enough to produce the desired result. Or take as many atoms of matter as constitute our world, not to mention the innumerable worlds floating in infinite space, and cast them forth to the mercy of fortuitous circumstance, and see how long it would require to produce in this manner a world like ours; a world of vales and forests and mountains, or birds and beasts and men. The mere suggestion of such a possibility is grotesque. There is indeed no solution of this problem but God.

It is pleasant, in this connection, to recall the testimony given by one of the most eminent scientists of our time, Professor Dana of Yale University. In his last interview with the Class of '67, he said, "Young men, let me say in parting with you, after our pleasant association in scientific study, that when you are puzzled and bewildered amid the conflicting views of human teachers, you can never go amiss if you will receive as your scientific ultimate the teachings of the Word of God."

But what is the practical bearing of such a discourse as this? Much every way. We stand facing two sphinxes; the one asking, "Whence?" the other, "Whither?" When we find an answer to the question of origin, we are not far from the solution of the problem of destiny. The same God who created us is caring for us.

I see two thrones: One is on the circle of the universe, where he sits high and lifted up, with veiled face, calling into being things that are out of those that were not. The other is on Calvary. Here the face is unveiled; the God of creation is the God of salvation. Behold, he is "the Lamb slain from the foundation of the world."

I hear two fiats: One is this, "In the beginning was the Word and the Word was with God and the Word was God; all things were made by him, and without him was not anything made that was made." The other brings us face to face with the incarnation and redeeming love. "The Word was made flesh and dwelt among us." Here are two august presentations of the Word of God, omnipotent on the one hand in the framing of the worlds, on the other in the salvation of the children of men.

> "'Twas great to call a world from naught,
> 'Tis greater to redeem."

When Dr. Simeon of Cambridge was dying he said, "I find my comfort in the word that is written, 'In the beginning God created the heavens and the earth.' He who originally framed the earth, can uphold and will never forsake me." Paul comforted the Christians of Colosse in like manner when writing to them of redemption through the Saviour's blood: "For by him were all things created that are in heaven and that are in the earth, visible and invisible, whether they be thrones or dominions or principalities or powers; all things were created by him and for him." Blessed be his name, who has thus joined together the remotest ends of history! We look for our deliverance and ultimate triumph to One who has demonstrated that nothing is too hard for him. "For God who commanded the light to shine out of darkness, hath shined in our hearts to give the light of the knowledge of his glory in the face of Jesus Christ."

"AS A REFINER OF SILVER."

"He shall sit as a refiner and purifier of silver."—Mal. 3, 3.

We are much given to asking, "Does God send trouble?" Why should he? We are born to trouble as the sparks fly upward. The French say, "Adversity comes in on horseback, and goes off afoot." All faces bear the marks of the plowshare. There are wrinkles and crow's-feet, the restless eye, hairs prematurely gray. All things are touched with sadness. There is ever a fly in the ointment, a cloud before the sun, a chill in the air. Is this God's doing? I do not believe it. By sin came all our woes. The order of the grim procession is: Sin, Death on the pale horse, and Hell following after with the mighty troop of human ills.

Shall we say, then, that our troubles are retributive? That depends. If I thrust my hand through a tradesman's window, two things follow: one is the sentence of the court, the other is a wounded hand. I may, for some reason, escape the sentence; but my hand is bound to bleed. So, in the course of human experience, we violate two laws, and pass under a double sorrow: one of these laws is written on God's statute Book, to violate which is to pass under the sentence of spiritual and eternal death; the other is written in the constitution of our nature.

We who believe in Jesus Christ have been delivered from all penalties; as it is written, "He hath blotted out the handwriting of ordinances that was against us and hath taken it out of the way, nailing it to his cross." In this sense, we are no longer under law, but under grace. Our Lord was wounded for our transgressions and bruised for our iniquities, in order that by his stripes we might be healed. He bore the penalty which was forensically due to us for violation of enacted law. But there are laws so interwoven with our being as to work automatically. If we violate them, we suffer the consequences here and now; and there is no escape. A man who breathes miasm will shake with an ague; and personal piety can not avert it. If he overeats, he must endure dyspeptic pangs, despite his faith in God. Such troubles are not the result of a forensic decree, and grace can not directly affect them. They are not penal, but consequential. In some measure they are due to heredity; in large measure also to personal folly. In either case they are inevitable, as being "ills that human flesh is heir to."

But what is the relation of God to such sufferings as these? "He sitteth as a refiner of silver." He does not kindle the fire beneath the crucible, neither does he quench it. One of the poets says:

> "Pain's furnace heat within me quivers,
> God's breath upon the fire doth blow."

But that is not true. God's breath does not fan the flame. Nor does his love quench it. He permits our sufferings; and he overrules them for our spiritual and eternal wellbeing. Paul prayed thrice that the thorn in his flesh might be removed; the answer was, "My grace shall be sufficient for thee." But still the question recurs, "Why does God permit his children to suffer?" It is not enough to refer the matter to his sovereign will. As Edward Payson lay on a bed of anguish, he was asked, "Do you see any reason for such a visitation as this?" "No," he replied; "but I am as well satisfied as if I saw a thousand; the will of my Father is reason enough." No doubt this should satisfy us, but somehow it does not. It has a hard, metallic ring. To say, "It is the Lord, let him do what seemeth him good"; or, "Who art thou that repliest against God?" is cold comfort. Our faith is not large enough to rest on such assurances. We want to know more; and, happily for our peace of mind, God stoops to reason with us. He makes quite clear the wholesome ministry of pain.

"Though losses and crosses be lessons right severe,
  There's wit there, ye'll get there, ye'll find nae itherwhere."

I. *Our troubles are divinely permitted in order that we may be weaned from the world.* We are constantly in danger of forgetting that we are not citizens of this world, but only pilgrims through it. "We look for a better country, even an heavenly, and for a city which hath foundations, whose builder and maker is God." But we incline to set our hearts upon the present life, and waste our energies on things that perish with the using. Our Father means that we shall not build houses here, but only tents to sojourn in.

His purpose is set forth beautifully in the parable of the eagle's nest. It was addressed to the children of Israel in their wanderings: "As an eagle stirreth up her nest, fluttereth over her young, spreadeth abroad her wings, taketh them and beareth them on her wings," so have I dealt with you. It is time for the eaglets to fly, but they will not. They are content in downy ease. Wherefore the mother-bird must needs disturb the nest; she breaks off twig by twig; she fluttereth overhead, chirping and calling upon her brood, in vain. Again she breaks off twig by twig, until the nest is wholly wrecked, and the fledgelings must fly or fall. Then she "fluttereth over them," and as their strength fails, she darts beneath and bears them up; then casts them forth again, and anon darts beneath, until at length they learn to fly.

The Jews dwelt in the land of Goshen as in a downy nest. They tilled their fields and multiplied their flocks; they were prosperous and, alas! content. Then the iron entered into their souls. The taskmaster came with his whip of scorpions and drove them into the brickyards. God saw him coming and allowed him to come. He meant his people not for the land of Goshen, but for another that flowed with milk and honey. The nest was thus broken up; the Jews, weary of the bitter bondage and unrequited toil of Egypt, were glad to journey toward the Land of Promise.

Did you make for yourself, my friend, a nest in prosperity? And were your earthly props and comforts taken away? Did there come a crash when your nest fell asunder? Did it seem as if God looked on, refusing to prevent it? Then, the world losing somewhat of its charm, you began to sing,

 " Rise, my soul, and stretch thy wings
 Thy better portion trace.
 Rise from transitory things,
 Toward heaven, thy native place!"

II. *We are allowed to suffer in order that we may seek the oracles.* This is what David meant when he said, " It is good for me that I have been afflicted, that I might learn thy statutes;" and again, "Before I was afflicted, I went astray ; but now have I kept thy word."

In our ferry boats there are placards directing attention to "Life-preservers under the Seats." You have seen the life-preservers there, unused and dusty. You have made a mental analysis, saying, "Cork and canvas." You have wondered as to the proper adjustment of the bands. But let an alarm of fire be heard, and you will learn more in a minute about life-preservers than you would in a thousand peaceful and contemplative trips across the ferry. So is it with the exceeding great and precious promises of Scripture. One-third of the Book has to do more or less directly with the rationale of trouble. But what are these promises to such as have never known adversity ? In the scorching sun we flee to the shelter of the great rock. When the tribes of the desert are upon us, we run into the fortress. Safe in the midst of danger, we say, "God is our refuge and strength; therefore, will we not fear, though the earth be removed and the mountains be cast into the midst of the sea." Let me put you in remembrance of the afflictions which have made precious such divine assurances as these: "Come unto me all ye that labor and are heavy laden and I will give you rest;" "He shall deliver thee in six troubles, yea in seven there shall no evil touch thee;" "He is a strength to the poor and to the needy in his distress, a refuge from the storm, a shadow from the heat, when the blast of the terrible ones is as a storm against the wall."

III. *The sorrows which we are divinely permitted to endure are great character-builders.*

> "Affliction is the good man's shining scene;
> Prosperity conceals his brightest ray;
> As night to stars, woe luster gives to man."

The two pillars on which character rests are *Faith in Christ as the Son of God*, and *Fellowship with Christ as the Son of Man*. We learn in adversity to trust Him as the Friend that sticketh closer than a brother. It is a familiar saying that no friend is worthy of full confidence until we have summered and wintered with him. We have summered with Christ on the slopes of Olivet, in the Mount of Transfiguration, in the upper room. But we have not fully made his acquaintance unless we have also wintered with him in the judgment-hall, at the olive press and on Golgotha. So are we enabled to say, "I know whom I have believed, and am persuaded that he is able to keep that which I have committed unto him against that day."

Thus also do we enter into fellowship with Jesus as the Son of Man; for we know that if we suffer with him we shall also be glorified with him. He was a Man of sorrows and acquainted with griefs. He goes before us through the wilderness of pain, like the pioneer in virgin forests, who breaks the twigs as he advances to mark the way for those coming after. As we follow in his steps,—footsteps marked with blood,—we enter into sympathy with Christ, and find a new significance in his word, "I will never leave thee nor forsake thee."

The truest beauty is the beauty of character; and the chiseling of pain completes it. There are faces that have a singular charm, not because of fair complexion or regular features, but by reason of an extraordinary light and sweetness that speak of perfection through suffering. This is indeed a reflection of that divine-human Face in which God revealed the beauty of his love.

And thus, *finally, our sorrows bring heaven near.* It is not unusual to hear it said, "This world is good enough for me." But indeed this world is not good enough for any child of God.

We are not fit for heaven until we have learned to long for it. Blessed are the homesick, for they shall inherit the Father's house. There are some of our most familiar hymns to which affliction only can attune our voices; such as

> O mother dear, Jerusalem!
> When shall I come to thee?
> When shall my sorrows have an end?
> Thy joys, when shall I see!
> Thy walls are made of precious stone,
> Thy bulwarks diamond-square,
> Thy gates are all of orient pearl—
> *O God, if I were there!*

I know a dear lady of above fourscore years, whose voice quavers and trembles as she sings her favorite hymn—an old-time hymn, precious to me from my cradle-days—a hymn that mellows with the remembrance of Baca and sweetens as the singer nears the border-land:—

"O when shall I see Jesus, and reign with Him above,
To drink the flowing fountain of never-ending love?
To see the saints in glory, and the angels stand rejoicing;
And the angels stand rejoicing, to welcome travelers home!"

We have reviewed some of the uses of adversity; enough, I trust, to satisfy us that God means kindly. There is no chance in our affliction, nor is there any stern decree. God saw the prodigal as he went over the hills to the far country. He saw him there wasting his substance in riotous living. He saw him going down step by step, through lawless pleasure to poverty and shame. He saw him putting off his fine raiment, donning a smock-frock and going into the fields to feed swine. He saw the fiend of darkness lashing him at every step until he reached the bottom. And he permitted it. He permitted it, because he knew that, sitting there in rags and hunger, the man's better nature would awake, and that in his shame and anguish he would cry, "I will arise and go unto my father!"

Ah, this is a sharp plowshare; but what matters that, if the harvest be sure? It is a bitter medicine, but, blessed be God if health shall come of it! It is a fierce fire, burning under the furnace, but behold how the Refiner watches the crucible, with what jealous love and care, until he sees his face reflected from the silver.

So, beloved, all is right. God knows what is best. We live forever, and our probationary years in this world are divinely adjusted and adapted to our deepest need. A great infidel has said, "Had I been intrusted with the making of a world, I could have made a better one." No doubt. And there are five hundred men in Sing Sing who feel the same way. Indeed, if this world were a rounded whole, we may well conceive how it might have been a better one. But our present life is only a handbreadth; death does not end all. We are getting ready for eternity, for our Father's house.

"Blest be the sorrow, kind the storm,
That drives us nearer home!"

One word more: *All depends on our way of bearing sorrow;* as it is written, " No affliction for the present seemeth to be joyous, but grievous; nevertheless, it worketh the peaceable fruits of righteousness to them that are exercised thereby"; that is, to those who are wise enough to profit by it. Lord Byron had a clubfoot, and it embittered his life. Walter Scott had a clubfoot also; but it sweetened his whole nature, so that all men love Sir Walter. The Lord help us to bear our afflictions in the right spirit, mindful of his great kindness in permitting and overruling them. It is not enough to say, "I will be patient and submit." Nay; let us be joyfully acquiescent. Let us catch the spirit of Paul when he cried, "We glory in tribulation, knowing that tribulation worketh patience, and patience experience, and experience hope, and hope maketh not ashamed, because the love of God is shed abroad in our hearts by the Holy Ghost which is given unto us."

The time is coming when God's providence will be made clear. "The bud may have a bitter taste, but sweet will be the flower." What we call troubles are mercies in disguise. We suffer for a little time, that we may reign forever. The day is not far distant when we shall know the full significance of those words: "Our light affliction, which is but for a moment, worketh for us a far more exceeding and eternal weight of glory;" and when, looking back over all the checkered experience of our wilderness journey, we shall strike the harp and sing with cordial joy and gratitude: "I reckon that the sufferings now past and gone are not worthy to be compared with the glory which is now and forevermore revealed in us!"

ONE RELIGION; ALL OTHERS FALSE.

"Sirs, what must I do to be saved?"—Acts 16, 30.

The deep longing of the universal heart was here voiced by the Philippian jailer. It took an earthquake to shake it out of him. Many of us are disposed to repress it; but all are sensible of sin. All feel the justice of the sentence, "The soul that sinneth, it shall die." All have learned from experience the utter futility of self-deliverance. So it happens that, deep down in every breast, the question throbs for utterance, "What shall I do to be saved?"

And here enters religion. The word is from *religare*, to bind back. The business of a religion is to restore the alienated soul to its original relation with God. The test of all religions, therefore, true and false alike, is this question, "What must I do to be saved?" We hear it said that one religion is as good as another if only there be absolute sincerity. To speak thus betrays a lack of comprehension of the problem. This will appear in a candid survey of the great systems which have come into contact with the one true religion; the touchstone of comparison being the question of personal salvation. We need have no misgivings as to the result. The gospel of Jesus Christ does not shrink from the closest and most searching scrutiny and comparison with other religious systems. It proposes to save sinners from the shame, the bondage and the penalty of their sin; and herein, as we shall discover, it stands solitary and alone. It is the one religion; all others are false. That is to say, the ethnic religions are man-made; Christianity alone is from God.

I. We begin with *the Religion of Egypt*, the oldest of all. Our knowledge of it is chiefly derived from the papyrus and byssus bands which are unrolled from the mummies. We are enabled thus to form a somewhat clear conception of the sacred book known as "The Book of the Dead."

1. The god of this religion was Ammon-Ra; that is, the sun, as center and source of life. He is represented as a hawk-headed man, his forehead encircled with the solar disk. He was worshiped by the priests in "mysteries," but to the people all forms of life were objects of devotion. The ibis, the crocodile, the scarabæus, the lizard and the snake,—all these were worshiped as proceeding from Ammon-Ra, the mystic Origin of Life.

2. The Egyptians believed in immortality. They carved upon their mummy crypts the image of the Phœnix rising from its ashes, and the lotus flower opening with the early sun. The dead were embalmed in the hope that, in the fulness of time, Ammon-Ra would revive them. The coffin itself was called "The chest of life."

3. They also believed in a final judgment. On many of their tombs the god Anubis is represented with balances in hand; a human heart in one scale, a feather in the other. Alas! the heart is lighter than

a feather! The teaching of the "Book of the Dead" is as clear with respect to final retribution as that of our own Scriptures: "We must all appear before the judgment seat of God, that every one may receive according to that he hath done, whether it be good or bad."

But what has the religion of Egypt to say in answer to the crucial question, "What shall I do to be saved?" The only preparation for judgment was obedience to the *Maat*, or rule of right living. It cannot be determined with precision what were the precepts in this elaborate code. This, however, is clear: In case of failure to obey the *Maat*, there was no remedy. It is this that stamps the Egyptian system as "the religion of despair." It contains no suggestion of forgiveness. Thus, while the Egyptians were the most mirthful people on earth, they were the saddest of worshipers. It is written, "They offered tears upon the altars of their gods." An illustrious lady, the wife of Pasherenptah, is represented as thus addressing her husband from the grave: "O my beloved, forbear not to eat and drink and drain the cup of pleasure while you live; for here is the land of slumber and darkness. We weep for the pleasures that have passed by."

II. *The religion of the Greeks.* They were, as Paul said, "exceedingly devout." In their pantheon we observe the exaltation of Nature. Zeus, the All-father, was the deification of æther. He reigned on the heights of Olympus; the lightning was the flash of his eye; and with his javelin, the thunderbolt, he hurled his foes down the mountain side. The minor gods and goddesses, who assembled about him, were personifications of natural forces. Apollo curbed "the fierce, flame-breathing steeds of day." Athene was the spirit of the morning, rising from the brow of the sky. A god was here for every river, a nymph for every brooklet. Troops of sirens came from the mossy clefts, and Oreads from the hills to claim their tribute of devotion; while dryads brought with them oracular secrets from the rustling oaks. It was a beautiful system, and should have been quite satisfactory and ultimate if it were possible for natural theology to satisfy the cravings of the immortal soul.

But the Greek deities, though made after a large pattern and endowed with extraordinary gifts, were only mortals projected on the skies. In their Olympian life they ate and drank, made war and love, quarreled and sinned, reveled and slept. Hermes was a thief; Aphrodite, a drab; Athene, an adept at billingsgate; Hera, no better than she ought to be; and Zeus, their worthy sire, a base deceiver who ofttimes drank too deeply of the mirth-inspiring nectar and was faithless to his wife, whom he "hung up in midheaven with anvils tied to her heels."

The festivals in honor of these gods were a magnificent display of utter sensual *abandon*. There were dances, tourneys, athletic sports, processions and chariot races. There were dramatic representations of the adventures of the Olympian gods in which lewd dancers, flushed with wine, ministered to the basest passions of men.

The failure of such a religion was a mere question of time. Doubt and inquiry arose. Lucian and the other satirists began to write ruthlessly against the gods. On went the unmasking of the tricksters.

The shrines were abandoned; the altar-fires were extinguished; and from the deep recesses of the forests the winds came wailing, "*Eleleu! Eleleu! — Great Pan is dead!*"

Then came the philosophers, lovers of wisdom. They were the protestants of their time, who fearlessly approached the stalking ghosts and spectres of the national religion and laughed them out of court. Plato founded the Academy and discoursed on virtue as the most desirable thing. Epicurus in his Garden exalted the emotions above the intellect; leaving to posterity the strange maxim, "Let us eat and drink, for to-morrow we die." Zeno, in his Painted Porch, founded the school of the Stoics; making expediency the highest rule of action. The Cynics, led by Diogenes, taught a philosophy steeped in gall. The Skeptics glorified doubt; they were the ancestors of our modern Agnostics, their chief dictum being, "We assert nothing; no, not even that we assert nothing." The Peripatetics, with Aristotle as their illustrious tutor, originated the inductive method of reasoning; and, drifting into practical materialism, rejected as unsubstantial all the great verities of the eternal life.

It will be observed that the philosophers failed, as utterly as the priests, to answer the great question, "What shall I do to be saved?" The earnest youths who walked amid the plane trees by the Ilissus had much to say of the Cardinal Virtues and the symmetry of a noble life; but they suggested no escape from the mislived past and left the doorway of the tomb shrouded in unbroken night. Socrates, the noblest of them all, with the fatal hemlock at his lips, could only say, "I take comfort in the hope that something may remain of man after his death." The priests and the philosophers gave no real comfort or positive assurance to those who longed for the endless life. Ixion was left bound to the wheel. The vultures still gnawed at the vitals of Prometheus, the prisoner of death and despair. Tantalus still abode in hell with the ever-receding waters close to his thirsty lips.

III. *Brahmanism.* An army of pilgrims coming from the great table-lands of the Caspian—so long ago that in our endeavor to trace them we lose ourselves in prehistoric mists—crossed the Hindu-Kush Mountains and took forcible possession of the banks of the Indus, announcing themselves as the superior race. In order to sustain this assumption, they invented the fable of Brahm issuing from the primeval egg, and creating from his head the Brahmans; from his breast the soldiers; from his loins the merchants; and from his feet the laboring class. Here was the beginning of that iron-banded system of caste which has prevailed in India for thirty centuries, crushing its best energies like the mountain resting on Typhon's heart.

The sacred book of the Brahmans is the *Rig-Veda*. As to its character we may safely accept the judgment of Max Muller, who apologizes for the deficiencies of his own translation by saying, that a complete rendering would have made him liable to prosecution under the English law against the publication of obscene literature. The three fundamental doctrines of the Veda are as follows:

1. Brahm, the inconceivable One. He is so far removed from all human understanding that "it can-

not be asserted that he is known nor yet that he is unknown."

2. Maya, or illusion. Nothing really exists except Brahm. Men are merely sparks from the central fire, separated for a time, to be absorbed at last. Our life with all its varied experiences is but "an illusory phantom such as a conjurer calls up."

3. Apavarga, the supreme good. This is to lose self-consciousness, in being finally merged into the ineffable One. The soul is like a drop of water, exhaled by the sun, floating for a time in vapor, at length falling into the sea.

What, then, shall the Brahman do to be saved? His only salvation is extinction. This is to be reached "by faith"; that is, by an unreserved yielding up of self to the contemplation of Brahm. If you would find a Hindu saint, search for him by the roadside. You will find him there crouching upon his knees, naked, with hair uncombed, the Vedas before him. His body is smeared with ashes and dung. His countenance wears a look of utter stupidity. He is intently contemplating one of his long finger-nails. This is "the twice-born Yogi," the consummate fruit of Brahmanism. And this is the answer the Vedas give to the question, "What shall I do to be saved?" The twice-born Yogi is losing himself in the Soul of the Universe. He has no longer any consciousness of guilt, no passion nor appetite. He moves not, speaks not, except when, with a spiritual pride which would be grotesque were it not so unspeakably pathetic, he lifts his dreamy eyes, and mutters, "I am God! I am God!"

IV. *Buddhism.* A child was born about 500 B.C.

in the royal city of Oude, who, as the oracles say, was destined for great things. At the moment of his birth he walked three paces and in a voice like thunder proclaimed himself the Fulfillment of Hope. The air was instantly filled with perfume, songs were heard in the distance, and lotus flowers dropped from the sky. The life of this wonderful child was thenceforth a continuous tale of marvels, until at length, in early manhood, he found himself under the sacred Bo-tree. While meditating there, the great truth—which indeed no living man can define —came to him like a sunburst; and he went forth to work Deliverance. At Benares he gathered a company of disciples about him, and, with their aid, compiled the sacred book known as *Tripitika*, or "The Three Baskets." It contains an amount of literature almost bewildering — about three hundred volumes folio. It is chiefly devoted to the importance of self-culture, or the development of the intellectual as distinguished from the carnal life. Its three fundamental doctrines are as follows :

1. Buddh; that is, the all-pervading Mind.

> " An immense solitary Spectre stands,
> It hath no shape, it hath no sound,
> It hath no place, it hath no time.
> It is, and was, and will be ;
> It is never more nor less, nor glad, nor sad;
> Its name is *Nothingness.*
> Power walketh high, and Misery doth crawl,
> And the clepsydron drips,
> And the sands fall down in the hour-glass ;
> Men live and strive, regret, forget,
> And love, and hate, and know it.
> The Spectre saith, '*I wait!*'

And at the last it beckons, and they pass ;
And still the red sands fall within the glass,
And still the water-clock doth drip and weep;
And that is all !"

The God of the Buddhists is indeed a specter; he has no eyes to see, no heart to pity, no arms to save. He is represented as sitting aloft in an imperturbable calm, unmoved by the pain and struggle of mankind —an inactive, impersonal, valueless ghost of a god.

2. Karma, or the Law of Consequences. As a man soweth, so shall he also reap. There is no escape. There is no pardon, no averting the doom. The law is automatic, administering itself; constant as one's shadow.

> The mills grind slow,
> But they grind woe.

3. Nirvana. This is the Buddhist's only heaven. It is defined as "the harbor of never-ending rest." It is indeed but another term for total annihilation. The path to Nirvana is through endless transmigrations. The Buddhist's noblest wish is to shorten the period of these successive cycles of existence, and lose his personality at last. To accomplish this he must conquer all feeling and attain to a sublime indifference to everything in life.

The moral code of Buddhism is contained in the Noble Eight-fold Path, which is: Right Belief, Right Feeling, Right Speech, Right Action, Right Means of Livelihood, Right Endeavor, Right Memory, and Right Meditation. To observe this Eight-fold Path will bring one to a final absorption in the soul of the universe. This is the answer which the Buddhist gives to the great question. His only conception of salvation is an utter loss of personal being, and even this is to be reached only by an absolute observance of law. In default of obedience, he must continue on the weary pilgrimage. The best that he can hope for is to breathe at last the odor of the lotus flower, and sink into oblivion like a raindrop in the sea.

V. *Confucianism.* Just outside the capital city of China stands an image, with a memorial tablet bearing this inscription, "*Kung-foo-Tse*, A king without a kingdom, yet reigning in hearts innumerable." The religion of the Chinese Empire, with its five hundred millions of people, is little more than a personal reverence for this illustrious man. He was superintendent of parks in the province of Lu, and, being brought into contact with much official corruption, was, as his biographer says, "frightened at what he saw." The times were out of joint; the Empire seemed hastening to its fall. K'ung Fu-tze, or Confucius, stood forth, saying; "I show you a more excellent way. It is foolish to speak of God and heaven and incomprehensible things. One thing we know; that is, present life and present duty. There is a region lying at our doors, where each may put forth his best energies for the public good." It will be seen that his purpose was not to originate a religious system, but to reform the present order. The sacred book is the "Analects of Confucius." Its central thought is The Kingdom. Christ also spoke of a Kingdom; by which he meant the Kingdom of Truth and Righteousness, the Kingdom of Heaven, the Kingdom of God. But the kingdom of which Confucius dreamed was of a far more material sort; it was the Chinese Empire. His "religion" is merely a system of civil economics. The Confucianist looks forward to no heaven; he dreams of no tabernacle descending from above in millennial glory. His Celestial Empire is China here and now. The three duties pre-eminently set forth in the Analects are as follows:

1. Filial Piety. The kingdom is regarded as a large family in which the Emperor is father of all. The prime duty of every citizen is reverence for his political father; after that for civil functionaries; then for his father in the flesh; finally for all his ancestors. In no other country are the obligations that flow from the filial relation more thoroughly respected than in China. There is no sentiment in this, however; its object is the conservation of the state.

2. Veneration for Learning. The scriptures of the Celestial Empire are a compilation of the wise sayings of the sages. These are purely secular. "When we know so little about life and its duties," said the great teacher, "how can we be expected to say anything about death or what comes after it?"

3. Reverence for the past. China has been at a standstill for twenty centuries. The old order changeth not. The ideas of the Chinese are musty and mildewed and—like their faces, their houses and their junks—all made after one pattern. As to the question, "What shall I do to be saved?" there is no voice nor answer nor any that regardeth. The word "Salvation" was rubbed out of their vocabulary by Confucius. They are a race of materialists, dull, plodding, heedless of eternity as moles.

> " To be content's their natural desire;
> They ask no angel's wings nor seraph's fire."

VI. *Islam.* The camel-driver of Mecca seems to have been at the outset a pure-minded and kindly-disposed dreamer of dreams; but in the year of the Hejira, A.D. 622, when he was driven out of his native city, his spirit was changed. As he issued from the gates of Mecca he unsheathed his sword and became a red-handed sensualist. The call to prayer was mingled with the summons to the Holy War. No quarter must be given to unbelievers. "Fight against them," said the prophet, "until not one shall be left to oppose us and the only religion shall be that of Allah the true God."

He gathered his disciples about him and produced the Koran. It is regarded as more than an inspired book, being "the uncreated Word of God." The angel Gabriel brought him the silken scroll on which it was inscribed, commanding him to read. He said, "I cannot read." Thereupon the angel shook him thrice and, lo, the inscription became as clear as light. He forthwith caused it to be transcribed on white stones, leather, palm leaves, the shoulder blades of camels and the breasts of men. The Koran consists of one hundred and fourteen surahs or chapters, each of which begins with the words, "In the name of the merciful and compassionate God."

The most succinct statement of Mohammedan belief is found in the *Kalima*, or creed; which is as follows: *La Ilah illa Allah; wa Muhammad Rusoul Allah*— "There is no god but God, and Mohammed is his prophet." The two propositions of this creed are called by Gibbon "The eternal truth and the eternal lie."

The Eternal Truth is this, "There is no god but God." It must be explained, however, that the God of Islam is the apotheosis of pure will. There is no love, mercy or sympathy in him. He is called by ninety-nine names in the Koran, but "Father" is not among them. The closest relation which a believer can sustain to this god is expressed in *Islam ;* that is, submission to the supreme will. Out of this conception grows the Moslem's belief in fate, or *Kismet.* All things being controlled by an infinite Will; what is to be must be, and there is no resisting it. Hence the desperate valor of the Moslems in battle. The day of a man's death is inscribed on his forehead and he can do nothing to avert it. The creation of the race is described as follows: Allah took into his hands a mass of clay, and dividing it in two equal portions, he threw one-half into hell saying, "These to eternal fire and I care not!" and, tossing the other upward, he added, "These to Paradise and I care not!" This is predestination with a vengeance.

The Eternal Lie is this, "And Mohammed is his prophet." The camel-driver of Mecca has come down through the centuries grasping a sword crimson with blood; he is attended on one side by the master of the harem, on the other by the Arab slave-driver. Thus in spirit he leads the Moslem host to-day as they push their conquests downward from the northern coasts of Africa among the barbaric tribes. In this Holy War the three historic evils of savagery are perpetuated : war, polygamy and slavery. Put over against this figure of the false prophet, the Christ of Calvary leading on his militant Church with no weapon save the sword of the Spirit which is the Word of God.

We have finished our brief survey of the six greatest of the false religions. There are some conclusions which we must have reached. *First:* There is a measure of truth in each of these religions. How could it be otherwise, since God has never left himself without a witness? There is gold in quartz, in the granite of the mountains, in auriferous sands, even in the waves that roll in upon the Pacific coast. But the question is, "Is it there in paying quantities? and can it be separated from the dross?" *Secondly:* There is somewhat of sound morality in each of the false systems, but in every case it is hopelessly mingled with the basest sentiments. By universal consent the ethical code of Christianity, as represented in its two great symbols, the Decalogue and the Sermon on the Mount, is absolutely perfect. There is nothing to be added, nor anything to be taken from it. *But thirdly:* The determining factor in our argument is the question, "What must I do to be saved?" To this the false religions give no answer. They all fail at the point where they are most needed. Not one of them has any suggestion to make as to our deliverance from the horror of a mislived past. Is there any escape? Can the record be blotted out? Aye! "The blood of Jesus Christ cleanseth from all sin."—"He that believeth on the Lord Jesus Christ shall be saved." This is *Spes Unica;* the only hope. "There is none other name under heaven given among men, whereby we must be saved." We look in vain among all the sacred books of the false religions for any doctrine corresponding to justification by faith.

> There is a fountain filled with blood
> Drawn from Immanuel's veins;
> And sinners, plunged beneath that flood,
> Lose all their guilty stains.

"I am not ashamed of the gospel of Christ; for it is the power of God unto salvation to every one that believeth." On this we build our confident hope that Christianity shall be the universal religion. It is the true religion, and the truth must ultimately prevail. The glory of the Lord Christ is destined to cover the earth as the waters cover the sea.

THE GLORY IN THE FACE OF JESUS CHRIST.

"For God, who commanded the light to shine out of darkness, hath shined in our hearts, to give the light of the knowledge of the glory of God in the face of Jesus Christ."—II. Cor. 4, 6.

The key of the argument is the word "For." Paul has been saying, "We preach not ourselves but Christ Jesus our Lord, and ourselves your servants for Jesus' sake." He was pre-eminently a Christological preacher. At the moment of his conversion he had asked, "Lord, what wilt thou have me to do?"—not that he had previously lacked employment, for as arch-inquisitor of the Sanhedrin he had been a very busy man. But the flash-light glimpse which he had caught of the face of Jesus, revolutionized his life. The things done in his past life were instantly seen to be not worth the doing. The vision, the dazzling light, the words, "I am Jesus," suggested a new mastership and drew from him the quick, acquiescent response, "What wilt thou have me to do?"

He was directed to go into Damascus, where in due time it should be told him what he must do. He was led, stricken with blindness, to a certain home in the street called "Straight"; and there he waited for the word which was to change the tenor of his life.

One day a disciple of Jesus came and, laying a kindly hand upon him, said, "Brother Saul, the Lord Jesus hath sent me that thou mightest receive thy sight and be filled with the Holy Ghost." He was then told of his appointment "as a chosen vessel to declare the name of Jesus before the Gentiles and kings and the children of Israel." This was his mission; this was his commission. Straightway he began to preach, accordingly, that Jesus is the Christ. In the synagogues, in the public streets, on Mars' Hill, in prison, on the steps of the Castle of Antonia, on shipboard, in palaces and judgment halls, his message was always the same, "This Jesus is the Christ!"

No doubt there were those among his hearers who would have heard the learned Rabbi discourse on other themes. He was competent to speak on the false philosophers of his time, on governmental science, on current events; but he was determined to "know nothing but Christ and him crucified." By reason of his familiarity with the arts of logic and rhetoric he might doubtless have made a mark for himself as the sensational preacher of his time; but to his mind there was nothing of more absorbing interest or more truly "sensational" than the great tragedy on Calvary. He was scourged, imprisoned, stoned, cast out of the synagogues, haled before magistrates; but he went right on preaching Christ. Why not? The love of Christ constrained him. The gospel filled the horizons of his life. Christ was around him like the air, over him like the dome of heaven, under him like *terra firma*. Christ had arisen in his soul like a morning sun, so that all minor lights cast a shadow. He could think of nothing but Christ, speak of nothing but Christ. And here is his apology: "For God, who commanded the light to shine out of darkness, hath shined in our hearts to give the light of the knowledge of the glory of God in the face of Jesus Christ."

I. *God had shined into his heart.* No greater revelation can come to any man. To know God—this is life eternal. It is easy to speak the word—a little word of three letters,—but what vast measures of truth are contained in it. Paul had been a religionist all his life. He had been graduated from the University of Jerusalem with the title Doctor of Divinity. He was familiar with the teachings of the Rabbis and an expert in the various schools of Greek philosophy. But he had never known God until the moment when this great light fell upon him. He had worn the cabalistic phrase, "Hear, O Israel, the Lord our God is one Lord," on the frontlet between his eyes. He was familiar with the conventional phrases respecting an "All-pervading Soul," a "Something-that-maketh-for-righteousness," and the "Essence of things." But now God had shined into his heart, and in this sunburst a new conception of life and duty and character had come to him.

He likens it to the original fiat: "Let there be light!" The God who had made himself manifest to him was the God who had "commanded light to shine out of darkness." The primeval world was a surging, steaming mass; elements in confusion; lightnings and thunderings; embryotic continents elbowing their way out of the roaring waters. Then the fiat; all nature felt it; life and beauty appeared; order and gladness; blooming flowers and singing birds.

> " God said, ' Let there be light ! '
> Grim darkness felt his might
>   And fled away.
> Then startled seas and mountains cold
> Shone forth all bright in blue and gold,
>   And cried, ' ' Tis day ! ' Tis day ! ' "

The unregenerate heart is like chaos: it is a world of crude and unorganized potencies. Will, mind and conscience are disordered. Paul says that he had sought in a pure conscience to serve God from His youth up. As he went forth from the hall Gazith to persecute the followers of the Nazarene, "breathing out slaughter," like a lion with red-stained lips, he "verily thought He was doing God service." But the light from heaven revealed his error. Bystanders, as they saw him led away, said, "He is blind"; but, though his fleshly eyes were closed, his inner vision was opened to behold things which he never had dreamed of. One truth was now as clear as day : "This Jesus is the Christ." Jesus, whom he had rejected, whose followers he had persecuted, was now and henceforth his Alpha and Omega, the beginning of every purpose, the end of every aspiration.

The shining of God into a human heart is always a revolutionary experience. It reverses all religious conceptions, and transforms character. The man who has seen the great light from heaven can never again be the same man; he cannot enter a sanctuary with the old feeling, he cannot go into his workshop with the old purpose. He has been born into the kingdom of truth and righteousness. His whole nature cries out, "What wilt thou have me to do?" Wealth, pleasure, personal emolument, all former pursuits, dwindle into naught. Old things are passed away; behold, all things are become new.

II. *To give the light of the knowledge of the glory of God.* But how could that be? Who can apprehend the glory of God?

The Jews say that Joshua, one of their ancient Rabbis, was summoned by the Emperor Trajan, who said, "You teach that your God is everywhere; show him to me." The Rabbi answered, "No mortal eye can behold him." "I am the emperor; show him to me." "No man can see God and live; but I will show thee one of his ambassadors." "Where is he?" The Rabbi pointed to the noonday sun. The Emperor exclaimed, "It dazzles me!" And Joshua said, "If thou canst not look upon one of his creatures, how canst thou behold him who is Creator of all?"

On one occasion Moses, being fearful and discouraged, prayed, "O God, show me thy glory!" And the Lord said, "I will make my goodness pass before thee, and I will proclaim my name before thee." And Moses hid in the cleft of the rock and waited. He heard the rustle of a garment, and saw a shadow pass by. That was all.

In the darkest hour of Jewish history the prophet Elijah fled into the wilderness, where the Lord appeared to enhearten him. A rushing wind swept over the mountain, but the Lord was not in the wind. Then the earth shook and trembled; but the Lord was not in the earthquake. Then a mighty conflagration; but the Lord was not in the fire. After that a still, small voice, and the voice said, "What doest thou here, Elijah? *Return to thy work.*"

The Prophet Isaiah, under similar circumstances, beheld a vision. He saw the Lord upon a throne high and lifted up; and his train filled the temple. He heard the seraphim crying to one another, "Holy, holy, holy is the Lord of Hosts!" and the house was filled with "the smoke of his presence." Then the prophet cried, "Woe is me! for I am undone; because I am a man of unclean lips: for mine eyes have seen the king!" In fact he had only seen the Shechinah, the luminous cloud in which God tempered the brightness of His glory; and it affrighted him. Then one of the seraphim came with a live coal from the altar, and laid it upon his lips, and a voice asked, "Whom shall I send, and who will go for us?" And the prophet, strengthened by his vision, replied, "Here am I; send me."

It thus appears that to catch a glimpse of the ineffable glory is to be mightily stimulated for service. We turn aside to frivolous pursuits, forget the great commission, squander our energies, lose heart, and fall into doubt and perplexity for lack of the vision. If to know God is life, to see his glory is a girdle of faithfulness. O that he would shine into our hearts to give the light of his glory!

III. *In the face of Jesus Christ.* At the moment when Paul was struck with blindness, this is what he saw—the divine glory shining in the face of Jesus Christ. Nowhere else can this glory be unveiled to human sight. We cannot look on God, in his essential being, and live; but in the incarnation he has condescended to reveal himself to us.

Paul had never seen Jesus in the flesh. He had heard of him as a carpenter, a man of the people, a setter-forth of strange truths. He had heard of his sermons, of his miracles, of his ignominious death, of his alleged resurrection: and he had doubtless taken all these with a grain of allowance. But now he saw him, heard his voice, saw God's glory shining in his face. He no longer wore a crown of thorns, no longer bore the marks of blood and spitting. His face was illumined with a light above the brightness of the sun. His simple word, "I am Jesus," born with it an irresistible force of conviction. No need of argument; the glory in the face of Jesus was enough. He whom Saul of Tarsus had despised as the crucified Nazarene was indeed "the brightness of the Father's glory and the express image of his person." In that moment Saul caught a glimpse of the mystery of the Incarnation, as the unveiling of the Infinite and Eternal One.

Is it not singular that in the inspired biographies of Jesus there is no description of his face? In vain have the great masters tried to portray it. Rubens, Murillo, DaVinci, Raphael, Titian, Guido, Angelo, Fra Angelico, all have attempted this in vain. But those who believe in Christ have something better than a portrait, better than a historic description, better than an artist's ideal. In the heart of every believer there is a face, bright with transcendent beauty, which words cannot describe; but day by day he lives in the light of it and rejoices in the glory of it.

And, however we may differ as to our conception of this divine face, there are some particulars in which all will agree: (1) *It is a pure face.* And herein it is unique. All human faces bear the marks of sin. What we call beauty is merely conventional. There is no beauty but the beauty of holiness; and this is never seen, in its perfection, in any human countenance. Sin ploughs furrows across the brow, corrupts the blood and blears the eyes. Retribution leaves its traces on the fairest features and heredity perpetuates the blemish. A photographer's negative must be "retouched," not because his art is imperfect, or the light is in default, but because the human face is unfit to bear the searching processes of the sun. In the face of Jesus, however, there was no defect. There was no guile in his heart, nor could there be outward sign of it. He is fairer than the children of men; grace is poured into his lips.

It is (2) *a strong face.* The mark of manly power is upon it. He wakes from sleep and, stretching his hands over the tempest, says, "Be still!" and the boisterous waves, like chastened children, sob themselves to sleep. He speaks to the demons who have possessed the soul of the Gadarene, "Come forth!" and the next moment the man has thrown himself penitent and weeping before him. To his enemies who seek him in the garden he suddenly appears; and before the brightness of his countenance they fall as dead men. Passing by the receipt of customs, he says to Matthew, "Follow me!" and the man without murmur or questioning, rises up and follows him. He preaches in the streets: "Come unto me all ye that labor and are heavy laden, and I will give you rest;" and one of his congregation—a lost, friendless, despairing woman,—follows him to his home and empties an alabaster box of precious oil of spikenard on his feet.

It is (3) *a loving face*. He alone of all the great teachers of history opens his arms to the children, saying, "Suffer them to come unto me." He weeps over Jerusalem at the very hour when its rulers and people are preparing to crucify him, saying, "How often would I have gathered you as a hen doth gather her brood under her wings, and ye would not!" In the agony of bitter death he turns his face toward the penitent thief, saying, "To-day thou shalt be with me in paradise."

It is hard to understand how any man can look thoughtfully and fixedly on the face of Jesus, shining thus with the divine glory,—the glory of holiness and power and love,—without yielding to him in humble submission, saying, "My Lord, my life, my sacrifice, my Saviour and my all!" But, alas! *we will not look fixedly and thoughtfully at him.*

One of our poets tells of a Brahman pundit who sat with the Shaster in one hand and the Bible in the other, hesitating between them "How may I know," he cried, "if this or this be God?" He had passed his life in the ancestral faith; but as he read the gospels, the magnetic power of Jesus came upon him. He formed a desperate resolution,—he would test Brahma at the dagger's point! That night he made his way into the temple; trembling in every limb, he crept along the colonnades of minor gods, fearful lest Brahma might at any moment lay a fierce hand upon him. He strengthened himself in the assurance that he came not to scoff nor to deny, but to know the truth. At length he reached the great image. Let the poet tell what followed:

" Full in the idol's breast the blade
Was plunged. There came no moan.
The Pundit dropped with stifling joy upon the pavement stone,
Sobbing, ' My Brahma is a lie; the Christ is God, alone !' "

A simpler, better test is this: to calmly ponder on Christ at Calvary,—to look upon his face, marred but divinely beautiful, until the eye shall affect the heart,—to look until the divine glory shall overspread it like a rising sun. The Cross is the touchstone of truth.

Domenichino, in his picture of the Crucifixion, represents a group of angels hovering above the cross. One of them, with a look of wonder and perplexity, is touching the points of the thorny crown. Aye, let him wonder, for never was love like this! And you, my comrade in the earnest quest of truth, gaze on this face of Jesus; for the great revelation is here and nowhere else. This is your East, whence the Sun of Righteousness must arise to find its shining way into your heart.

" O could I speak the matchless worth,
O could I sound the glories forth,
    Which in my Saviour shine;
I'd soar and touch the heavenly strings,
And vie with Gabriel while he sings
    In notes almost divine."

And here is the beginning of the Christian life; to see the great Sacrifice, to hear the voice that Paul heard, saying, "I am Jesus." As we look, the eyes of Jesus, filming in death, beam with an unearthly love; his lips, parched with the last fever, are moving, and his hands, nailed to the accursed tree, are stretched out. "His hands are stretched out still!" Did we say once, "He hath no form or comeliness, and there is no beauty that we should desire him"? Ah, he is the "chiefest among ten thousand, the one altogether lovely." And if we behold him thus in his humility, wearing the glory of heaven on his face, how will he appear when he sitteth on his throne high and lifted up?

"Well, the delightful day will come
When my dear Lord will bring me home,
And I shall see his face;
Then with my Saviour, Brother, Friend,
A blest eternity I'll spend,
Triumphant in his grace."

THE DIGNITY OF LABOR.

"And the Lord God took the man and put him into the garden of Eden to dress and keep it."—Gen. 2, 15.

Why was not Adam placed in an automatic garden that would dress and keep itself? Had the matter been left to him, he might have chosen to sit under the trees listening to singing birds and murmuring brooks, watching the panorama of clouds sweeping by, saying sweet nothings to Eve and building castles in the air. But the Lord knew best. He knew that under such conditions the man would run to adipose tissue and fail to develop the possibilities that were within him. He knew also that "Satan finds some mischief still for idle hands to do."

It is the fashion in these times, in certain quarters, to look on manual labor as "bad form." It must shock the sensibilities of some people to reflect that their remotest ancestor was a workingman; and, alas for them! the second Adam also was a workingman. In one of the famous satires of Celsus directed against the Christian religion, he says, "It is abominable to suggest that God should have sent his only-begotten Son into the world to be a carpenter." On the contrary this is precisely what we should expect. If the only-begotten Son is to assume our humanity, it is natural that he should take the form not of the lowest nor of the highest, but of the average man. This is precisely what he does. The effort to adorn him with a luminous halo is quite futile; he could have no more fitting crown than the workman's cap. He belongs to the Third Estate; he is distinctly a man of the people, a man among men.

I speak of the Dignity of Labor. It is a mistake to suppose that a curse was originally put upon labor by reason of Adam's sin. The ground was indeed "accursed for his sake." All nature bears the mark of attainder. "I went by the field of the slothful and, lo, it was all grown over with thorns; and nettles had covered the face thereof, and the stone wall thereof was broken down." It is the curse of indolence. Industry must lift the ban. Our present purpose is to show that labor is every way blessed and, like matrimony, "honorable in all."

I. *It is the ordinance of nature.* "In the sweat of thy face shalt thou eat bread" is the primal law. The apostle puts it in negative form, "If any will not work, neither let him eat."

God never made a loaf of bread. He made a man and a field: and to the man he said, "Behold, I have made a field; you must do the rest." If the man refuses to till the soil, reap the harvest, grind the corn and bake the flour, he shall not eat bread.—God never made a coat. He made a man and a sheep; and to the man he said, "Lo, I have made a sheep, and wool to grow upon its back; you must do the rest." If the man will not shear the fleece, and card the wool, and spin and weave it, his back will go bare.—God never made a house. He made a man and a forest; and to the man he said, "Go into the forest, fell a tree and make for yourself a house; or you shalt have no roof to shelter you."

The man who will not work is out of harmony with nature. The world is a vast laboratory; air, earth and water are ever busy in the work of decomposition and reconstruction. Listen and you may hear the sounds of the formative processes; wheels revolving and dynamos at work. The furnaces are never extinguished. Force is being turned out in various forms and applied to its manifold uses. Bees are making honey, birds are building nests, lions are hunting their prey, beasts of burden are plodding along the beaten paths. The indolent man is a loose pin in the machine. The order of nature would be better without him.

II. *Labor is the safeguard of society.* What is society? A mutual organization with a common fund. All members of this organization are bound to be producers,—that is, contributors to the common fund.

The great sociological problem is how to deal with the non-producers. We have jails and reformatories for criminals, and asylums for the helpless; but what shall be done with the non-producing classes—those who violate no law but the primal law of industry?

There is the multitudinous army of tramps. The sum total of their philosophy is, "The world owes me a living." In fact the world owes no man a living; it owes him merely the opportunity to make a living for himself. In this particular they do not serve who "only stand and wait."

A still more difficult class is the idle aristocracy. The world groans under its burden of respectable ne'er-do-weels. I am sorry for a rich man's son. As a rule an inheritance is a curse. There are splendid exceptions; but a youth must have a brave heart, broad shoulders and a strong vertebral column, in order to bear up under a patrimony and not be ruined by it. It is a mistaken kindness in fathers to relieve their sons of the responsibilities of common toil. We are told that nine out of ten sons of wealthy men, in the struggle of commercial life, are driven to the wall. Who are the successful men in New York? A few years ago most of them were living on the farm, rising at five in the morning and drawing on woolen mittens to do the chores and water the stock. In due time, moved by a splendid ambition, they came to the metropolis, seeking a larger field of labor. And, while the scions of rich fathers were waiting on the ground floor for an elevator to carry them up, these brawny youths climbed the stairway, three steps at a time, to the "room at the top."

A word also as to our young ladies. It is greatly to the credit of many that they are able to meet the trials and temptations of society with no sacrifice of true womanhood. But there are others whose lives are utterly giddy and frivolous; who turn night into day and day into night; devote their noblest energies to formal calls, novel reading, embroidery, the elaborate duties of the toilet and "social functions." Miss Flora McFlimsy, who "had nothing to wear," has passed out of vogue; but multitudes are left who, more unfortunately, have nothing to do. Their business is "to amuse and to be amused, to see and to be seen, to follow in the train of fashion, to turn life into a pageant or a song." The summit of their aspiration is reached when they go decked and smiling to the connubial altar; for what is better than to be a beautiful ivy with a stalwart oak to cling to? And when the end is reached, there is nothing behind save the memory of giddy hours; and before? The judgment day. The end of all is a tombstone whereon should be inscribed, "Vanity of vanities."

III. *Labor is the secret of happiness.* The song of the toiler is the melody that has gladdened the earth. Who are the people that complain of the blues and the doldrums, of jaundice and melancholia? Who are the woebegone and discontented, the grievers and complainers, *les miserables?* You will not find them in busy shops and counting rooms, but among those who have nothing to do. The happy people are those who go whistling to their tasks. They have no leisure for fret and worry; and their fare is too simple to induce dyspepsia. It is a true saying, "The heart of the toiler has throbbings that stir not the bosom of kings."

IV. *Labor is the key to success.* This is our objective point—success. The men whom we meet along the thronging thoroughfares are all addressing themselves to it.

It cannot be too strongly emphasized that there is no "Northwest Passage" to this Eldorado. "The longest way around is the shortest way there." As a rule, success comes to those who deserve it.

You are making a mistake, young man, if you think that you can "live on your wits." The effort to circumvent the ordinary methods of gaining a livelihood or winning a fortune are quite futile. I know an honest artisan who ruined himself by inventing a washing-machine. He left his bench and devoted himself to the development of his idea. It was a good machine—barring only the trivial fact that it would not wash. The inventor went hither and yon, searching for capital to back his enterprise. He talked nothing but washing-machines, dreamed only washing-machines. He grew threadbare and hollow-cheeked. The last I heard of him he was still pursuing his will-o'-the-wisp.

It is an equally grave mistake to resort to speculation. A commission merchant in Detroit recently said, that probably one-third of the young business men of that thrifty city are crippled by investing in options. Poor Micawber! It should be understood that it is manifold easier to turn something up than to wait for something to turn up. Poor Colonel Sellers! His counterparts are many; dining on turnips and water, while planning great enterprises with millions in them.

Are you thinking of the Klondyke? Be well-advised. *Festina lente* is a good motto. Stick to your bench; plod; a day's wage is better than the philosopher's stone. The latest advices tell of two men who were found frozen on their sledge, returning over the Skaguay trail. On their persons were a hundred thousand dollars in yellow dust. What dreams died with them! What wasted labors and privations were theirs! We may imagine that, as they set out on the return, one said to the other, "Well, it's been drudgery, but worth while; I have fifty thousand dollars in my belt." And his friend replied, "So have I. This is success." But what shall it profit a man?

And then there are many youths who lean on

patronage. They come to you with their pockets full of credentials. Blessed is the youth who asks no other assistance than that of his ten fingers, which are his ten best friends. It is manly to shift for one's self. It is knightly to win one's spurs. Who would be a potted plant, shielded and watered and trained on a stick? Better be an oak. Put an acorn into a crevice, and it will strike its roots downward and reach forth its tentacles, searching for a grip—the grip that is always better than a pull—and clasp the rock and brace itself in defiance of wind and tempest. Get your resolution from the force of resistance, my friend; strengthen yourself in your own brave purpose for the fierce struggles of life.

Are you ambitious to be as great as Franklin? as successful as Edison? as eloquent as Whitfield? as immortal as Handel? Do you mean it? Would you condescend to push a wheelbarrow through the streets of Philadelphia, as Franklin did? Have you patience to talk into a cylinder eighteen hours a day for seven weary months to get one aspirated sound? If not, you cannot be as successful as Edison: for that is precisely what he did. Would you be willing to black the boots of your fellow-students at school? If not, you cannot expect to emulate Whitfield; for that is what he did. Could you practice on a harpsichord day after day, night after night, until the keys were hollowed like a spoon under your industrious fingers? If not, you can never become as great a musician as Handel; for it was thus that he won his claim to immortality.

V. *Labor is the basis of character.* For what is character but a well rounded and thoroughly developed bundle of energies. Ask an electrician why the armature of his great magnet is loaded with weights, and he will tell you that it loses power when it has nothing to dô. So is it with a man; he grows by exercise. In indolence he runs to seed.

This is true of national as of individual character. Industry is the measure of civilization. Savages refuse to work. They have no agriculture; they prefer to live on what grows of itself. They have no manufactures; a stone hatchet is easier to get than a Damascus blade. They have no commerce; a hollow log will answer their indolent needs. The moment you furnish a dugout with sails and rudder, that it may venture farther from the shore, you are passing from barbarism to civilization.

A few years ago, while we were camping among the Sioux, above Lake Superior, the Indians often came with berries to sell. They approached in Indian file, the braves trotting in front—tall, stalwart and empty-handed, and after them the squaws, bending under the heavy mokucks of berries. It was beneath the dignity of the braves to perform any sort of manual toil.

The effect of indolence upon a nation finds an apt illustration in Spain. No country on earth has a richer soil; they say, "If you tickle it with a hoe, it laughs with a harvest." But, unfortunately for the Castilian race, they have a prejudice against the hoe. They are given to bull-fighting and fan-flirting and love-making. Once there were twelve thousand villages along the Guadalquiver; now there are but eight hundred—the land has fallen into innocuous desuetude. The people are a race of beggars, more or less respectable. There is no greatness in Spain.

If the kingdom were to perish from the earth, it would leave no laws, no literature, nothing as a legacy to posterity. The pride of the Spaniards is vast and ludicrous. Their strength has been bluster for centuries. Little Holland, with less than three millions of people, fought Spain, one generation taking up the fight where the last had left it, until Philip III. begged for an armistice. They are unable even to subdue Cuba. Poor, famished Cuba! What a pathetic farce is this; that the grandees of Spain, with their fleets and their armies, should be successfully resisted by a few brave islanders, whose ranks are decimated by slaughter, famine and plague!

We, on the contrary, have been derided as "a nation of shopkeepers and artisans." Our glory is in the truth of that imputation. Alas for us, when we consent to look on labor with Spanish eyes! If war must be declared against Spain—which God forfend—let us rejoice that a call for volunteers would be answered, as it was when Lincoln made his historic appeal for a "hundred thousand more," not by volunteers from the street corners and drawing-rooms, but from the fields and the workshops. Here is the source of our greatness; here the hope of our perpetuity. The true American is neither the alms-taker nor the gentleman of leisure, but the man of whom Longfellow sings:

> "Under a spreading chestnut-tree
>   The village smithy stands;
> The smith, a mighty man is he,
>   With large and sinewy hands,
> And the muscles of his brawny arms
>   Are strong as iron bands.

"His hair is crisp and black and long;
  His face is like the tan;
His brow is wet with honest sweat—
  He earns whate'er he can;
And he looks the whole world in the face,
  For he owes not any man."

Two thoughts in conclusion: *First, Our work is all for God.* This is the clause which "makes drudgery divine." The most menial of duties is glorified if it be performed as in the great Taskmaster's eye. And *Second, Our supreme work is in the Kingdom.* We are in constant danger of concentrating our energies upon the getting of a livelihood to the neglect of our real life. The Hindus, at one of their festivals, pay divine honors to the implements of their trades. The blacksmith brings his hammer, the carpenter his saw and plane, the husbandman his rude plow; and they bow down and worship them. We are in danger, amid the absorbing competitions of secular life, of falling into a similar idolatry. Let us be diligent in business, fervent in spirit, but always serving the Lord. And while faithful in our bread-and-butter work, let us ever remember that our supreme interest is in the pursuits of the higher life.

The only-begotten Son of God came from heaven to save men. In due time he entered the carpenter shop and toiled as other men; but *he never forgot his supreme work.* The villagers brought in their furniture, the farmers their plows to be mended; and the Carpenter of Nazareth gave honest work for honest wages. But the thought of his great mission was never out of mind. "I have a baptism to be baptized with; and how is my soul straitened until it shall be accomplished!" When he had reached and passed the consummation of his great purpose on Calvary, he gathered his disciples about him and said, as he had said before to them, "As the Father sent me into the world, so send I you." That is, the disciples of Christ are ever to regard themselves as laborers with him in the great mission of delivering this world from sin. Be faithful, my friend, in your workshop; but, in the name of our dear Lord, let not its four walls confine you. Let your soul be larger than your shop. Seek first the kingdom of God and his righteousness. This is the glory of Christian living. The man who fails to apprehend this,—that he belongs to two worlds and must be ever doing two things, busy in the shop yet ever busy in the affairs of the kingdom,—misses the opportunity of his life. Thanks be to God for the exalted privilege, for the inestimable honor, which he has put upon us; in that we are permitted to stand in the great harvest, wielding our sickle by the side of his well-beloved Son!

A PLEA FOR FANATICISM.

"But when Sanballat the Horonite, and Tobiah the servant, the Ammonite, and Geshem the Arabian, heard it, they laughed us to scorn, and despised us, and said, What is this thing that ye do?"—Neh. 2, 19.

The Jews who returned from the Babylonian captivity were a feeble folk, like the conies—feeble in numbers, but great in courage and steadfastness. They met with serious opposition when they set themselves in earnest to restore the ruined city. The heads of the surrounding tribes at first accused them of conspiring against the king; this, however, was easily refuted by the decree of Artaxerxes. They then invited the Jews to submit the matter of controversy to arbitration; "Come, let us meet together in some one of the villages in the plain of Ono;" the answer was, "We are doing a great work, so that we cannot come down." The hardest thing the exiles had to bear, however, was ridicule. Their opposers "were wroth, and took great indignation, and mocked them." Sanballat said, "What do these feeble Jews? will they fortify themselves? will they accomplish their purpose in a day? will they revive their city out of the rubbish heaps?" And his comrade Tobiah laughingly said, "If a fox go up, he shall even break down their stone wall." But on went the work until the walls were finished and dedicated "with thanksgivings and singing, with cymbals and psalteries and harps." They laugh best who laugh last.

The sharpest weapon of Antichrist in our time is derision. His bow is laughter and his arrows are epithets. We no longer stand in terror of the ax, the fagot, and the dungeon; but we are always in danger of being laughed down. A boy at school finds it easier to bear the discipline of the birch than to be told that he is restrained by his mother's apron string. The pointed finger is a deadlier weapon than the naked sword. The height of courage is to stand at our places in the building of the wall, regardless of sneers and reproaches, of taunt and invective, of hissing and vituperation. These are the things that try the soul of a man.

At the beginning of the last century a few youths in Oxford came together for the study of the Scriptures. They were dubbed "The Holy Club"; but they smiled and pursued their work. In due time the members of this association carried their zeal out into the larger world of affairs; then they were derisively called "Methodists." But they stood to their principles and glorified God in that name. Among them were the two Wesleys and Whitfield. They accepted the derisive epithets that were applied to them as Samson shouldered the gates of Gaza and carried them away to the mountain.

Up from the fens of England came a company of stalwart yeomen to the defense of civil and ecclesiastical freedom. They wore no frills or furbelows. Unlike the cavaliers, whose curls fell over their shoulders, their hair was cropped. They were greeted with the epithet "Roundheads." They made no uncivil reply, but marched on to Marston Moor; there, with the shout, "God with us!" they set the cavaliers aflying like chaff before the wind.

In 1666 a company of Dutch nobles appeared before the Regent to protest against the impositions of the Council of Trent. Count Berlaymont, observing the Regent's trepidation, said, "Fear not, your Majesty; they are but a pack of beggars." They forthwith hung about their necks the beggar's wallet, and marshaled an army against the legions of Spain. Their cry, "Oranje boven!" rang through the Hollow-Land, and "The Water Beggars" became a name to juggle with.

The fiercest of the weapons turned against our Master was ridicule. Some of the finest things that were ever said of him were said in epithetic form. They called him "The Carpenter"; accepting the title, he gave dignity to common toil, and became for all time the champion of the Third Estate. They called him "The friend of publicans and sinners"; not resenting it, he chose for an apostle Matthew the publican, and said to the Magdalene, "Go in peace." They crowned him with thorns and bowed before him in mock obeisance, saying, "Hail, King of the Jews!" The epithet was inscribed on the titulum which was nailed to the cross. He is honored and worshiped to-day as King of the whole Israel of God.

Blessed is the man who, in defence of his principles, can thus turn to advantage the weapons of his foes. When some one said to Diogenes, who lifted his voice against the sensuous pleasures of his time, "Thine enemies deride thee," he answered bravely, "Nevertheless, I am not derided!" The man who is sensible of right intention and high aspiration can afford to rise superior to puerile opposition. Shall we expect to be exempt? "Woe unto you when all men speak well of you."

I. You have opinions; and because they are deeply grounded in mind and conscience and heart, you are tenacious of them. My friend, *you are a bigot!* The "liberals" will tell you that Christianity is not doctrine, but life. They will quote with unction,

> "For forms of faith let canting bigots fight;
> His faith cannot be wrong, whose life is right."

They cannot understand why you should be a stickler for a creed. If you still insist, they will tell you frankly that you are narrow and intolerant. Do not flinch, now. Do not resent it. Plead guilty, and, as a bigot, proceed to glorify God.

For, what is a bigot? Webster says, "One who is stubbornly wedded to a particular creed." So be it. There are some truths which, when a man has accepted them, are so interwoven with the very fibers of his being that he cannot keep his manhood and surrender or qualify them.

You believe in God; a personal God; a God whom you can call, "Our Father"; a God who has eyes to see, a heart to pity, and hands to help. A scientific friend comes to you, saying, "I also believe in God; an all-pervading force, a something-not-ourselves that-maketh-for-righteousness, the essence of things. Why, then, can we not walk together?" And what can you answer? "Nay, friend, there is a great gulf between us. I am stubbornly wedded to my faith in a personal God."

You believe in Jesus Christ as the manifestation of this God. He is the brightness of the Father's glory, and the express image of his person. He that hath seen Christ hath seen the Father. He is very God of very God. A Unitarian friend appeals to you: "Why should we not walk together? I also believe in Christ; he was the noblest man that ever lived. Shall we not, then, abide in fellowship?" What can you say? "Friend, we differ at the vital point. The divinity of Jesus Christ is not one of the non-essentials. It is the root and foundation of all. I cannot surrender it for friendship's sake."

You believe in the Bible; you have taken it as your only and infallible rule of faith and practice; you say, It is the Word of God; and you are not juggling with words. A friend, who favors the Higher Criticism, comes to you saying, "I too believe in the Bible; not as a true book, indeed; but as a book true in spots. Why should we part company on so trivial a matter?" What must you answer, as an honest man? Tell him the Bible is the only historic witness of Jesus Christ; and that a man, therefore, cannot part company with the Bible and keep company with Christ. Tell Him that the Bible is inspired, that is, "God-breathed," and that God could not have breathed a lie.

You believe in Justification by Faith; the great doctrine of the evangelical Church; "*articulum ecclesiæ stantis aut cadentis.*" A rationalistic friend says, "What difference does it make? All ways lead to Rome. There is good in all religions and philosophies. Some people are saved by works, others by penance, still others by liturgical forms. Let us hope, however, that we shall all come together at heaven's gate." Are you loyal to your Christian profession? Tell him, then, all ways may lead to Rome, but there is only one way that leads to heaven; to-wit, the royal way of the Cross. "For there is none other name under heaven given among men whereby we must be saved."

In taking such positions you will be charged with intolerance. Nevertheless the world will respect you. In the end you will sacrifice no friendships, but win the profound regard of those who differ with you. In any case we must be true to our convictions. We must stand for what we believe. We cannot compromise.

A few years ago a black man came to the ticket office of the Albany Line, in this city, registered his name, and asked for a stateroom. The clerk was much embarrassed on perceiving that the name was "Frederick Douglass, Negro." He said, "I am extremely sorry, but the rules of the company require that colored men shall sleep on the lower deck. But if you will kindly allow me to substitute 'Indian' for 'Negro,' I can give you a stateroom." Mr. Douglass replied with indignation, "No, sir! Put me down Negro, plain Negro, and I will sleep in the hold." He who does not respect such courage as that, lacks the spirit of a man.

II. You have a conscience; you have a clear apprehension of the difference between right and wrong; you are scrupulous in avoiding whatever is contrary to this rule of conduct. My friend, *you are a Puritan!* This is what your free-and-easy friend will tell you. And, I pray you, do not begin to deny or to apologize. Do not enter any defense. Plead guilty to the charge, and proceed to justify it.

Who were the Puritans? The best men of their time. They had their faults; they walked with a measured gait, wore a too melancholy visage and spoke with a nasal twang. They inveighed against the Maypole and deemed it sacrilege to eat plum pudding on Christmas day. But there was a sweet kernel in that rough nut. We can forgive the Puritans for leaning a little backward in their devotion to conscience, when we remember the lax morals of those days. It is better to err on the side of strict morality than to be lax and lawless. Better be a precisian than a Parisian; better be strait-laced than rickety. Hands off the memory of the Puritans! No braver men ever lived. Macaulay says, "No man ever despised them who had met them in debate, or crossed swords with them on the embattled field."

For two great principles they stood with a patient and unswerving courage:—*First*, for the sanctity of the Moral Law. They believed in the Decalogue as it is interpreted in the Sermon on the Mount. They denounced the custom of profanity, so current in their day. We are largely indebted to them for the institution of the Christian home; the family altar with the Bible on it and the household gathered around it. We are greatly indebted to them, also, for the preservation of the holy Sabbath. They denounced the "Book of Sports" which represented the loose morals of the Stuart family—the meanest family that ever wielded sceptre or wore crown—which finds its exact counterpart in the diluted piety of those who favor our Sunday newspapers and athletic games on the Lord's day.

Second, they contended for the freedom of the individual conscience as against all interference of civil or ecclesiastical authority. At this point they set themselves distinctly against the fashions of their time. "Non-conformity" was their shibboleth; as it is written, "Be not conformed unto this world, but be ye transformed by the renewing of your minds"; and again, "Come out from among them and be ye separate, saith the Lord"; and again, "He gave himself for us, that he might redeem us from all iniquity, and purify unto himself a peculiar people zealous of good works"; and again, "Ye are the light of the world; let your light so shine before men that they may see your good works and glorify God."

In all this the Puritans are worthy of imitation. Our religion is not a matter of sentiment, but of principle. If we have entered into God's fellowship, we must needs love what he loves and hate what he hates. No man can be a true Christian who fears scrupulosity in the avoidance of sin.

All the world knows how the French people, at the conclusion of the Franco-Prussian war, refused to hold fellowship with their foes. I stood once in a rose-garden, in a little town in Brittany-by-the-Sea, and heard an old baroness,—whose son, a general in the French army, had recently been slain in battle,— relate how she had refused to accept the courtesies of Von Moltke in an apartment of a railway car. Her eyes flashed, her bosom heaved, her lips trembled while she told it. "But, Madam," said I, "why could you not accept courtesy even from your foe?" With a splendid and pathetic dignity she said, "Why, sir, his hands were red with the blood of my only son!" Would that we might manifest some of that spirit in our attitude toward sin! God hates it. God hates it with an utter loathing and abhorrence. How could it be otherwise? It nailed to the cross his well-beloved Son. Our abhorrence of sin is the sure token of our fellowship with him.

III. You are in earnest; you think it means something to be a follower of Christ; you are constrained by his love; the thought of his great mercy and of the sinfulness of rejecting him forbids that you should hold your peace. My friend, *you are a fanatic!* All the world and many of your Christian friends will tell you so. But do not resent it. Stand to your guns. It is a glorious thing to be in dead earnest for the right.

Why is it that earnestness is commended in everything else but religion? There was Archimedes the mathematician, who, when the enemy, at the capture of Syracuse, rushed in upon him with uplifted sword, was so intent upon a geometric figure drawn upon the floor that he merely said, with a deprecating gesture, "Wait a moment! just a moment, until I solve this." Such concentration of purpose is admirable in any cause. Why not, then, in ours?

(1.) We believe there is a real danger. All have sinned. The soul that sinneth, it shall die. Hell is an awful fact. Our Lord coupled it with the figures of the unquenchable fire and the undying worm. And those who reject the Lord Jesus Christ are rushing headlong towards it. He that believeth not in

Jesus Christ, shall be damned. If these things are so, how can we forbear to warn those who are in jeopardy of life? If a man passing on Fifth Avenue were to see flames issuing from the roof of this sanctuary, he would rush through the door without ceremony, crying, "Fire! Fire!" Would you blame him? Would you say, "My friend, you are interrupting the service?" Nay, you would praise and thank him for it.

(2.) We believe also in a way of escape. The lifeline is thrown out from Calvary. It is the one plan of salvation. It is simple and effective. It is offered on the sole condition of faith. "He that believeth, shall be saved." If so, it is of the utmost importance that our friends shall close in with its overtures. A few days ago one of our great steamships came into port with her engines disabled. She reported that for three days she had drifted about in mid-ocean, in great peril, and that her signals were unheeded by an inbound steamer passing by. There was great indignation. On a sudden, however, the matter was hushed up; the reason being that the passing steamer was a sister ship of the same line. There can be but one opinion as to the utter turpitude of such a course. But what shall be said of Christian people living in close fellowship with those whom they believe to be in danger of spiritual and eternal death, members even of their own households, whom yet they warn not?

In the year 66, Festus, the governor at Cæsarea, was visited by King Agrippa and his mistress, Bernice. For their entertainment Paul was brought out of his dungeon, wearing his chains, and required to display his eloquence. He did so with tremendous effect. He told the simple story of his conversion on the Damascus highway, of the sunburst that changed the whole tenor of his life, of the voice saying, "I am Jesus," of his blindness and the subsequent revelation of truth. And as he thus spoke, Festus said with a loud voice, "Paul thou art beside thyself; much learning doth make thee mad!" He answered, "I am not mad, most noble Festus, but speak forth the words of truth and soberness." Mad? O, would to God there were more fanatics like Paul! The truths we profess are so solemn, the issues involved are so stupendous, that it seems as if, should we keep silence, the very stones must cry out.

Just forty years ago a man arose in our Fulton Street prayer meeting, in the presence of a large assemblage of business men, and read these words, which he had written during the previous night:—

> "Where'er we meet, you always say,
>   What's the news? what's the news?
> Pray what's the order of the day?
>   What's the news? what's the news?
> Oh! I have got good news to tell;
> My Saviour hath done all things well,
> And triumphed over death and hell,
>   That's the news! that's the news!

> "The Lord has pardoned all my sin—
>   That's the news! that's the news!
> I feel the witness now within—
>   That's the news! that's the news!
> And since He took my sins away,
> And taught me how to watch and pray,
> I'm happy now from day to day—
>   That's the news! that's the news!"

At this moment we are all profoundly interested in "the news." Our hearts are moved by rumors of approaching war; we can scarcely wait for the issues of the daily press. But to one who has really and adequately grasped the great verities of our religion, is there any current event to be compared with the tragedy on Golgotha? or any happening that can so profoundly concern him as this revelation of God's mercy to his own soul?

A wave of patriotism sweeps over our country which has obliterated Mason and Dixon's line and united all our people in devotion to the Republic. The unfurling of the starry flag in any public place of assemblage is the signal for an immediate outburst of enthusiasm. Why not? Is there any national emblem that can compare with it?

> " When Freedom from her mountain height
> Unfurled her banner to the air,
> She tore the azure robe of night
> And set the stars of glory there!"

Ah, yes, friends, there is a standard dearer to our hearts than "Old Glory." We are enlisted under the red banner of the cross. It stands to us for truth and righteousness, for mercy and eternal life. If we love Christ, let us be loyal to it. Let not Sanballat and Tobiah laugh us out of our convictions. Let us not be ashamed of the Gospel, for it is the power of God unto salvation to every one that believeth. Let us be true. Let us be in dead earnest. Let us be loyal to Christ!

THE WITHERED HAND.

"And he entered into the synagogue; and there was a man there which had a withered hand. And they watched him, whether he would heal him on the Sabbath day; that they might accuse him. And he saith unto the man which had the withered hand, Stand forth. And he saith unto them, Is it lawful to do good on the Sabbath days, or to do evil? to save life, or to kill? But they held their peace. And when he had looked round about on them with anger, being grieved for the hardness of their hearts, he saith unto the man, Stretch forth thine hand. And he stretched it out: and his hand was restored whole as the other."—Mark 3, 1-6.

The second year of our Lord's ministry was drawing to a close. The clouds were gathering dark about him. There was a widespread interest in his preaching; as it is written, "the common people heard him gladly." But the rulers were against him; and not without reason.

To begin with, he utterly failed to meet their cherished views of the Messiah. They expected him to come in royal state, but Jesus was the son of a carpenter; "a root out of a dry ground; he had no form nor comeliness that they should desire him." Another reason for their opposition was his denunciation of their darling sins; for, in spite of their ceremonial sanctity, they were given to usury, uncleanness and a general disregard of the true spirit of the Moral Law. He found them parading before the people in broad phylacteries and with scriptural frontlets between their eyes; he cried, "Woe unto you, mask-wearers! Ye are as whited sepulchres; fair without, but within full of dead men's bones and all uncleanness." Little wonder that they opposed him! Moreover, he was "the friend of publicans and sinners." This was a notorious charge; and—the more shame—he apparently gloried in it. He said, "They that be whole need not a physician; I am come to seek and to save the lost." The words with which he closed the parable of the Prodigal Son cut to the quick,—"For I say unto you, there is more joy in the presence of the angels of God over one sinner that repenteth, than over ninety and nine just persons that need no repentance." A still further offense was his claim of Godhood. He said, "I and my Father are one;" and again, "He that hath seen me hath seen the Father"; so, repeatedly, making himself equal with God. He claimed to forgive sin, which was plain blasphemy; as the Pharisees said, "Who but God hath power on earth to forgive sin?"

But the crowning offense of Jesus in their eyes was his contemptuous disregard of their *Toldoth*, or Sabbath prescripts. The Sabbath was their fetish. They had made it a weariness to the people by adding a vast number of burdensome requirements. It was unlawful to walk upon the greensward on the Sabbath, lest, the grass being in seed, the act should be construed as threshing. A radish must not be left in the salt, lest it should prove to be pickling on the Holy Day. A man must not feed his poultry more than was absolutely necessary, lest the remainder of the grain should germinate, and he might be justly charged with sowing. The Lord Jesus had no patience with these *Toldoth;* he said to the Pharisees,

"Ye have made the law to be of none effect by your vain traditions"; and again, "Ye lade men with burdens grievous to be borne."

On the morning of the Sabbath of our context he had permitted his disciples, as they were passing through the fields, to pluck the ears of grain and rub them in their hands. They were called to an account for this as a specific violation of the Sabbath law. He vindicated them in a brief reply, concluding with the words, "The Sabbath was made for man, and not man for the Sabbath; wherefore, the Son of Man is Lord also of the Sabbath."

It was the afternoon of the same day when he entered into the synagogue; a great company was assembled; and there was a man there with a withered hand. The enemies of Jesus watched him— for, knowing his humanity, they expected him to heal this man, despite their traditional prohibition. He perceived what was in their hearts and said indignantly, "Is it lawful to do good on the Sabbath days, or to do evil? to save life, or to plot murder as ye are doing now?" And they held their peace; for what could they say? He looked round on them with indignation, being grieved for the hardness of their hearts; and then he healed the man.

What is the lesson? For, let it be understood, the miracles are not mere singular acts of healing; they are acted parables, for the setting forth of spiritual truth. We know what Jesus meant when he fed the five thousand: "I am the living bread which came down from heaven, of which if a man eat he shall never hunger." We know what he meant when he wiped away the leper's spots: "Come now, let us reason together; though your sins be as scarlet, they shall be white as snow; and though they be red like crimson, they shall be as wool." We know what he meant by the raising of Lazarus from the dead: "I am the resurrection and the life; he that believeth in me, though he were dead, yet shall he live; and whosoever liveth and believeth in me shall never die. But what is the meaning here?

(1) This miracle teaches, at the outset, *the compassion of Jesus.* The man who had the withered hand is said, in one of the Apocryphal gospels, to have been a stone-mason, with a wife and children dependent upon him. It was a case indeed to move a compassionate heart. Our Lord pities all the distressed. If the roofs of our city were to be lifted, we should hide our eyes at the pitiful sight. O, the pain and sorrow! The multitudes who toss on beds of languishing; the shame, the despair, the breaking hearts! But the roofs *are* lifted before him; and he sees and pities all.

(2) It teaches, also, *the true spirit of Sabbath observance.* There are foolish people who hold that Jesus swept away the sanctions of the Fourth Commandment. How grievously they misunderstand him!

Let us hear a parable of the Lord of the Castle. He went his way and sojourned for a season in a far country. On his return he found a fantastic group of harlequins in possession of his mansion. They had set up their implements of jugglery in its chambers, and hung their fantastic banners on its outer walls. They had permitted thorns and thistles to grow along its garden paths, and had collected heaps of rubbish in its gates. He was filled with indignation, and cried, "Away with these implements of your magic! Tear down yon banners! Clear out the garden paths, and remove the foul débris from the gates!" Was this destruction? Nay, it was restoration. So did our Lord cry out against the *Toldoth*, the "vain traditions" of the elders, because they had made the Sabbath a burden and weariness to the people. As Lord of the Sabbath, he claimed the right to restore the sanctions of the original law.

(3) But there is another lesson here, which I desire to emphasize particularly, as to *our relation to great spiritual truths*. The Lord spoke twice to the man with the withered hand, and both words were unnecessary to the work of healing: "Stand forth," and "Stretch forth thy hand." Both were intended to stimulate the man to self-exertion. Our Master's teaching on this, as on other occasions, was like the blast of a pibroch in the Scottish hills above a sleeping village. We are all too dull and apathetic; he comes to awaken, to invigorate and stimulate us.

I. "*Stand forth;*" literally, "Forth into the midst!" This meant publicity. The man was here subjected to a trying ordeal; for chronic sufferers are usually diffident. Nevertheless, the Master did not spare him. "Forth into the midst!" It suggests that the religion of Jesus is not for the cloister. God's remedies are sunlight and mountain air. The Christian is not called to be a silent cenobite, but above all a man among men.

(*a*) He who seeks salvation is required at the outset to make a frank acknowledgment of sin and an open confession of his belief that Christ can save him; for "with the heart man believeth unto righteousness and with the mouth confession is made unto salvation." Is this unreasonable? Christ in our behalf was nailed upon a tree, the tree was raised upon a hill, the hill overlooked the city; so that he was made a gazing-stock before all.

> "Jesus, and shall it ever be,
> A mortal man ashamed of thee?
> Ashamed of Jesus? yes, I may,
> When I've no guilt to wash away,
> No tear to wipe, no good to crave,
> No fears to quell, no soul to save.
> Till then—nor is my boasting vain—
> Till then I boast a Saviour slain ;
> And O, may this my glory be,
> That Christ is not ashamed of me."

(*b*) So in the building of character. As Christians we are eager to grow in grace and in the knowledge of our Lord and Saviour Jesus Christ. There is nothing nobler than this aspiration; yet, to our shame be it said, we are oftentimes loath to acknowledge it. You have seen young artists in the gallery of the Louvre, seated before such masterpieces as "Ecce Homo," or "The Immaculate Conception," laboriously copying every line. Did they blush to have it known that they were trying to catch the spirit of the illustrious masters? Why should we be reluctant to show our earnestness in the imitation of Christ? There is nothing better than character, and the summit of character is Christ-likeness.

> "Howe'er it be, it seems to me,
> 'Tis only noble to be good."

(*c*) And furthermore, in Christian service. We are

too fearful of being thought over-zealous or fanatical. We have much to say of modest service and of quiet ministry. We lay great emphasis on the Master's words, "And thou, when thou prayest, enter into thy closet and shut to the door;" and, "When thou doest alms, let not thy left hand know what thy right hand doeth." There is indeed a time to go alone into the trysting-place and to hide our beneficence from human eyes; but there is also a time to brave publicity in doing good. Remember the word of the Lord Jesus how he said: "Let your light so shine before men, that they may see your good works and glorify God."

At the battle of Cassova the impetuous Bajazet, seeing a circle of baggage-wagons and kneeling camels arranged as a breastwork, cried out, "Have the sons of Othman ever feared to meet their enemies face to face? Shall we, who have conquered Asia, shelter ourselves behind our camels? Are such artifices worthy of a divine cause?" It is proper to inquire if much of our assumption of modesty is not a mere subterfuge of cowardice. How else shall we account for the multitude of professed Christians who stand idle in the market-place while the fields are yellow for the sickle? Is it more reprehensible to be a zealot than a good-for-naught? Let us prove our sincerity and earnestness by working in the open. Forth into the midst, O disciples of Christ!

II. "*Stretch forth thy hand.*" It need scarcely be said that Jesus could have accomplished his purpose without requiring any personal effort on the part of this man. Not only so, but the thing which he demanded was impossible; for the word rendered "hand" is comprehensive and includes the entire arm. The man might have answered, "Good Rabbi, how canst thou say, 'Stretch forth thy hand?' Dost thou know paralysis? Every nerve and tendon here is atrophied. In vain have I sought to move my arm. If I lift it with my left hand, thus, behold, it falls again as if it were dead. 'Stretch it forth!' Nay, Rabbi, that were impossible; surely thou mockest me." Nevertheless, it is written, "He stretched it forth." How could that be? "God helps those who help themselves." He makes no unjust exaction. He ever gives power with the effort to obey him.

Sin is paralysis. Mind, conscience, heart,—the whole moral nature is atrophied.

> "Our weakness in this emblem, we,
> Our total inability
> Of doing good, may find."

Nevertheless we are required to use mind, conscience and heart in holy endeavor; and God enables us to do this. Here is the token of his wise goodness: that he makes us, by an infinite condescension, co-laborers with himself in our restoration and upbuilding. We dwarf our children, in mistaken kindness, by doing everything for them. God stimulates us by this word, "Do for yourself, and I will work with you."

(a) At the beginning of the Christian life we are required to believe. This is the condition of life. Let us say that God could deliver us without any effort of our own; he does not deliver us in that way. No truth of Scripture is clearer than that he has affixed the condition of personal faith to the gift of eternal life. We must stretch forth our hand to accept the gift, else we shall not receive it. God might have healed the serpent-bitten Israelites with a gracious word; he did indeed, but that word was a call to effort, "Look and live!" Our Lord was pleased to use this as a silhouette of the plan of salvation: "For as Moses lifted up the serpent in the wilderness, so also must the Son of Man be lifted up; that whosoever believeth in him should not perish but have eternal life."

(*b*) And again, in character-building. God could doubtless create a perfect saint in the moment of conversion, were he so disposed; as Minerva is said to have sprung full-armed and panoplied from the forehead of Jove. But, instead, he is pleased to call us into a splendid fellowship with himself in the working out of character. We are adjured to "work out our own salvation with fear and trembling, because it is God that worketh in us." It is precisely as when a father sets up his son in business. He buys a stock of goods and says, "Now, my son, I have given you a start; work this out, until you shall make a competence or a fortune for yourself. Meanwhile, I will stand by you; should you be involved in difficulty, call on me." Our conversion is merely a start in the great business of life. God says to us then, "Work out your salvation to the very uttermost." For salvation is more than a mere deliverance from the penalty of death; it comprehends all the graces of character and all the vast possibilities of usefulness. In the attainment of these we are assured that God will co-operate with us. How kind, how gracious, how conducive to the highest development of our own powers, is this condescension on our Father's part ! How it exalts our manhood to be thus assured that we are "laborers together with God!"

(*c*) And, still further, in Christian service. The same God who caused light to shine in chaos, might, no doubt, at any moment illuminate our sin-stricken world by a similar fiat, "Let there be light!" But instead, he has wisely chosen to use us in the work of his kingdom; that is, in the restitution of all things. Our Lord said to his disciples, "As the Father hath sent me into the world, so send I you." And after his crucifixion he returned and said again, "All power is given to me in heaven and on earth; go ye, therefore, and declare the evangel." Oh, the riches of the wisdom and grace of God ! Blessed be his name, that he thus dignifies our humanity in calling us into copartnership with himself. The world waits for us to appreciate and grasp the high honor. The world lieth in darkness, groaning and travailing, until we shall apprehend not the duty merely, nor the grave responsibility, but the sublime privilege of joining with God in restoring the nations to truth and righteousness, and in bringing in the Golden Age.

Let us be grateful to-day, if the words of our Master have stirred any compunctions within us. For pain is the antithesis of palsy. Did you ever awake in the middle of the night to find that your arm was asleep ? You were alarmed; because you knew that men are sometimes stricken with palsy in the night. You rubbed your arm briskly until you felt a tingling; and then you knew that all was well. "Woe to them that are at ease in Zion." Blessed is the man who feels his infirmity, and deeply longs for a better and nobler life.

Finally, let our awakened energies be newly consecrated to Christ. It is safe to say that, when this man of Capernaum went out of the synagogue he never again thought of his restored hand in the same way. It was thenceforth Christ's hand. It grasped the trowel to do honest work for the Master who had healed it. It ministered to the poor, for Jesus' sake. We profess to be Christians; we are sinners saved by grace. We are healed of impotence, body and soul, hands and feet, by the power of Christ. What shall we say, then? Let us glorify God with our bodies and spirits, which are his. "Take my life and let it be consecrated, Lord, to thee!"

THE BEACON ON BETH-HACCEREM.

"O ye children of Benjamin, gather yourselves to flee out of the midst of Jerusalem, and blow the trumpet in Tekoa, and set up a sign of fire in Beth haccerem: for evil appeareth out of the north, and great destruction."—Jeremiah 6, 1.

To Jeremiah was assigned the unpleasant duty of bewailing the sins of the nation and giving notice of coming retribution. "O that my head were waters," he cried, "and mine eyes a fountain of tears, that I might weep day and night for the slain of the daughter of my people!" It was a time of apparent prosperity. The religious leaders were much devoted to the superficial forms of the ceremonial law; they complacently said, "The temple of the Lord, the temple of the Lord are we!" But the prophet must needs utter his note of warning. He represents Israel as "a comely and delicate woman," adorning herself, simpering, posing for adulation; while her priests and princes, like lovers, congratulate her, saying, "Peace, peace." Meanwhile, the Chaldean army appears in the prophet's vision, sweeping downward along the northern roads, its banners waving, its horses like eagles. They come to kill and spoil as a grape-gatherer enters his vineyard, basket in hand. And alas! Israel heeds it not! The sound of the trumpet is now heard on the summit of Tekoa.

On high Beth-haccerem the signal-fire streams upward into the night. "Peace?" cries the prophet; "there is no peace, but war; dark, bitter, bloody, relentless war!"

The people of America are apparently on the verge of portentous events. The sky is red and lowering. It is the part of wisdom to observe the signs of the times. Let us stand for a while under Beth-haccerem and, in the light of that flaming beacon, meditate on War.

I. *It is an awful Fact.* Milton says:

> " . . . Black it stood as night,
> Fierce as ten furies, terrible as hell,
> And shook a dreadful dart."

On a May morning in 1879 General Skobeleff visited the battlefield of Shipka Pass. A year had passed since the close of the Turco-Russian war. He paused and uncovered at a wooden cross, marking the grave of a heroic standard-bearer. Then he silently surveyed the field. The snow was melting; the shallow graves had been uncovered by the sweeping winds of winter, and dogs and wolves had wrought grim havoc. Here and there were torn uniforms and human bones. He said to his aide-de-camp, "See how these skulls are grinning at us." Then, after a pause, he added:

> "The drying-up a single tear has more
> Of honest fame than shedding seas of gore."

The Duke of Wellington said, "There is only one thing in the world more melancholy than a battle lost; that is, a battle won." And a greater than Wellington—whose fame is destined to grow brighter with advancing time—at the close of a military career marked by singular success, left this word as his best heritage to prosperity, "Let us have peace !"

II. If the *History of War* could be adequately written, what a red chronicle it would be !

(1) It came in with sin. The first proclamation of war was also the first prophecy of ultimate peace. It was the protevangel; in which God said to the serpent, "*I will put enmity between thee and the woman, and between thy seed and her seed ; it shall bruise thy head, and thou shalt bruise his heel.*" The author of this proclamation was God Almighty; but the instigator of war is the Prince of Darkness. It is his flaming torch; it is his dripping sword. God is the Author and Promoter of Peace; but God's peace is only to be accomplished by the overthrow of Satan and the extirpation of sin.

(2) War has been as constant as the succession of time. I see the form of a man passing out of the primeval shadows, wielding a bludgeon stained with gore. It is Cain; the red mark on his forehead; his hand against every man.—I see the enemies of truth and righteousness falling in behind him and marching down the ages.—I hear the clash of arms in the vale of Siddim where Abraham, the father of the faithful, has gone out against the kings of Canaan for the rescue of his kinsman.—I hear the battle-song of Miriam and her daughters beside the sea: " Who is like unto our God, glorious in holiness, fearful in praises, doing wonders ! "—I see the hosts of Israel arrayed against Og of Bashan and Sihon of the Amorites, contending for their homes, wives and children, life and freedom. — In quick succession come the judges, Othniel, Ehud, Shamgar with his

ox-goad, Barak with Deborah raising the anthem, "The stars in their courses fought against Sisera!" Gideon and Jephthah; and Samson lifting his rude battle-song, "Heaps upon heaps, masses on masses, a thousand men!"—Then the procession of the kings: Saul casting away his dishonored shield on the heights of Gilboa; David lamenting, as countless parents have bewailed their slain in succeeding ages, "O Absalom, my son, my son! would God that I had died for thee!"—Now Israel marches against her barbaric foes; again the tribes are arrayed against each other; but always war, war, war, until at length it rages fiercely at the very gates of doomed Jerusalem!—Then long processions of captives are led in chains toward the East, where, hanging their harps on the willows, they weep when they remember Zion. The Old Economy closes thus amid the clang of weapons and rattle of chains. Its glories fade into the twilight of the exile, and then into deep darkness, as of an Egyptian night.

But now the Sun of Righteousness arises with healing in his wings. Surely war will cease forever at the coming of the Christ. For is not his name Shiloh, "Prince of Peace"? Was ever a sweeter birth-song than this: "Glory to God in the highest; on earth peace, good will toward men"? Was ever a more irenic proclamation than his Golden Rule? Was ever a more pronounced "peace policy" than that which he marked out for his Church on the last night of his earthly life, "Put up thy sword into the sheath; for they that take the sword shall perish by it"?

But the coming of Christ by no means meant an

immediate cessation of war. That was indeed its ultimate purpose; but the thing which he instantly did was to rend the Theocracy asunder. Up to this time the union of Church and State had been perfect and absolute in the Theocracy; now they were separated. Jesus said, "My kingdom is not of this world." Henceforth Church and State were intended to go down through history in parallel lines, each as a divinely ordained power doing its own appointed work in its own appointed way. The Church was commissioned to evangelize the nations, using no weapon but "the sword of the Spirit which is the Word of God." The State, however, was still burdened with the responsibility of carrying on the great conflict against the Prince of Darkness, meeting fire with fire on the high places of the field.

We see Nero, accordingly, at the beginning of the Christian era, unsheathing his sword against the followers of Christ. Constantine goes out under the red-cross banner against Maxentius, the herdsman emperor. Kings and dynasties rise and fall; but the struggle goes on. It is still war, war unceasing. There is an inevitable and irrepressible antagonism between truth and error, light and darkness, civilization and barbarism. When shall the end be?

(3) The end can only come with the overthrow of sin. No makeshifts or subterfuges can avail. When arbitration has done its best, there are still questions which can only be submitted to the grim tribunal that meets on the embattled field. No temporary arrangement can extirpate a deep-rooted evil. Lincoln said truly, "Nothing is settled until it is settled right." Right and wrong cannot be compromised. No earthly

court can intervene between Jehovah and the Prince of Darkness. No earthly government can heal the rupture between tyranny and oppressed humanity with an armistice. Let the issue be joined: and God defend the right!

In an old-time fable it is related that a wolf came to the flock saying, "Why need there be enmity between us? The trouble is with those wicked dogs. If you will but muzzle the dogs, all will be well." The dogs were muzzled; and, lo, the sheep were at the mercy of the wolf. As between the sheep and the wolf a truce, however fair-seeming, is always dangerous. It is the business of Christian governments to defend the right, to champion the weak, to lay siege to the strongholds of iniquity and batter them down; and this must go on until the head of the serpent is mortally bruised, and until (to use the figure of the Psalmist) iniquity is shaken out of the earth like crumbs out of a napkin.

The last proclamation of war will summon the nations to Armageddon. The Prince of Peace, in garments stained with blood, will lead his white-clad cohorts to the field. The world will tremble beneath the clash of arms. Amid the rattle of chains, the Red Dragon will be hurled into the bottomless pit. Then earth and heaven will join in the shout, "Babylon the great is fallen, is fallen!" and the reign of "peace with honor" will begin upon the earth.

III. As to the *Ethics of War*. It will probably not be questioned that most of the bloodshed in history has been for insufficient cause. In Southey's poem on "The Battle of Blenheim," a scarred veteran tells the story to a wondering lad:

> "'And everybody praised the Duke
> Who that great fight did win.'
> *But what good came of it at last?*
> Quoth little Peterkin.
> 'Why, that I cannot tell,' said he,
> 'But 'twas a famous victory.'"

It is never justifiable to make war for selfish ends. The duello for the vindication of honor is as questionable in governmental as in personal affairs. The real dignity of men and nations can stand much hammering. To fight for the avenging of a real or fancied affront is usually to pay "too dear for one's whistle." The wars that have been waged for personal glory are an ineffaccable blot on the history of our race. In the Wierts gallery at Brussels there is a picture called "The Welcome of Napoleon to Hell." As the great commander enters the gate he is met by a leering company of his victims, some with scarred faces, others with handless arms ; and haggard mothers holding up their dead infants to greet the author of their woes. And this is "glory."—Nor can anything better be said for wars of conquest. Was it wrong for Ahab to seize on Naboth's vineyard as an annex to the royal garden? Then, manifold more, is it wrong for Russia and Germany and England to hover along the shores of China awaiting an opportunity to add new territory to their vast domains. Is it said, by way of counterpoise, that God authorized the conquest of Canaan ? There never was such a "conquest." The word is a misnomer. The children of Israel went up from Egypt to recover a land which, by virtue of previous occupancy, already belonged to them.

It is right, on occasion, to wage war in self-defense. A man who, finding a burglar or ravisher in his apartments at night, will not defend himself and his household, is something less than human. By the same token, the people of Leyden were justified in resisting the Spanish siege. Let them hurl down stones upon their enemies! Let them pour blazing pitch on their heads! Self-defense is the first law of nature. And this is true of nations as of men.

It is right, also, to make war for principle. The Vaudois, the Huguenots, the Beggars of Holland, the Puritans, are justly honored for adventuring all in defense of great verities which were dearer than life. In our single century of American history we have had two magnificent wars. One of them was provoked by an unjust stamp law. Shall the sword then be drawn to resist a mere tax upon tea? Aye; for over against that small imposition is the manifesto, "No taxation without representation"; and within that manifesto is the living germ of civil and ecclesiastical freedom. Our other war was for the overthrow of slavery. A million men were slain; a thousand millions of money were sunk in an ocean of blood. But it was a splendid investment. It was in direct pursuance of the mission of Christ himself, who came to break all chains and bid the oppressed go free.

Noblest of all is the war for humanity. It asks no vindication. Men and nations are at their best when striving for the defense of the weak and helpless. When Moses had smitten an Egyptian in sudden anger, God suffered him to be driven away to the desert of Midian. But forty years after, the Lord met him there at the burning bush and said, "The time has come. The cry of my people has come unto mine ears. Go, deliver them, and I will be with thee!"

At this moment we are praying for divine guidance in our relations with Spain. The sinking of a man-of-war though done with malignant intent, is an offense that might possibly better be overlooked than avenged. But there are other considerations which go deeper far. For three years the armies of Spain have desolated the neighboring island of Cuba. We are the one great nation of the Western World, and it is for us to say whether or no this shall continue. We cannot evade the responsibility. It is unthinkable that God should desire us, a Christian people, to speak no word, to lift no hand, while massacre, with an indescribable accompaniment of famine and pestilence, goes on for years under our very eyes.

A scene of dramatic interest was witnessed in the Senate last Tuesday when Mr. Thurston spoke on the Cuban situation. He referred to the fact that "not less than four hundred thousand simple, peaceable, defenseless country people had been driven from their homes and imprisoned upon the barren wastes outside the Cuban cities." "A conservative estimate indicates that two hundred and ten thousand of people have perished from starvation." "In the meantime the government of Spain has not contributed one dollar to house, shelter, feed or provide medical attendance for these sufferers." The speaker said, after a somewhat circumstantial statement of the horrors of the Spanish invasion, "I shall refer to these things no further. They are there. God pity me, I have seen them! They will remain in my mind forever. And this is almost the twentieth century! Christ died nineteen hundred years ago, and Spain is a Christian nation; she has set up more crosses, in more lands, beneath more skies, and under them has butchered more people than all the other nations of the earth. Europe may tolerate her existence as long as the people of the Old World wish. God grant that before another Christmas morning the last vestige of Spanish tyranny and oppression shall have vanished from the Western hemisphere!" Is there one among us who will not cordially echo that wish? It is granted that intervention on our part may mean war with Spain. But what are Christian governments for, aside from the protection of their own peoples, if not to vindicate the rights of humanity and protect the weak? This is the very essence of Christianity as I understand it.

"In the beauty of the lilies Christ was born across the sea,
  With a glory in His bosom that transfigured you and me;
  As He died to make men holy, let us die to make men free;
    For God is marching on."

IV. *War can be concluded only by the evangelization of the world.* The nations must first acknowledge by common consent that the Lord is God.

Meanwhile the two great powers, State and Church, must proceed along parallel lines, doing their appointed work. If the Church had been loyal to her responsibilities, the State would long ago have been relieved of all necessity for making war.

Let us be grateful that God's people are beginning to realize, in some measure, the importance of the Great Commission. The Church is mobilizing her forces every day. I recently stood in the presence of a great convention of "student volunteers." There were forty college presidents, three hundred and sixty professors of various educational institutions, and more than two thousand students, pledged to go forth for the evangelization of the world. A like assemblage would have been impossible at any former period in history. It means that the Bride of God, so long asleep in the city gates, is hearing at length the Bridegroom's voice, "Awake! awake, O Zion! Shake thyself from the dust and put on thy beautiful garments."

At a single session of our national legislature, recently, an appropriation of fifty millions of money was voted without a dissenting voice, for purposes of war. If God's people, as they are represented in the Christian churches, would, with corresponding unanimity and enthusiasm, set apart an equal sum for the purposes of Christian conquest, we should be able to build, forthwith, a church on every hilltop, a Christian school in every valley, with bell-towers at such frequent intervals that the chimes of Shiloh's coming should ring in unbroken melody around the world.

War will cease when Jesus comes to reign. It is for the Christian Church to say when that shall be. In that consummation of history the prophecy of Zechariah shall be fulfilled. He saw the Captain of our salvation standing among the myrtle-trees; and behind him an angel troop. "Who are these?" the prophet asked. "We have returned," they answered, "from going up and down in the earth; and, behold, the whole earth is at rest!" But the end is not yet. "Watchman, what of the night?" And the watchman said, "The night cometh!" Alas! the night seamed with the lightnings of hatred and bloody strife. "But the morning, also!" God's truce is coming, the daybreak of peace and good-will on earth.

May he hasten it in his time! Then shall be heard again the primal chorus, silenced so long amid the clash of arms, in which the morning stars sang together and all the sons of God shouted for joy.

A CERTAIN NOBLEMAN.

"So Jesus came again into Cana of Galilee, where he made the water wine. And there was a certain nobleman, whose son was sick at Capernaum. When he heard that Jesus was come out of Judea into Galilee, he went unto him, and besought him that he would come down, and heal his son: for he was at the point of death. Then said Jesus unto him, Except ye see signs and wonders, ye will not believe. The nobleman saith unto him, Sir, come down ere my child die. Jesus saith unto him, Go thy way; thy son liveth. And the man believed the word that Jesus had spoken unto him, and he went his way. And as he was now going down, his servants met him, and told him, saying, Thy son liveth. Then inquired he of them the hour when he began to amend. And they said unto him, Yesterday at the seventh hour the fever left him. So the father knew that it was at the same hour, in the which Jesus said unto him, Thy son liveth: and himself believed and his whole house."—John 4, 46-53.

I have something to say about Faith. We speak of the doctrine of Justification by Faith as the "article of a standing or a falling church"; it is more, it is the article of a living or a dying soul. We are saved by faith in Jesus Christ. You say, "It is Christ himself who saves; to him alone be the glory!" True. He is our Saviour; but faith is the instrumental cause. It is on this wise: A railway train is waiting to be drawn to Albany. The engine is ready and quite competent; but it must be coupled with the cars or they will never reach their destination. Christ saves; but faith is the coupler that binds us in vital union with him.

"The just shall live by faith." This is the truth that came, like a sunburst, to the soul of Luther as he was climbing *Sancta Scala*, trusting in penance and self-righteousness.—" This is the victory that overcometh the world, even your faith." If ever we enter the gates of the heavenly city, it will be with the banner of faith flying over us.

But what is faith? The Latin word is *fides*; which we have in "diffidence" and "confidence"; the former denoting the minimum, and the latter the maximum, of faith. The word in the Hebrew is cognate with *Amen*,—which to our every prayer affixes the seal of personal emphasis. Faith is "substance"; faith is "evidence" (Heb. 11, 1). There are various kinds and measures of faith. At this point we call in a certain nobleman* of Capernaum to help us.

First. *The Faith of Hearsay.* The child of this nobleman is lying at the point of death. A passer-by in the narrow street sees shadows crossing the window; he gives the matter but a heedless thought; sickness is so commonplace. But it makes a great difference which side of that window you are on. Turning the leaves of a book but yesterday, I came upon these words:

> "We watched her breathing through the night,
>   Her breathing soft and low;
> As in her breast the wave of life
>   Kept heaving to and fro."

On the margin was written, "July 4, 1880, 1 a.m." O melancholy date! The next morning the shadow was over the home.

One touch of nature makes the whole world kin. It is an easy matter for those who have passed through a similar experience, to imagine the anxiety

---

*It is conjectured with much probability that this nobleman was Chuza, whose wife, Joanna, was a devoted follower of Jesus (Luke 8, 3). This opinn is held by Trench, Lightfoot, Chemnitz and others.

of tnat sickroom at Capernaum. The mother sat watching by the little sufferer; stroking his hair, bathing his fevered lips. Near by stood our nobleman. He was steward in the king's palace. He had wealth and influence, but they were unavailing here. The family physician had done his best. Perhaps a consultation had been held; and the leeches had shaken their heads ominously. "The black camel knelt for his burden." No hope!

Presently the father said, "Wife, it is rumored that your Nazarene rabbi has come again into Galilee and is now at Cana."

"Jesus at Cana? O husband, if you could but see him! He has power to heal. You do not believe; but indeed he has wrought many wonderful works. Go, I pray you, and entreat him to heal our little lad."

"I will send a servant," he said. "It is a long journey; and who knows whether he can help us? But it can do no harm. I will send and entreat him."

"Nay, nay, Chuza; go thyself and see him face to face. He will not refuse thee!"

It was a journey of twenty miles, and up hill all the way. But, hoping against hope, the nobleman went. And, as he journeyed, he reasoned within himself: "I greatly fear this is a fool's errand. It is hard to believe that the Nazarene carpenter can succeed in a case where the court physicians have failed. It would indeed require a miracle; and only the unlearned believe in miracles. Nevertheless, to please my beloved wife, I will appeal to him. Who knows? Perhaps some good may come of it."

In the meantime the faithful Joanna, watching by the bedside of the little patient, knelt again and again, praying, "O God, bless my husband on his errand. Let Jesus heed his request. And let my dear man see the beauty and the power of Christ, and learn to love and follow him."

Shall we blame this nobleman for his little faith? There were many difficulties in the way. To begin with, Cana and Capernaum were so far apart. A physician must needs come to the bedside and make his diagnosis, feel the patient's pulse and prescribe the remedy then and there. How was Chuza to know that Jesus was superior to all limitations of time and space? Indeed his child so critically ill might have passed away ere now. How was he to know that Jesus loved to exercise his superhuman skill on desperate cases? There were rumors, indeed, of his healing chronic invalids, bedridden cripples, lepers and demoniacs; but these rumors must be taken with a grain of allowance. As yet Chuza had nothing but the faith of hearsay. Seeing is believing. He will trust nothing short of the testimony of his senses. So the courtier probably reasoned along the way.

All of us have the faith of hearsay. What shall be done with it? We have heard of Jesus from our mothers' lips. We have read in our Bibles the story of his wonderful life. We have listened to the preaching of his gospel for years. The whole world is talking about Jesus. His name and renown are in the air. Thus all have the faith of hearsay. But what shall be done with it? Let us live up to it, as Chuza did. Let us go to Cana and, face to face with Jesus, confirm the rumor, or refute it. This is the part of wise men.

Second. — *The Faith of Approach*, or of personal

audience with Christ. It was seven o'clock in the evening when the nobleman reached Cana. He found Jesus, probably, in the home of Nathanael, conversing with his friends. At once he said, "Come down, and heal my child!" No words were wasted in ceremony; a matter of life and death is heedless of conventionality. No door-bell gets such hard usage as that of the physician. An anxious heart forgets punctilio.

And Jesus said, "Except ye see signs and wonders, ye will not believe." Here is a commingling of rebuke and encouragement. The man, however, was in no mood for didactics. It was true, indeed, that his faith, lacking the confirmation of signs and wonders, was only a broken reed; but his importunity used it like a scepter. The vision of his little son burning with fever was before his eyes.

"Sir, come down," he cried, "ere my child die!" The heart of the compassionate Christ was touched. What could he do?

"And he saith unto him, Go thy way; thy son liveth!"

And the man believed the word that Jesus had spoken unto him, and he went his way. He seems to have had no misgivings. He went his way at a leisurely pace, not reaching Capernaum until the next day. "He that believeth, shall not make haste." He took Jesus at his word. *Dictum, factum.* The word of the Master was enough for him. He tarried at an inn somewhere that night. As he lay down to rest, he may have soliloquized on this wise: "I cannot account for it; but I feel quite sure that my little lad is delivered from death. There was something in the face of Jesus which inspires me with a great confidence. A most singular man! Who can he be? Is Joanna right? Is he the very Son of God?"

And while Chuza sleeps at the inn, lulled to rest by his confidence, let us observe that he has graduated from the faith of hearsay and come into that clearer confidence which is reached only by looking into the face of Jesus. An earnest man, realizing that the great question is, "What think ye of Christ?" will not be satisfied with rumors. The part of reason is to seek a personal interview; and we can always meet Jesus at the mercy-seat and confer with him.

Do you want anything? Our life is a bundle of wants. John Quincy Adams, quoting the familiar lines—

> "One wants but little here below,
> Nor wants that little long,"

was moved to add,

> "'Tis not with me exactly so,
> Though 'tis so in the song."

We are doubtless all of a similar mind. We want health, vigor, long life, influence, wealth, pleasure, wisdom, friends, reputation, life, everything. Our faculties are like the family of the horse-leech, all daughters, and every one crying, "Give! Give!" Eyes and ears, hands, palate and heart, are ever unsatisfied.

There is one alone who can supply our need. Go tell it to Jesus. Make a clean breast of it. If your desire is wrong, he will kindly reason with you; if right, he will exceed your fondest hope. Do not be over-particular as to your liturgy. "Come down!" said the nobleman. It was brief and abrupt; but

Jesus knew. Be sincere and in earnest. You are bearing a burden; he can lift it. You are discouraged; he can bind a girdle of strength about your loins. You are under conviction of sin, oppressed with "a certain fearful looking-for of judgment." I congratulate you, my friend; you are not far from the kingdom of heaven. But do not make the mistake of trying to save yourself. Do not let the adversary get the better of you with suggestions of personal merit. "Go and tell Jesus." Cry earnestly unto him. He loves the cry of a returning prodigal more than all the *misereres* of the chanting Pharisees. He will say, "Go in peace; thy sins be forgiven thee!"

Third.—*The Faith of Experience.* It was bright and early the next morning when the nobleman arose. He set out upon his journey with an accelerated step; he had confidence that his son was healed; but, with a father's love, he longed to meet him. As he drew near to Capernaum, he saw in the distance some of his servants approaching; they had been sent out doubtless by his faithful wife to reassure him. We should expect him to ask, "What of the lad?" But he says nothing. The servants, impatient of delay, cry aloud, "Thy son liveth!" He manifests no surprise; it is just as he expected.

"Tell me," he inquires, "the hour when he began to amend."

"Yesterday at the seventh hour," they reply, "the fever left him."

Yesterday at the seventh hour! It was the very hour when Jesus had said, "Go thy way; thy son liveth." A strange coincidence. Is that all? Then the earthly life of Jesus was crowded with coincidences.—One morning he went down to the shore of Gennesareth and found a company of fishermen there. "Have ye caught anything?" he asked. "Nay; we have toiled all night and taken nothing." "Push out from the shore," said he, "and let down your nets on the right side of the ship." They did so, and, behold, their nets came in full of fishes.—On another occasion he lay asleep in a little boat when a tempest arose, and the boatmen, being at their wits' end, awoke him, crying, "Master, carest thou not that we perish?" He arose, stretched forth his hands, said, "Peace, be still!" and instantly there was a great calm. A strange coincidence!—He went down to Bethesda where there were a great number of lame and withered and halt; and finding there a man who had been a hopeless cripple thirty and eight years, he said to him, "Rise up and walk." Yonder he goes with his mattress on his shoulder. Another strange coincidence!—As Christ was journeying he heard the lamentable cry of ten lepers, standing in the distance with their fingers on their lips. "Unclean! unclean! have mercy upon us!" He bade them go show themselves to the priest for their cleansing; and as they went, lo, the scales of their leprosy fell off. A marvelous coincidence!—And, again, Jesus stood before the grave of Lazarus, who had been dead four days, and cried, "Come forth!" Yonder he comes, issuing from the sepulcher, bound hand and foot with grave clothes. Again a coincidence!—You have known a man addicted to an unconquerable habit; a poor inebriate who had tried everything, turning over "new leaves," signing pledges, taking the gold cure; at length he sought the presence of

Christ, who lifted him up and made a man of him, "clothed and in his right mind." Call that a coincidence, if you will.—You yourself were a sinner and profoundly felt it ; one blessed day you came to Christ beating upon your breast and crying, " Be merciful!" He said, "Thy sins be forgiven thee"; and ever since you have gone singing, "Bless the Lord, O my soul." Great coincidences, these! All history is crowded with them. Christ is the wonder-worker. Nothing is too hard for him.

But let us get back to our nobleman. As he approached his home, perhaps the little lad ran out to meet him. And when the loving father held him in his arms, the last remnant of his doubt vanished. The faith of hearsay had become the faith of personal experience. He passed through the doorway of his home and Joanna met him. "Now I know," said he, "that this Jesus is the very Christ. I believe in him not because of your words, but because I have seen and proved him. Henceforth, I will follow and serve him."

"And himself believed and his whole household." Here we leave him; kneeling with wife and son and servants at the family altar. This is the nearest approach to heaven. We can overhear his prayer: "I thank thee, Father, for the healing of our child. And I thank thee for the opening of the eyes of my understanding. We of this household do revere Jesus as thy well-beloved Son. Help us faithfully to serve him." And Joanna said, "Amen."

What is our lesson ? *Christ is the mighty to save.* Was it a great thing to restore the little lad to health? It was greater to open his father's eyes. Of all the marvels in the world, there is none comparable with the deliverance of a soul from spiritual and eternal death. In the harbor of Havana lies the wreck of "The Maine;" a rent and tangled framework of iron. They say that all the wreckers on earth cannot raise her. If now a wonder-worker were to wave his wand and call that battle-ship to the surface of the water, with pennant flying and all her crew alive and at their posts on her decks, what a marvel that would be! Yet Christ is doing greater wonders constantly before our eyes. He restores the soul of a sinner, whose faculties are in utter ruin, girds him with the glorious strength of manhood and sets his lips atremble with the song of salvation. Faith does this; that is, the contact of the dead with the living, a sinner with the Prince of Life.

On the ceiling of the Sistine Chapel is Angelo's picture of The Creation of Man An insensate body is reclining on a verdant knoll; the Omnipotent is reaching down from above; from God's finger to the uplifted hand of man is passing an electric spark; and, lo, he becomes a living soul Reach up your hand, my friend, and feel the electric thrill that comes from God. Stand upon your feet a new man in Christ Jesus; a sinner saved by Christ through faith; as it is written, "He is able to save unto the uttermost all that come unto God by him."

THE FORTUNATE ANGEL.

An Easter Meditation.

"And behold, the angel of the Lord descended from heaven and came and rolled back the stone from the door, and sat upon it."—Matt. 28, 2.

The unseen world is nearer than we think. We are prevented by our physical limitations from communicating with its inhabitants; but there are reasons for believing that they are familiar with events transpiring here. In our childhood we sang :

" There is a happy land
Far, far away."

The hymn has gone out of fashion, yielding to a general and just opinion that heaven is in close touch with us.

On the heights of Bethel a lonely man, fleeing from the wrath of a wronged brother, lies down to rest with a stone for his pillow. He dreams; and lo, a ladder is let down from heaven to earth; and angels are going upward with the wanderer's prayers and coming down with blessings upon him. "Far, far away"? Oh, no. The man awakes to realize that ministering spirits, at the divine behest, are ever near to guide and succor him.

> Thus let the way appear,
>   Steps unto heaven;
> All that Thou sendest me,
>   In mercy given;
> Angels to beckon me
>   Nearer, my God, to Thee,
>   Nearer to Thee!

We are apt to view the doctrine of Angel Ministrations with misgiving. And little wonder, considering its unwarranted uses. So-called "Spiritualism" is a grotesque and stupendous fraud. The inhabitants of the unseen world are surely in better business than tipping tables, posing as ghosts in darkened rooms and talking transcendental nonsense to short-haired women and long-haired men. But we must not, on this account, be frightened out of a most helpful doctrine. No truth is without its *reductio ad absurdum*. The devil misquoted Scripture to our Lord; "He shall give his angels charge concerning thee: and in their hands they shall bear thee up, lest at any time thou dash thy foot against a stone." But this truth is none the less precious for the devil's garbling it. The angels are ambassadors between heaven and earth; as it is written, "Are they not all ministering spirits, sent forth to minister for them who shall be heirs of salvation?"

> How oft do they their silver bowers leave
>   To come to succor us that succor want!
> How oft do they with golden pinions cleave
>   The flittering skies, like flying pursuivant,
>   Against foul fiends to aid us militant!
> They for us fight; they watch and duly ward
>   And their bright squadrons round about us plant:
> And all for love and nothing for reward.
> Oh, why should heavenly God to men have such regard?

The Old Testament is full of their service. A man is threshing wheat by a wine-press in Oprah, fearful of the Midianites who have overrun the land. An angel appears to him saying, "The Lord is with thee, thou mighty man of valor; go, save thy people, saith the Lord; have not I sent thee?"—A man is sitting in the gateway of Sodom; two wayfarers draw near, dusty with travel; he invites them to tarry all night with him. In the morning they lay aside their disguise and admonish him; "Arise, take thy wife and daughters and escape; look not behind thee nor stay in all the plain!"—The prophet Elijah, fleeing to the wilderness from the fury of a woman scorned, weary and famishing, casts himself under a juniper tree, crying, "It is enough, O Lord, take away my life!" He sleeps; presently an angel awakes him, saying, "Arise and eat;" and, behold "a cake baken on the coals and a cruse of water at his head."—A bond slave, driven from home, wanders in the desert with her child who is perishing of thirst; she lays him in the shadow of a shrub to die and weeps aloud: an angel speaks, "What aileth thee, Hagar? God hath heard the voice of the lad;" and the murmur of a fountain falls upon her ears.— At the time of the evening oblation, Daniel, clothed in sackcloth for the sins of his people, kneels in prayer: "O Lord, righteousness belongeth unto thee, but unto us confusion of face; let thine anger be turned away from thy Holy City, and cause thy face to shine upon thy desolate sanctuary; incline thine ear; O Lord, hearken, and defer not!" The words have scarcely fallen from his lips ere an angel stands beside him with the assurance of the coming of Messiah in fulness of time.

How far is it, then, from heaven to earth? The journey was made while Daniel was on his knees. It is written of the angels, "They excel in strength!" A cannon ball would require five hundred years to pass from our world to the sun; but who shall estimate the speed of an angel of light? By what spiritual clairvoyance do these celestial beings surmount the difficulties of time and space? They seem to traverse the interstellar distances in the twinkling of an eye.

The angels are represented as having a special interest in the earthly life of Jesus. One was chosen to make the annunciation to Mary; "Hail, thou that art highly favored, the Lord is with thee!" A group of them were appointed to sing the birth-song, "Glory to God in the highest, and on earth peace, good will toward men!" Others were sent to minister to him after his temptation in the wilderness. Two of the saints triumphant, Moses and Elias, held converse with him in the Mount of Transfiguration "concerning the decease which he should accomplish at Jerusalem;" showing that the inhabitants of heaven are cognizant of earthly events. There were "legions of angels" above his cross, waiting at his word to draw the cruel nails and bear him in triumph to his throne. When the great tragedy was over, they still lingered, invisible, while the crucified One was carried to his grave.

And Pilate said to his servitors, "Go, make the sepulcher as fast as ever you can; see that the stone is secure; seal it up." Seal it up? Seal up the dayspring! Seal up the fountains of the mighty deep!

Bring hither the waters of the ocean in a calabash! Measure the air in a wine-skin! Who is this that would seal up the Author of life in a sepulcher? He that sitteth in the heavens shall laugh! For hath he not said, "I will not leave thy soul in Sheol; neither will I suffer my Holy One to see corruption"?

In heaven a messenger is wanted; "Who will go to Joseph's garden and roll away the stone?" All heaven is full of volunteers. One is chosen. O fortunate angel! "Go carry the message of the resurrection! Go roll away the stone! Go break the seal! Put powers and principalities to shame! Release my well-beloved Son!"

It is the darkest hour of the night. In Joseph's garden the sentinels are passing to and fro. The moment is at hand. What sudden light is this? With the speed of lightning the messenger has come; one glance, and the guards are fallen upon their faces as dead men. He touches the stone; it rolls away. He loosens the shroud; unwinds the napkin from the wounded brow; and, lo, Jesus comes forth! His chariot waits; He mounts aloft. God is gone up with a shout! From the distance comes the song, "Lift up your heads, O ye gates; and be ye lifted up ye everlasting doors, and let the King of Glory enter in!"

I. *The angel of the resurrection was fortunate in being permitted to serve the King.* Need it be said that Jesus could have dispensed with this service? He had "power to lay down his life and power to take it again." The rolling away of the stone was a small matter to One who by his indwelling energy was able to overcome the King of Terrors. But here we note the blessed condescension of our Lord: he invites men and angels to become "laborers together with him."

A man is busy in his workshop. His little son is playing among the chips and shavings. "Come, my son," he says, putting a saw into his hand, "help me." Proud lad; to be helping his father! It is proper training for the serious business of life. So God sees us playing with yellow dust and chasing thistledown; and he calls us to fetch and carry for him. It is our apprenticeship for eternity. It is glorious preparation for the larger tasks of the kingdom of God.

The world believes in Christ. It believes in him as an historic fact; it credits the story of the manger and the cross; but, as for the story of the open sepulcher? Just there the eyebrows are lifted. The world believes in a dead Christ. The stone is still against the door of the sepulcher. It is for us to roll it away. The King asks this service of us.

The truth of the resurrection is God's sign-manual on the work of redemption; as it is written, "He was delivered for our offenses and raised again for our justification." Without this the gospel is like the story of Edwin Drood; it lacks a *denouement*. Tell it out, therefore, that he who was dead is alive and liveth forevermore. Tell it in your walk and conversation; show it by the glory shining in your face; sing it with heart and understanding:

> "From the dark grave he rose,
>   The mansions of the dead;
> And thence his mighty foes
>   In glorious triumph led.
> Up through the sky the Conqueror rode,
> And reigns on high the Savior God!"

II. *The angel of the resurrection was fortunate, also, in being permitted to render a special service to the Church.* As yet the Church was but a little company of "feeble folk like the conies." The heart went out of them when Christ was crucified. John and the three Marys stood on Calvary with their faces fallen upon their breasts. At the window of the upper room in Salome's house there were others who looked off toward the hill; saw the strange darkness, and then the returning light, and saw through their tears the dark effigy against the sky. He whom they had expected to redeem Israel was dead. "I go a-fishing," said Peter; the others said, "We also go with thee." Why not? Their hopes were dashed; their Lord was lying in his grave.

As they were dragging their nets in the early twilight of the morning they saw One walking on the shore. They whispered, "It is the Lord." Then Peter, throwing off his fisher's coat, cast himself into the water and swam to meet him. The fishing days of Peter and his friends were over. Jesus was risen from the dead. The work of his kingdom must thenceforth engage their every thought.

Now it was the Day of Pentecost; in the power of the Spirit the disciples were speaking with other tongues. The on-lookers asked, "What meaneth this?" Some said, "It is the power of new wine." Peter was on his feet at peril of his life, to speak of Jesus. "New wine!" he cried, "Nay, this is the prophecy of Joel, 'It shall come to pass in the last days, saith the Lord, I will pour out my Spirit upon all flesh.' Ye men of Israel, hear these words: Ye took Jesus of Nazareth and crucified him with wicked hands; and behold, God hath loosed him from the pains of death: He, therefore, being at the right hand of God exalted, hath breathed his Spirit upon us!"

A little later we hear Peter saying, "Blessed be the God and Father of our Lord Jesus Christ, who according to his abundant mercy hath begotten us again" (as if a begetting into the faith of Christ crucified were not enough) "unto a living hope by the resurrection of Jesus Christ from the dead!" And the time came when this man, who once trembled and fell before the pointed finger of a maid-servant, went forth without a tremor to be crucified beyond the city walls, rejoicing in hope of the crown of martyrdom made for his devotion to the truth.

The doctrine of the risen Christ is our inspiration. It is the inspiration of the Church in her great propaganda. The world is to be won by the doctrine of a living Christ. Scotland was once saved by an army following a golden urn which contained the embalmed heart of Robert the Bruce. The Captain of our Salvation is the Conqueror of Death. He gave the watchword on Olivet when he said to the assembled disciples, "All power is given unto me in heaven and in earth. Go ye, therefore, and evangelize; and, lo, I am with you alway, even unto the end of the world."

III. *A distinct and glorious service was rendered by this fortunate angel to all the children of men.* Blessed is the bearer of glad tidings! In the early dusk a group of women set out for the sepulcher with spices to embalm their Lord. They went with leaden feet; asking by the way, "Who shall roll us away the stone?" As they drew near, however, they perceived that the stone was already rolled away, and the angel was there, sitting upon it. "The Lord whom ye seek," he said, "is not here; he is risen!" A moment later they were running to tell the disciples. What cared they for decorum? One of them was the wife of the royal steward. On she ran, eyes bright, face flushed, lips trembling, heart beating wildly! Oh for winged feet to bear them now! Run! Run! Tell the world that Christ is risen!

The world has enough of dead gods. Zeus and Apollo, the gods of Walhalla, dreamy-eyed Buddh, all are dead. They have eyes, but they see not; ears, but they hear not; hands, but they help not. We dwell in a great pantheon full of dead deities. Blessed is the man who knows his commission and hastens to say, "There is One that liveth, One that is mighty to save; One that hath at his girdle the keys of death and hell!"

The word for Easter is *Sursum Corda!* Up with your hearts, O followers of Christ! Hallelujah! "The Lord is risen, indeed." It gladdens our lives, it glorifies our faith, it makes the gospel the power of God unto salvation.

Do you cherish among your treasures a letter, worn and tear-stained, written by one who long ago passed out of your life? What if, as you sit reading it, a hand should be laid upon you, and, looking up, you should hear him say, "I am alive; weep not!" The story of Christ crucified is such a letter. Read it to-night with a new expectancy. Listen for his step; lift up your eyes; he speaks. It is the voice of the Shepherd come to awake and woo his bride: "Rise up, my love, my fair one, and come away; for, lo, the winter is past; the rain is over and gone; the flowers appear on the earth, and the time of the singing of birds is come. Arise, my love, my fair one, and come away!"

THE PRIDE OF NAAMAN.

"So Naaman came with his horses and with his chariot, and stood at the door of the house of Elisha. And Elisha sent a messenger unto him, saying, Go and wash in Jordan seven times, and thy flesh shall come again to thee, and thou shalt be clean. But Naaman was wroth and went away, and said, Behold, I thought, He will surely come out to me, and stand, and call on the name of the Lord his God, and strike his hand over the place, and recover the leper. Are not Abana and Pharpar, rivers of Damascus, better than all the waters of Israel? may I not wash in them, and be clean? So he turned, and went away in a rage."—II. Kings 5, 9-12.

The keynote of the life and character of Naaman is pride. And why should he not be proud ? He was a mighty man of valor; brave, cautious, energetic. He was the commander-in-chief of the Syrian armies. The time was when Ben-hadad commanded in person; but now he was old and Naaman was his trusted helper. Surely, the king's favorite, the wealthy aristocrat, the successful captain, had reason to be proud.

Nor was he singular in this. Pride is our universal failing. An East Side missionary says that the families of his congregation who have but a single chair in their tenements are scarcely recognized by the others. On Cherry Street it is a question of chairs; on Fifth Avenue, of birth and culture and wealth. In some of the Alpine valleys the people are proud of their goiters; on the Congo, of their thick lips.

In any case, however, pride is irrational. A gnat having alighted on a bull's horn said, "I'm afraid

I'm heavy; if I trouble you, say so and I'll be off." "Oh, never mind," was the reply; "I shouldn't have known you were there if you hadn't mentioned it." Strange what a small amount of capital will set a man up in this business. "Why should the spirit of mortal be proud?" Naaman was no worse than the rest of us.

But there was a minor note; "he was a leper." This was the crook in Naaman's lot. The white scale was on his forehead. Had he been an Israelite it would have disqualified him for public service; not so in Syria. As yet, the disease had not reached its malignant stage; his visor would hide it. Ah, but he knew, his household knew; it began to be rumored among his soldiers, his servants gossiped about it. A little maid in his home, a captive out of the land of Israel, had ventured to say, "Would God my lord were with the prophet that is in Samaria, for he would recover him of his leprosy." She spake better than she knew. The wife of Naaman reported this saying to her husband and prevailed upon him to visit the prophet. It is our present purpose to follow him on that journey, and to observe *how his pride was brought low.*

He is just setting out. There is a stir at the mansion. Naaman is in his chariot; the outriders are before it; a retinue of soldiers follows after, with a company of slaves. He is going in state, so as to make a suitable impression. He is arrayed as becomes a great captain, and he takes with him ten changes of raiment. He carries ten talents of silver and six thousand pieces of gold,—about sixty thousand dollars—a most generous physician's fee,—

for he will accept nothing without pay. Still further, he bears a letter from his king, Ben-hadad, addressed, not to the prophet—indeed it would have been beneath the dignity of the Syrian king to notice a mere prophet—but to Jehoram, the king of Israel. This letter is couched in the imperative mood: "Behold, I send herewith Naaman my servant to thee, that thou mayest recover him of his leprosy." Jehoram had met Ben-hadad in battle and knew the temper of his steel. Let him fail to heal Naaman at his peril!

Thus arrayed in worldly pride, the great captain sets out upon his journey; plumes waving, armor glistening in the sunlight, the procession moves on. His devoted wife watches his departure through the lattice; beside her stands the little captive maid, her lips moving in prayer to her God.

The next day Naaman presents himself at the palace of Jehoram with his letter. The king trembles as he reads; knowing the spirit of Ben-hadad, he cries, "Am I God, to kill and to make alive, that this man doth send unto me to recover a man of his leprosy? See how he seeketh a quarrel against me!" He rends his garments in token of dismay. At this juncture a messenger arrives from Elisha, saying, "Fear not, O king, send Naaman unto me, and he shall know that there is a prophet in Israel."

Now the cortége of Naaman lines up before the door of the prophet's humble home. The captain has no intention of dismounting, but awaits the prophet's appearance. The delay irritates him. A servant appears. Here is a studied affront, which the forthcoming message merely aggravates:—"Go and wash in Jordan seven times, and thou shalt be clean." What wonder that Naaman "was wroth"? Was ever such discourtesy put upon a mighty man of valor? To the Jordan forsooth? "Are not Abana and Pharpar, rivers of Damascus, better than all the waters of Israel?" Abana, gushing from the rugged side of Anti-Libanus, spreading over the beautiful glens, then bursting through a gorge, and dividing itself into seven crystal streams. And Pharpar, pure and limpid, called *Chrysorrhoas*, the "River of Gold"! What is Jordan to these? shallow and turbid Jordan, flowing out of a marsh and emptying into a pool! Indeed, there is something admirable in Naaman's patriotic indignation.

> "Lives there a man with soul so dead,
> Who never to himself hath said,
> This is my own, my native land?"

They tell of the Rhine with its cliffs and castles; but what of our glorious Hudson? They tell of the Thames; but what of our "Father of Waters"?

> My native country, thee,
> Land of the noble free,
>   Thy name I love;
> I love thy rocks and rills,
> Thy woods and templed hills;
> My heart with rapture thrills
>   Like that above!

But worst affront of all was the injunction to bathe. To bathe seven times! It seemed like a studied attempt to make sport of him.

All this was very different from what the man had expected: "Behold, I thought, He will surely come out to me, and stand, and call on the name of the Lord his God, and strike his hand over the place, and heal me." He had regarded the prophet as a necromancer,—one likely to be impressed by his pomp and circumstance,—had supposed that he would say, "Presto!" and perform the cure. At the center of this imposing scene, he himself would be the observed of all observers. "Go to the Jordan," indeed! This was not at all according to the program. There would be no éclat in such a performance. The prophet was facetious, was making a jesting-stock of him. Little wonder that he "fell into a rage." Doubtless it was a genuine military rage, full of oaths and imprecations. But the prophet knew what was best for this mighty man of valor: he must be emptied of his pride before God could help him. So must you; so must I.

Thus the errand of Naaman came to the very verge of failure. He turned to his charioteer and said, "Drive to Damascus; we will reckon with this prophet in due time." His leprosy was still upon him; pride was still raging in his heart. The prophet was a charlatan. The journey to Samaria was for naught.

But what is this? A conference among the servants; they whisper together. One of them, as spokesman, draws near to the chariot and falls upon his knee. "My father," he cries. In that word we are introduced to a better side of Naaman's character. His servants loved him; on occasion they might venture even to take liberties with him. They did not tremble at his martial aspect; they knew that under his corselet beat a kindly heart, and that back of his hot temper was sound reason. But what will this servant say? "My father, if the prophet had bid thee do some great thing, wouldest thou not have done it? Wast thou not ready to pay him ten talents of silver and six thousand pieces of gold? How much rather then wilt thou do this little thing that he saith, Wash and be clean"? There is something in that. Naaman yields to his sober second thought. "Drive to the Jordan!" he cries; "it can do no harm. We have come so far; let us go through with it."

And here they are at the bank of Jordan. He lays aside his armor, puts off his outer garment, steps down into the river. He dips himself in the water once, twice, thrice; then turns to see his servants watching from the bank. He is indeed the "observed of all observers", but not as he had thought. Four times, five, six, and still no change! Why should he thus be made a gazingstock for naught? He will go no further with the dumb show. "Dip again, Master," cry his servants, "once more, once more!" He dips the seventh time; lifts his hand to his forehead as he emerges from the water; and a cry comes from the bank, "Master, the white scall is gone!" Behold, his flesh is become again like the flesh of a little child.

His leprosy was gone. More yet, his pride was gone; something better had come to supplant it. As he entered his chariot there was a conflict of strange emotions within him.

"Where now, Master?" asked his charioteer. "To Damascus?"

"Nay; back to Samaria." It was out of his way, indeed; but a true man must make his just acknowledgments.

And as they rode, he pondered. He had been a worshiper of Rimmon. But could Rimmon heal him ? The power that had been manifest upon him must be the power of the true God.

He is again at the prophet's door. He descends from his chariot with a low obeisance. Elisha sends no servant now, but comes forth himself to greet him.

"Now I know," says Naaman, "that there is no God in all the earth but the God of Israel." The passing of his leprosy was the slightest change in this man. He had changed his God. It was right that he should confess it.

"Take, therefore, a blessing of thy servant," he continues. His attendants are unloading the strong boxes.

"As the Lord liveth," replies the prophet, "I will receive nothing from thee." The man must be taught that the God of Israel is not a merchant, that he should sell his commodities, but a Giver, a great Giver, a royal Giver, whose gifts are without money and without price.

"Give, then, to thy servant two mules' burden of earth, that I may build an altar on holy ground; for thy servant henceforth will sacrifice unto none other but the true God."

The request is granted, and, making his grateful farewells, the Syrian captain sets forth. But a look of perplexity gathers on his brow. He turns back. A question of grave importance has occurred to him: "The Lord pardon thy servant," he says, "for this thing; but what shall I do ? When my master goeth unto the house of Rimmon to worship there, he leaneth on my hand; and when he boweth, I also have been wont to bow. What now shall I do?"

It was a hard question. "Go in peace," said the prophet; that is, simply, "Farewell." He must settle the problem for himself. He has henceforth a conscience to reckon with. This is the first evidence of regeneration. No sooner does a man begin the better life than he confronts great questions which before were of little moment to him. "Go in peace; the Lord will direct thee; this is a matter to be determined between thee and God."

In due time Naaman reached his home. His faithful wife, awaiting him, saw her lord's company as they drew nigh on the Lebanon road; her heart was beating fast in suspense; she shaded her eyes to see whether he were a leper still, but his helmet hid his face. As he, at length, descended from the chariot, he lifted his visor,—the white scall was gone! We may be sure she sobbed forth her joy in her husband's arms. And as for the little captive maid? No doubt they overlooked her; but she had done, by her timely word, what Ben-hadad and Jehoram could not do. The mouse had gnawed the lion out of his net. Such deeds are their own reward. She saw the great captain healed of his infirmity and quietly thanked her God.

Here the curtain falls. Naaman had many marvelous things to tell his wife that day. "We have worshiped Rimmon," he said, "but Jehovah alone is God." In the court of his mansion he sprinkled the two mules' burden of earth and reared an altar. A lamb was laid upon it and the captain and his wife knelt in worship. In the light of that sacrifice we draw our practical lessons:

1. Sin is leprosy; an incurable dis-ease. The scall is in all flesh. All men are conscious of it, and equally conscious that its penalty is spiritual and eternal death.

2. There is a God in Israel. In healing leprosy he gives token of his power to forgive sin. Of this we have definite assurance in the gospel of his well-beloved Son. A fountain is opened at Calvary for all uncleanness. This stream has healing power beyond all the rivers of Damascus. "Come now, saith the Lord, and let us reason together: Though your sins be as scarlet, they shall be as white as snow; though they be red like crimson, they shall be as wool."

3. Our pride alone stands between our sins and God. Pride is buttressed by prejudice. "I thought," said Naaman. So say we, as we turn our eyes toward the cross. "Behold, I thought my penance would atone for sin. I thought to earn my way to heaven by good works. I thought by outward forms and ceremonies to commend myself to God." "I thought! I thought!" God save us from such preconceptions. The question is not what we think, but what God thinks as to this matter of the endless life. "I will not" has slain its thousands, but "I thought", its tens of thousands. God's thoughts are not as our thoughts, nor his ways as our ways. His thought is expressed in the announcement, "God so loved the world that he gave his only-begotten Son, that whosoever believeth in him should not perish, but have everlasting life."

His thought as expressed in the cross is simplicity itself. Yet this very simplicity is an offense unto us.

Christ crucified is "foolishness to the Greek, and to the Jew a stumbling block; but to them that are saved, it is the wisdom and the power of God." Here is our only hope of salvation. Let us put away pride and prejudice and address ourselves to the saving truth as God hath revealed it. "He resisteth the proud, but giveth grace to the humble." He offers eternal life on the sole condition of faith in the atoning blood of his Son. The gift is without money and without price. Bow low, my friend, to receive it. Put away thy thought; let God have his way with thee. If you and I are ever saved, it will be because we come to Christ as Wesley did, saying,

> "I'm a poor sinner and nothing at all;
> But Jesus Christ is my all in all."

THE HANDS OF JESUS.

"And when he had thus spoken, he showed them his hands."—Luke 24, 40.

The "Art of Palmistry" is compounded of one grain of truth and ninety-nine of artifice; the only doubt being as to the single grain. The father of the so-called "Art" in its modern form was Lavater, an eccentric priest. The work assigned to him, as a candidate for holy orders, was to stand at the doorway of the chapel, holding a velvet bag for offerings. His eyes were downcast, in pursuance of his vow of humility; thus he became perforce a close observer of hands. It was indeed a matter of little skill to read the character of the giver in this way. A hand of velvet, plump and unctuous, told unmistakably of worldly ease. A hard, horny hand was indicative of honest toil. A thin hand, armed with talons, said, "Shylock is casting in an alms." It was but clever guesswork.

We need no conjurer's art or artifice for our present task. We are to contemplate the hands of Jesus. The lessons they teach are plain and simple and for practical uses.

Observe, first,—They were a man's hands. The crucifixion was over. The disciples were met in the upper room; and the doors were shut "for fear of the

Jews." There were rumors that Jesus had risen from the dead. In this company were certain women, who said that they had seen him. But some doubted. On a sudden he stood among them, saying, "Peace be unto you." They were dazed, terrified, supposing it to be his disembodied spirit. Then he said, "Behold my hands and my feet, that it is I myself; handle me and see; a spirit hath not flesh and bones." Thus they were convinced that it was the very Jesus who had lived and walked among them.

He was, on earth, a veritable man. He took our nature—"not the nature of angels, but of men." A sect arose called *Docetæ*, who, in order to evade the difficulties of the incarnation, held that the body of Jesus was a phantasm; his alleged humanity was an optical illusion. The truth, however, is that he was flesh of our flesh, our real kinsman, being in all points such as we are, only without sin.

And so he remains forever. Let us emphasize this fact. The incarnation was not a temporary expedient. In the theanthropic person of Jesus there was a perfect union of Godhood with humanity. When he came from heaven to earth he did not empty himself of his godhood; nor when he returned from earth to heaven did he lay aside his manhood. As he ascended from Olivet his fleshly body was sublimated, etherealized, adjusted to the necessities of the spiritual world; but that fleshly body furnished the seed (1 Cor. xv. 35-57) or material for his spiritual body; so that he abides through all eternity the God-man. Here is infinite comfort: he remains the first born among many brethren, the Elder Brother of us all. The true statement of this doctrine, as given in one of our venerable symbols, is this: "The Eternal Son of God became man by taking to himself a true body and a reasonable soul, and so was and continues to be God and Man in two distinct natures and one person forever."

Second,—They were pure hands. "Who shall ascend unto the hill of the Lord ? or, who shall stand in his holy place ? He that hath clean hands and a pure heart; who hath not lifted up his soul to vanity nor sworn deceitfully." Where shall we find such an one ? Is it you ? Is it any of your friends or acquaintance ? Nay, there is no difference; all have sinned. There is none that doeth good; no, not one. "Will all great Neptune's ocean wash this blood clean from my hands?" Jesus claimed an absolute sinlessness. Here is his challenge: "Which of you convinceth me of sin ?" Of all the accusations brought against him, not one impeached the spotless purity of his character and life.

And his claim was strangely conceded. The man who betrayed him returned to the hall Gazith, where he had received the price of treachery, and casting down the pieces of silver before the rabbis cried, "I have betrayed innocent blood!"—The man who sat in judgment over him and sentenced him to death brought him out to Gabbatha, the place of Judgment, and, in sight of the assembled multitude, said, "I find no fault in him at all."—The centurion who had charge of his execution, looked toward the cross when the tragedy was over, and testified, "Verily, this was a righteous man." Were ever such tributes paid to the virtue of another ? Some have, indeed, claimed perfection; but the world has laughed them to scorn. The world has lauded others for their perfection; but they have repudiated it. In Christ alone the claim and the testimony are united. Behold the Man!

Third,—They were callous hands. What went ye out for to see? A man with soft, white hands? Nay; such are in king's palaces and in the mansions of those who can live without labor; or else in the market-places and at the corners of the streets, where idlers say, "The world owes me a living." But Christ belonged to the Third Estate, the honorable company of working men. He was a man of the people, an average man. It is written of Buddha that, at the beginning of his ministry, he left his palace and took his place under the sacred Bo-tree to meditate. On the contrary, Jesus entered a carpenter-shop and became the brother of all who give themselves to labor as the fulfillment of the primal law.

It was now three years since he had crossed the threshold of his shop in Nazareth to engage in the distinctive work of his ministry. But hands that have once known handicraft are marked forever with its imprint. Once a toiler, always a toiler. Our Lord in heaven is as truly the sympathetic Friend of workingmen as when he made plows for the farmers of Galilee and mended the furniture of the people of Nazareth.

The great problem, destined to be the last which civilization shall solve, is that between capital and labor. We are addressing ourselves to its solution by such devices as arbitration. So far, so good. But who shall be arbitrator? Pope, or bishop, or archbishop? Nay, call in the Lord and Master of them all. It is greatly to be feared, however, that an objection would be entered against him on the ground of probable bias. His sleeves were not of lawn. Nevertheless it remains for him to solve the problem. All classes must be blended, all middle walls of separation broken down, by the application of his Golden Rule: "Do unto others as ye would have them do unto you."

Fourth,—They were strong hands. Not strong with a mere knotted muscularity, like those of an athlete, disciplined to strike a blow; but hands that spoke of courage and authority, of a perfect physical and moral symmetry.

The right hand of Jesus is the hand of judgment. It is written, "His fan is in his hand and he will thoroughly purge his floor; he will gather the wheat into his garners, and burn up the chaff with unquenchable fire." This is the hand that wrote in Belshazzar's hall, ' *Mene, Tekel,*" Weighed and found wanting!

This right hand is the hand of a King. It holds the scepter of heaven and earth. His enemies put an impotent reed into it, and paraded before him with mock obeisance, crying, "Hail, O King!" They shall see him reigning in light and glory unapproachable. His scepter is a right scepter; his dominion is for ever and ever.

This right hand of Jesus is the hand of salvation. It can pluck a sinner from the depths. It made the worlds and spun them out upon their orbits in infinite space; a work so great that in celebration of it the morning stars sang together and all the sons of God shouted for joy. But that was not his greatest work; indeed, it was no more for him to frame the worlds than for a lad to blow bubbles into the air. His master-work is Redemption. For this he is represented as "making bare his arm," like a workman about to address himself to a tremendous task.

"'Twas great to call a world from naught,
'Tis greater to redeem."

Fifth,—They were friendly hands, the kindest and most helpful. They were ever employed in doing good.

On one occasion he called little children to him, laid his hands upon them and blessed them, saying, "Suffer them to come unto me." No such record is made of any other of the world's illustrious teachers. He loved children; he recognized the truth, "The child is father of the man."

On another occasion a leper cried, "Lord, if thou wilt, thou canst make me clean!" Jesus approached him.—Take heed, good Rabbi, lest thou come too near! Here is infection; here is ceremonial uncleanness.—He put forth his hand and touched him, saying, "I will; be thou clean!" This man was so pure that soul and body alike were proof against defilement. The evil had no part in him.

On another occasion a demoniac boy was brought for healing. "Thou dumb and deaf spirit," he cried, "come forth!" The lad, rent by the parting demon, fell as dead. And Jesus "took him by the hand and lifted him up and he arose." Such is his custom. How many a soul, afflicted once by sin and trouble, can say, "He took me by the hand, he lifted me up!"

The Evangelist in Patmos saw him in the midst of the golden candlesticks, clothed with a garment of authority, girt with a golden girdle, his face shining like the sun. "And when I saw him," he writes, "I fell at his feet as dead. Then he laid his right hand upon me, saying, 'Fear not!'" John knew the voice; he knew the touch of that right hand. "Fear not!" The trouble of his soul was gone. Here was the Friend on whose bosom he had pillowed his head in former days.

Sixth,—They were wounded hands. It was thus that the prophet Zechariah saw him five hundred years before his Advent. In amazement he asked, "What are these wounds in thy hands?" The vision answered, "They are those with which I was wounded in the house of my friends." Let us thrust our fingers into these nail-prints and be not faithless but believing. They have a wonderful story to tell. They are eloquent of God's love; he so loved the world that he gave his only-begotten Son to suffer and die for it.—They are eloquent of God's justice; as it is written, "Awake, O sword, against my fellow." He so hated sin that, being unable in the nature of the case to overlook it, he must needs send his well-beloved to expiate it in his own body on the tree.—They are eloquent of God's wisdom; in all the religions of the world there is no other plan of deliverance from the penalty of a misspent life. The blood of Jesus cleanseth; and without the shedding of blood there is no remission of sin.—They are eloquent of God's power; by these wounds we are given to believe that he is able to save even to the uttermost. These hands were nailed to the cross;

but even there they did not lose their cunning. A thief in penitence cried out, "Remember me!" and Jesus saved him.

He saved the dying thief! The world objects: "Shall a malefactor, who has passed his years in crime, be carried to heaven *in articulo mortis?*" O, mean and grudging world! Cruel, implacable world! Narrow, bigoted world, thus to deny a poor sinner his only chance. Now or never it must be. In an hour this thief will be in eternity, his character fixed, and repentance forever too late. Blessed be God for his grace; free grace and unto the uttermost! By the power of his pierced hands let it be known and preached that he rescues thieves and Magdalenes. Nothing is too hard for him.

Seventh,—They were uplifted hands. He stood in the midst of his disciples and blessed them, saying, "Peace be unto you." The last glimpse they caught of him, as he was received by the opening heavens, he was still stretching out his hands in benediction over them.

Better still, they are uplifted in intercession for us. The high priest, on the Great Day of Atonement, with the names of the tribes written on his breast, entered the Holy of Holies to sprinkle the mercy-seat with blood and plead for the pardon of the people's sin. So Christ has entered into the holiest by a new and living way. Our names are written upon his hands, close to the nail-prints. Thus he makes an all-prevailing plea: "O Father, these have sinned; but I have made atonement for them. Behold these wounds in my hands! Let these guilty ones enter into life for my sake." And from all the mercy-seats, the sanctuaries, the trysting-places of earth, is heard an echo of that intercession, "For Jesus' sake."

> Arise, my soul, arise,
> Shake off thy guilty fears ;
> The bleeding Sacrifice
> In my behalf appears;
> Before the throne my Surety stands
> My name is written on his hands.
>
> Five bleeding wounds he bears,
> Received on Calvary ;
> They pour effectual prayers,
> They strongly plead for me:—
> Forgive him, O forgive, they cry,
> Nor let that ransom'd sinner die.

Finally,—They are outstretched hands. He stands in an attitude of invitation. The gospel is in this word, "Come." " Ho, every one that thirsteth, come."— "Come now, saith the Lord, let us reason together; though your sins be as scarlet, they shall be as white as snow."—"Come unto me, all ye that labor and are heavy laden, and I will give you rest."—" The Spirit and the Bride say, Come; and let him that is athirst, come; and whosoever will, let him take the water of life freely."—Come! Come! Come!

His hands are stretched out still. O infinite patience! "All the day long have I stretched forth my hands unto a disobedient and gainsaying people." There is still opportunity of closing in with his overtures of mercy. But he will not save us in spite of ourselves. In this he pays tribute to the dignity of our manhood. We are made in the likeness of God, with sovereign wills. We can yield or resist. If he draws us, it must be "with the cords of a man." It takes two to make a covenant. Faith is the condition of salvation. His arm has been made bare for us. His right hand is reached from heaven to save us. Grasp it, and enter into life?

THE STRENGTH OF A YOUNG MAN.*

"I have written unto you, young men, because ye are strong, and the word of God abideth in you, and ye have overcome the wicked one."—I. John, 2, 14.

I bring a message from a centenarian. John was a hundred years old when he wrote this letter. " Let the multitude of years show wisdom." His life covered the world's most eventful century. His fellow-apostles had been led, one by one, to the stake, the headsman's block or the amphitheatre; and he alone was left. He had outlived twelve emperors; had been haled before Nero and escaped out of the mouth of the lion; had seen Titus lay siege to Jerusalem and reduce it, rearing crosses on the surrounding hills in awful fulfillment of the prophetic malediction, "His blood be on us and on our children!" He had now returned to Ephesus from his exile, old and feeble. The candle was slowly burning to its socket.

I. "I write unto you, *young men.*" In the heart of the aged evangelist there was a warm place for young men. It is related of him in one of the early legends, that once he went out from Ephesus along a dangerous road. In the depth of the

---

*This sermon was preached Sunday, May 1st, 1898, on the tenth anniversary of the founding of the Brotherhood of Andrew and Philip.

forest he paused and listened, leaning on his staff. In the distance was heard the sound of horses' hoofs and then the clang of steel. He should have been afraid, but his face was lit with joyful expectancy. A moment later the robbers were upon him. He smiled a kindly greeting, saying, "Take me to your captain." They led him to an open space. There sat on a horse a young man bravely equipped with helmet and breastplate. Then a strange thing happened. At sight of this old man the robber chief uttered a cry of mingled pain and terror, threw himself from his horse, and fell prostrate before him. The evangelist lifted him to his feet, saying, "My son, if any man sin, we have an advocate with the Father, even Jesus Christ the righteous." They had last met at the sacramental altar at Ephesus. The youth had broken his vow; had mingled in the merry dance of Aphrodite around the midsummer fires; had cast restraint to the winds. But here was his reclamation. He cast away sword and helmet and returned with John to Ephesus, a trophy of God's redeeming grace.

II. "I write unto you, young men, *because ye are strong.*" There is profound pathos here. I see the evangelist as he writes; his eyes are dim, his hands tremulous; the characters are wayward and irregular. Time was when he wrote a clear, bold hand. Time was when he ventured forth with his comrades on the boisterous lake, rejoicing in the whistling wind, the bellying sail, the creaking mast. Time was when he stood by his brethren in the forefront of Christian service, his eye kindling at the thought of dangerous enterprise. Now his blood runs slow;

'his manly voice, turning again towards childish treble, pipes and whistles in his sound." The grasshopper is a burden. He shakes himself, like Samson, to find that his locks are shorn. The infirmities of age are upon him.

And there is so much to be done! The world is bright with promise. Doors are opening on every hand. The followers of Christ are multiplying. The Roman eagle has begun to build its nest in the cleft of the Rock of Ages. O for youth and strength and courage to mingle in the stirring events of history! It is as if John said, "Young man, know your privilege. The future calls as with beckoning hands. The fields are yellow unto the harvest. Thrust in the sickle and reap. Be eager, be ambitious. Follow your Leader to the high places of responsibility and usefulness. Use your strength for God!"

What is the strength here referred to? *Not physical*, surely. Ask the average boy, "Who was the greatest man?" and he will answer, "Samson, who rent asunder the jaws of a lion as if it had been a kid; who carried away the great gates of Gaza to the hilltop; who laid his hands upon the columns of Dagon's temple and brought the great fabric rattling down in ruin about him." Or ask, "Who is the leading man at college?" and the lad will answer, "The captain of the 'Varsity crew." But give him time and he will revise his judgment. He will learn that physical strength alone goes for little in the earnest world. The glory of the college athlete, if it be alone, soon lapses into desuetude. "Bodily exercise profiteth little." . . . . . Or, *did John refer to mon-*

etary strength? You are ambitious, mayhap, to be "a young Napoleon of finance." You mean to win a fortune. Suppose you succeed? "We brought nothing into this world and it is certain we can carry nothing out." This is but a transient and superficial sort of strength at best. "A man's life consisteth not in the abundance of the things which he possesseth." A child who wearies himself in chasing a butterfly, ends by brushing a little yellow dust from his fingers. "So, also, shall the rich man fade away in his ways." . . . . . Or is the reference to *that spectacular power which comes from living in the public eye?* You covet a little brief authority. But is it worth while? Louis XIV., as he lay dying, called the Dauphin to his bedside and said, "My son, I might have lived a better life; profit by my errors; and remember this: kings die like other men." . . . . Or is the reference to *intellectual strength?* It is a true saying, "Knowledge is power." Every time a boy learns a lesson, he generates force and adds to the possibilities of his personal usefulness. But "knowledge ceaseth." The valedictorian of my class, dear fellow, broke down under his mental exertions, before he had fully entered upon life's responsibilities, and died in an asylum. It is a true saying, "Much study is a weariness of the flesh." And when we have learned our utmost, it still remains that "the wisdom of man is foolishness with God." . . . . No; the strength which the evangelist had in mind was beyond and above all these. *It was moral strength*, or character. The word itself is significant. The original meaning of *character* is a stamp or graving tool; that which makes an impression. Our true strength or moral value is not to be measured by natural gifts and endowments, but by what we are and what we do. In 1798, when our country was facing the possibility of war with France, the President wrote to Washington at Mount Vernon, "We must have your name; it will be of more value to us than a standing army."

How shall we estimate the importance of a man? We cannot weigh him, as we do beef cattle, on a platform scale. Put him there, if you please, as so much avoirdupois; fill his pockets with gold; place a jeweled crown on his head; fill his hands with books and parchments; still you are not weighing the man. What of his faith, his virtue, his high ambition and noble aspiration? These and kindred graces and attributes go to make character; and character is the Archimedean lever which lifts the world.

III. *Whence comes this power?* The apostle tells us,—from "the word of God." Here is the secret of influence. The strongest man in the world is the best Bible-Christian; he who most sincerely believes the Book and most consistently lives up to it.

I confess to an utter weariness of Biblical controversy. For twenty years the Bible has been practically a closed book; yet we boast of living in an age of Bible study. We have been studying *about* the Bible; about its age and authorship; about its chronology and style and hypothetical construction; all about the outside of it. Is it not time, in the name of the living God who inspired it, to open this venerable book and learn its contents? If we do not believe it, that ends the matter; if we do, then let us rest awhile from noisy strife and read it. For out of this volume are the issues of eternal life and death. "Search the Scriptures," said the Master, "for in them ye think ye have eternal life, and these are they which testify of me."

It is from these Scriptures that we derive *our views of spiritual truth*. The business of all earnest men is to have definite convictions as to the great verities. A lad of sixteen recently said in my hearing, "I am an agnostic." He probably did not even know the meaning of the word. An agnostic is one who knows nothing and is proud of it. We are living in a time that calls for vertebrates; for men who can stand erect on their two feet, with their faces toward heaven and say in a tone of utmost conviction, "I believe." Be anything, my friend, rather than an agnostic. Be an atheist; be an infidel; be something. Know where you stand. If you are "an honest doubter," go to God's oracles as thirsty men to a spring of living water. Hear what they have to say of God and duty and immortality. These are the postulates of life. Believe them and be able to give a reason for the faith that is in you.

Out of the Scriptures we also derive *our moral code*. They tell us how to determine, as Plato said, "betwixt the worse and better reason." Like a fingerboard at the crossroads, they direct us where to go. Our conscience answers, "Yea" and "Amen", to their moral determinations. A man who passed through our Civil War has a Bible which he cherishes as marking the turning-point of his life. It bears the scar of a bullet which found its way half-way through the volume, to the eleventh of Ecclesiastes, where it left a black mark of emphasis against this verse: "Rejoice, O young man, in thy youth, and let thy heart cheer thee in the days of thy youth; and walk in the ways of thine heart, and in the sight of thine eyes: but know thou, that for all these things God will bring thee into judgment." Blessed is he to whom a "Thus saith the Lord" has been thus forced home, like a bullet to its mark. Truth must have a lodgment; it needs a background. The man who can meet the Scripture half way is bound to make life tell. The energy that comes to us out of the old-fashioned Book formulates itself into faith and principle, and expresses itself in the duties of life.

But the benefits of Scripture are only to be gotten by appropriation. We grow strong not by virtue of a Bible on the study-table, but by "the Word of God abiding in us." We profess to receive it as our infallible rule of faith and practice. Its truths are thus transmuted into moral power. We grow rich as we search it for hid treasure; we grow wise as we find in it the mystery of godliness; we grow strong as we welcome it into our hearts and consciences and give it expression in nerve and sinew, in walk and conversation, in all the duties and responsibilities of life.

IV. And when we have acquired this strength, *what shall we do with it?*" The apostle tells us; we are to use it for "the overcoming of the wicked one." Is there, then, a Wicked One? The doctrine of a personal devil is rarely preached nowadays; but it is impossible that men should disbelieve it. Sir Thomas Browne quaintly says, "When I see cities deserted, homes demolished, mothers and children in rags and beggary, I say, 'The Spaniard hath been here.' And, by the same token, when I see men's lives blighted, their hearts defiled, their consciences seared as with a hot iron, I say, 'The devil hath been here.'"

You need not go far afield in search of him. Turn your eyes inward and you shall find the evidences of his malignant presence. The symptoms are three: "the lust of the flesh, the lust of the eyes, and the pride of life." What is the lust of the flesh? Let us have no euphemism here; the words mean just what they say. What is the lust of the eyes? Our eyes are the organs of envy and covetousness: they are never satisfied; they reach forth, like the horse-leech's daughters, crying, "Give! Give!" And what is the pride of life? It is satisfaction with the things that perish with the using; a sordid content with life here and now. A soul that surrenders itself to these three is under the dominion of the Evil One.

He is everywhere abroad in the world. If it ever could be truly said, "He goeth about like a roaring lion, seeking whom he may devour," it is true just now. Our Lord and Master came "to destroy the works of the devil"; and he has laid the same commission upon us, to tear down the strongholds of iniquity and cast out the Prince of Darkness from the hearts and homes of the children of men.

Our war against Spain is justifiable only on this ground. For three weary years the destroyer has relentlessly wrought his cruel purposes among the Cuban people. They have groaned under tyranny; they have struggled in vain. Some hundreds of thousands of innocent victims have meanwhile died of hunger and exposure. I saw last night two pictures side by side, in startling contrast. They were called, "The Two Mothers." One showed the Queen Regent of Spain, and by her side the youthful king in royal apparel. The other represented a hollow-cheeked Cuban mother with her gaunt and starving boy. It was easy to imagine, between the two pictures, the malignant face of the wicked one. Our armies and fleets go forth under a divine commission to destroy his works. Their watchword is, "The Spaniard must go!"

But there is a broader view. The malignant power of the Prince of Darkness is seen everywhere about us. Crimes and oppressions, sensuality, Sabbath desecration, intemperance; all these are works of the wicked one. There are seven thousand dramshops on Manhattan Island! These are open mouths of hell. There is not a right-thinking or respectable man in any community that will undertake to defend the saloon. It fills our prisons and workhouses, our asylums and hospitals. It has wrought evil and only evil, and is to-day the most potent and universal expression of Satanic influence on earth. Do we say, in view of long-continued tyranny and oppression in Cuba, "The Spaniard must go?" Where is our sense of just proportion that we do not add, with united voice, "The dramshop must go!"

Our young men cannot all enlist in this national campaign. But God calls upon them all to go forth on a crusade against the wicked one, and none is exempt. This is the Holy War. The man who does not enlist, misses the splendid opportunity of life. When the Northern kings, under Sisera, came down against Israel, the beacons were kindled on the mountain tops and the tribes were summoned to go forth. The roll was called: "Judah." "Here!"—"Ephraim." "Here!"—One by one they answered to their names.—"Meroz." There was silence. Where was Meroz? Among the sheepfolds listening to the bleating of the flocks.—On went the army to the defence of Israel. The great battle was fought by the waters of Megiddo. But in the song of victory there was a minor strain: "Curse ye Meroz, curse ye bitterly the inhabitants thereof, because they came not to the help of the Lord, to the help of the Lord against the mighty!"

The Captain of our salvation comes this way. He speaks to every earnest youth, "Follow me! Follow me to the Holy War! To him that overcometh will I give to sit together with me in my throne." He awaits your answer. Will you waste your energies in the pursuit of perishable things, or will you hear the summons to a better, nobler life? God grant that it may be written of you, "And he arose and followed him."

THE SWORD OF GOLIATH.

"And David said unto Ahimelech, And is there not here under thine hand spear or sword? for I have neither brought my sword nor my weapons with me, because the king's business required haste. And the priest said, The sword of Goliath the Philistine, whom thou slewest in the valley of Elah, behold, it is here wrapped in a cloth behind the ephod: if thou wilt take that, take it; for there is no other save that here. And David said, There is none like that; give it me."—I. Samuel 21, 8-9.

The sword here mentioned had an interesting story. The armorer who forged it was doubtless advised that no common blade would answer the needs of Goliath of Gath. "Make me a mighty sword," said the giant, "with a hilt to fit this brawny hand, a point for a mortal thrust and a double blade, sharpened like a razor's edge. Make it strong, yet not too heavy; well tempered and pliant, yet not too brittle, lest it snap and betray me; nor yet too soft, lest it turn its edge. In a word, let it be the weapon for a warrior of six cubits and a span."

It hung in the scabbard, strapped to Goliath's thigh, in the valley of Elah, when he proclaimed his challenge to the armies of Israel: "Why are ye come out to set yourselves in battle array? Am not I a Philistine? Choose you a man and let him come down to me!" Day after day, brandishing his spear, he uttered those boastful words; and, lo, all Israel was dismayed. On the morning of the fortieth day, he saw coming toward him a ruddy youth of a fair countenance, with no weapon but a leathern thong. His pride was affronted. "Am I a dog that thou comest to me with staves?" And he cursed the young athlete by his gods. It was a brave word that rang back across the valley, "Thou comest to me with a sword and with a spear and with a shield, but I come to thee in the name of the Lord of hosts! This day he will deliver thee into my hand, and I will give thy carcass to the fowls of the air and the beasts of the earth; that all the earth may know that there is a God in Israel!" And even as Goliath laughed his derision, a smooth stone from the leathern thong smote him and he fell headlong. Then the youth ran, bent over him, drew the champion's sword from its scabbard, cut off his head; and with the dripping sword in one hand and that gory trophy in the other he returned to Saul's pavilion; while the valley rang with acclamations, "There is a God in Israel!"

In due time the sword of Goliath was placed in the tabernacle, not as a trophy of David's prowess, but as a thank-offering to God. It was meet that he should thus express his gratitude, for the battle was the Lord's. He had no reason to suppose that he would ever see that sword again; indeed he seems to have quite forgotten it. How many things had happened since he carried it to the Holy Place! He had known the vicissitudes of life in a palace; he had distinguished himself on the high places of the field; he had been driven into exile by his jealous sovereign and hunted like a partridge over the hills.

THE SWORD OF GOLIATH. 311

He now presented himself at the door of the tabernacle, a lonely fugitive. In his adventurous life he had lost his simple faith. He begged for food. The priest had none to offer but the loaves of shewbread. Necessity knows no law. David satisfied his hunger; and then, being unarmed, begged for a weapon. The priest said, "The sword of Goliath is here wrapped in a cloth behind the ephod; if thou wilt take that, take it; for there is none other." And David said, "*There is none like that; give it me.*"

He knew the weapon well. It was a tried and trusty blade. True, an enemy had forged it and a hostile hand had wielded it; but David knew its weight, its temper and the sharpness of its edge. *Experientia docet.* Why shall he not use this weapon now in self-defense?

Here is our lesson. The adversary has forged many a sword against us; we may wield them to our own advantage, by the help of God. The key to a manly career is in knowing how to turn the tables on the enemy. Macaulay says, "The secret of success is to triumph over environment and prove one's self superior to adverse circumstance." This is possible, if God be with us.

"I like the man who faces what he must
  With step triumphant and a heart of cheer;
  Who fights the daily battle without fear;
 Sees his hopes fail, yet keeps unfaltering trust
 That God is God; that somehow, true and just,
 His plans work out for mortals; not a tear
 Is shed when fortune, which the world holds dear,
  Falls from his grasp; better, with love, a crust
 Than living in dishonor; envies not,

Nor loses faith in man; but does his best,
Nor even murmurs at his humbler lot;
But with a smile and words of hope, gives zest
To every toiler; he alone is great,
Who by a life heroic conquers fate."

The enemy is digging a pit to ensnare us. Let him dig it deep and wide; the deeper, the better; for, please God, he himself shall fall into it. He is rearing a gallows on which, like Haman, he means to hang us. Let him make it fifty cubits high; for in God's providence he himself shall dangle from the rope's end. He is forging a weapon. Let him temper it well and whet it to a razor's edge; for, by the truth of Jehovah-jireh, he himself shall test the sharpness of it.

I. *The sharpest sword that ever was forged against a mortal man is Sin.* All have felt it. Where is the man who does not bear its scars? Some of us can show unhealed wounds. But even sin, fierce and terrible though it be, may be turned upon the foe to our own advantage. For, is it not written, "All things work together for good to them that love God"? But whoever would use this weapon must grasp it aright. There are three conditions; if we meet them, the victory is ours.

(1). *Confession.* We must admit at the outset that we are sinners. Let there be no mouthing of excuses nor disguising of the dreadful fact. The Orientals say that when an elephant is about to bathe, he muddies the water, that he may not see the deformity of his feet. We are in danger of making our confession in the same way. It is impossible to exaggerate the sinfulness of sin. The iron has entered into our souls. We are under the deserved wrath of God. Let the prayer of David be ours: "Have mercy upon me, O God, according to thy loving kindness: according unto the multitude of thy tender mercies blot out my transgressions! For against thee, thee only, have I sinned and done evil in thy sight."

(2). *Absolution.* God has made an abundant provision for our pardon: "The blood of Jesus Christ his Son cleanseth us from all sin." There is no reason why any, listening to these words, should for another hour abide under the penalty of the broken law. Christ has been crucified for us. He has borne our sins in his own body on the tree. Look and live! There is no condemnation to them that are in Christ Jesus. Though your sins be as scarlet, they shall be as white as snow. Put away pride and prejudice, and close in with the overtures of mercy. He that believeth in the Lord Jesus Christ shall be saved; sin shall have no more power over him.

3. *Renunciation.* "Go and sin no more." Have the grace to profit by experience. If you have visited Edinburgh Castle, you will remember a path along the precipitous cliff where the enemy climbed up on a dark night and scaled the wall. But only once; for just there the wall was trebled and a watch tower set up. You know your besetting sin. The breach in the wall reveals your immediate duty. Station sentinels there. Be on the watch. Are you prone to avarice, love of pleasure, unholy ambition, sensuality? Know your infirmity; guard the breach; sin no more.

The man who has attended to these three—confession, absolution, renunciation—is in a coign of vantage, where he may get the better of his sin. The place nearest to the heavenly throne is reserved for those who have fought their way heavenward with this weapon. The angels sing, "Holy, holy, Lord God Almighty!" but sinners saved by grace,—the penitent thief, Mary the Magdalene and a great multitude whom no man can number—sing a sweeter song: "Worthy is the Lamb that was slain; for he has redeemed us by his blood and made us to be kings and priests unto God!"

II. *Adversity also is a weapon forged against us.* How shall we regard it? As cowards who lie down and suffer the torrent to overwhelm them? As stoics who say, "What can't be cured must be endured"? Nay; rather as Christians, who believe that affliction worketh for them a far more exceeding and eternal weight of glory.

Are there hot, fierce fingers clutching at your heart? O the sharpness of pain and disease! But here is the making of manhood. Paul's thorn in the flesh was "a messenger of Satan sent to buffet him." He prayed thrice that it might be removed, and God answered, "My grace shall be sufficient for thee." He lived to render thanks for the ministry of that thorn; saying, "If I must needs glory, I will glory in tribulation; for when I am weak, then am I strong." It is a true saying, "No affliction for the present seemeth to be joyous, but grievous; but in the end it yieldeth the peaceable fruit of righteousness unto them which are exercised thereby." The leprosy of Naaman was his deliverance from death. Not a few were driven to Jesus during his earthly ministry by their acquaintance with the ills that human flesh is heir to. A great musical critic was asked his opinion of the singing of a young debutante; he said, "It lacks the depth of sorrow, the passion of tears. If I were a young man, I would court her, marry her if possible, maltreat her, break her heart; and in six months she would be the greatest singer in Europe."

Are you a prisoner of poverty? Even poverty has its compensations. Our best men are those who have worked their way. There was a penniless lad in Dartmouth, out at knees and elbows, who received from a well-meaning friend a recipe for oiling shoes; to which he replied, grimly, "I would thank you for a recipe to keep out water and gravel-stones." Yet this youth, Daniel Webster, spurred on by difficulty, blazed a way for himself to a foremost place in the ranks of successful men.

But you have tried and failed? what then? There is deep pathos in the words, "*Receiver's Sale,*" above a tradesman's door. It tells of fruitless toil, of anxiety and buffeting, of honest effort come to naught. Nevertheless, defeat may lead to noblest triumph. If Russia is a great power to-day, it is because Peter the Great was defeated two hundred years ago by Charles XII of Sweden, who marched against him with a paltry twenty thousand. By that event the Czar was stimulated to drill and mobilize his undisciplined armies; and the result is seen in the commanding position of the Russian empire at this day.

The worst of failures is in Christian living. Have

you tried there, my brother, and failed? Be not disheartened; to your knees, and make defeat an omen of success. Profit by experience. No man ever failed more ignominiously than the apostle who denied his Lord thrice with a bitter curse. But he never denied him again. The man of impulse and vacillation, throwing himself at Jesus' feet, rose up the Man of Rock. Our extremity is God's opportunity. His strength is made perfect in our weakness. The sword of the enemy in a brave hand, backed by a believing heart, is the best of weapons for an earnest life.

III. *But what shall be said as to the sharpness of Death?* This also is a weapon of Satan's forging. God never meant that we should speak of Death as "the King of Terrors." Were it not for sin, our dissolution would be as peaceful as that of Moses, of whom the Rabbis say, "God kissed away his breath"; as triumphant as that of Elijah, who ascended in a chariot of fire to his heavenly home. We are affrighted at death only because of that which lies beyond. The thought of the Great Day, the possibility of an endless night, appal us. Yet the anticipation of death may be made a mighty stimulus to earnest endeavor and a noble life. How may we thus turn it to advantage?

(1) Face the fact. Why should we be cowards? We are bound to die. Let us feel the edge of this weapon, as Jesus did in Gethsemane. The purple cup which was placed to his lips was full of the horror of death. He trembled as he looked upon it. "O my Father," he prayed, "let this cup pass from me!" And again, "O my Father, if it be possible let this

cup pass from me?" And again, "O my Father, if it be not possible, thy will, not mine, be done." And, in appreciation of its full significance, he drank it.

(2) Prepare for it. "The sting of death is sin." Christ came into the world to destroy that sting. Go to the cross and behold him conquering death by death; enduring in his own soul its bitterness for you. Go to the open sepulcher and sing your triumph: "O death, where is thy sting? O grave, where is thy victory? The sting of death is sin, and the strength of sin is the law; but thanks be to God who giveth us the victory through our Lord Jesus Christ!"

(3) Do your appointed work. There is no time to waste. "Say not, There are yet four months and then cometh the harvest; lift up your eyes and see; behold, the fields are already white unto the harvest." There is character to build; there is good to be done; there is trouble to assuage; there are souls to save; there are strongholds of evil to be broken down.

"Make haste, O man, to live,
 For thou so soon must die;
 Time hurries past thee like the wind—
 How swift its moments fly."

Do your work; do it well; do it now. The King's business requireth haste. And you shall face the great mystery at last, as Paul did, with joyful anticipation. He had ended his journeys among the Macedonian hills; he had finished his preaching in cities, in synagogues and in prisons. What more remained? "I am now ready to be offered, and the time of my departure is at hand; I have fought the good fight, I have finished my course, I have kept the faith; there is, henceforth, laid up for me the crown of righteousness which the Lord the righteous Judge shall give to me at that day!"

Thus we learn the lesson of Goliath's sword. All things work together for our good. We win our triumphs with arrows from the quiver of the enemy. Samson's riddle is solved: "Out of the eater cometh forth meat, and out of the strong cometh forth sweetness."

And here, as everywhere, Christ is our example. The cross was intended for his overthrow. It was called "the accursed tree." But Christ assumed it, bore it patiently, triumphed over it, and is now conquering the world with it. The cross gleams on innumerable spires, is worn as an amulet over the hearts of believers and stands in history as a divine symbol of victory.

"In the cross of Christ I glory,
  Towering o'er the wrecks of time."

It is probable that when David left the tabernacle that day, grasping the sword of Goliath, he lay down to rest in a lonely place. He placed the sword beside the stone which served as his pillow, and kept his hand upon it. In the watches of that night memory was busy. It seemed but yesterday that he had gone forth against the champion of Gath. He heard again the challenge ring across the valley. He remembered the prayer with which he winged the smooth stone as it flew from the leathern thong. He heard the shouts of the Israelites as he bent above his fallen foe. He felt again the grateful pride with which he had presented himself at the royal pavilion. And, alas! he bitterly recalled his forgetfulness of divine mercy. He had wandered on the dark mountains far from God. When he awoke, his hand was still upon Goliath's sword; he drew it from the scabbard and looked along the blade. Was it rusted with blood? It seemed as if the weapon had been reforged while he slept. What is this that he reads upon it? "There is a God in Israel." This should henceforth be to him not the sword of Goliath but the sword of the Lord. And he arose in newness of faith and went upon his way.

If God be upon our side, my friends, the weapon has never been forged that can hurt or destroy us. If God be for us, who shall be against us? All hope of success lies there. Look upon the giant's sword again. Read there the divine promise: "All things work together for good to them that love God." All things! Aye; pardoned sin, sorrow, and death's sharpness, all must serve thee. Go forth in this thy might. Be strong; be of good courage; for the sword of Goliath has become for thee "the sword of the Spirit which is the word of God."

THE GOSPEL OF CERTAINTY.

"For we have not followed cunningly devised fables, when we made known unto you the power and coming of our Lord Jesus Christ, but were eye-witnesses of his majesty. For he received from God the Father honor and glory, when there came such a voice to him from the excellent glory, This is my beloved Son, in whom I am well pleased. And this voice which came from heaven we heard, when we were with him in the holy mount. We have also a more sure word of prophecy; whereunto ye do well that ye take heed, as unto a light that shineth in a dark place, until the day dawn, and the day star arise in your hearts: knowing this first, that no prophecy of the Scripture is of any private interpretation. For the prophecy came not in old time by the will of man: but holy men of God spake as they were moved by the Holy Ghost.—I. Peter 1, 16-21.

The greatest of current questions is this: What think ye of Jesus which is called the Christ? It behoves every thoughtful man to address himself at once and with all earnestness to this consideration; for herein are the issues of life and death.

At this point we observe a grave difference of opinion. There are millions of people who believe in Christ as their Lord and Saviour, who regard him as chiefest among ten thousand and altogether lovely, and have accordingly surrendered all their powers of body and soul to him. There are other millions to whom he has no form nor comeliness that they should desire him; who reject his Messianic claims and overtures of mercy, saying, "We will not have him to rule over us."

It is passing strange that there should be such a divergence of opinion in a matter involving our eternal destiny. If the doctrines of the Christian religion are false, then the believers of the past have walked in a dream, they that have fallen asleep in Christ are perished, and we are but drowning men grasping at straws. Then the Church is a masterpiece of folly, history a bewildering puzzle, Christendom a blot on the map of the world, the progress of these nineteen centuries a phosphorescent gleam in the blackness of darkness, life a labyrinth without a clew, and death a plunge into an unbroken night.

But if the claims of Christianity are true, what then? All other systems are false and pernicious, for "he that believeth shall be saved and he that believeth not shall be damned"; scepticism is blindness, indifference a fatal mistake, rejection of Christ an unpardonable sin, and a great multitude, among whom are many of our dearest friends, are fatuitously hurrying on, lockstep, quickstep, to spiritual and eternal death.

In view of such considerations it should be the first business of every earnest man to determine this question, pro or contra, without delay. There is no neutral ground. Indifference is the height of folly. There are many who claim to be "honest doubters." Let them put themselves to the test, for there is a serious misapprehension here. "Doubt is either the agony of a noble soul or the trifling of a fool." It is greatly to be feared that many who think themselves truth-seekers are self-deceived. Are they doing their best, with all aids at command, to determine the great problems of life? An honest doubter is one who, realizing the importance of the issue, rests not day nor night until he arrives at truth. He puts away all preconceptions and, with a clear conscience and a single purpose, addresses himself to the point at issue. He seeks no neutral ground. He perceives that there is only one alternative: either to receive Christ at his word—in which case he will close in with his overtures and devote his life to him—or else to reject him outright as a self-deluded fanatic or wilful impostor, unworthy of faith or countenance. "How long halt ye between two opinions; if the Lord be God, follow him; if Baal, then follow him."

If, then, my friend, you are an honest doubter, you will weigh the evidence at once, and determine upon it. You will not be satisfied to hold judgment in suspense. You will do one thing or the other, accept Christ or reject him. And, pending the settlement of this question, you will not sleep soundly or go about your secular tasks with a light heart; for that would be to trifle with destiny. You are standing at the crossroads; the responsibility of choice confronts you. Cæsar at the banks of the Rubicon was under no more immediate constraint than you just now. How long did he pause? Only long enough to weigh the argument. To remain where he was meant failure; to cross would plunge the nation into civil war; he passed over, saying, "The die is cast!" Great problems do not await our convenience; to solve them without fear, delay, or vacillation, is to quit ourselves like men.

But how shall we decide? View the evidence candidly, fearlessly, and at once. The gospel appeals to reason. If the testimony offered in its support is inadequate, reject it. But go into court, and remain there until you have heard the case through and passed upon it.

In our text Peter sets forth the lines of evidence in favor of Christianity. They are three: Oral Testimony, Scripture, and Personal Experience. "A threefold cord is not quickly broken."

I. *As to Oral Testimony.* He says, "We have not followed cunningly devised fables, when we made known unto you the power and coming of our Lord Jesus Christ; but were eye-witnesses of his majesty." He is speaking to those who had not seen Jesus in the flesh. He himself had heard his sermons, seen his miracles, witnessed his wonderful life. In particular, he had been with him in the Mount of Transfiguration, had seen the garments of the Nazarene flutter aside for a moment, revealing the royal purple, and had heard a voice from heaven saying, "This is my beloved Son." This was no dream, no fable, no hallucination; he had seen and heard it. And there were others who, as eyewitnesses, were prepared to testify as to the divine character and mission of Christ. This sort of testimony is still offered to sustain the gospel claim. But you say, "This is mere hearsay." We answer:

(1) Such evidence has valid weight. We are all the while accepting it. How do we know that light travels at the rate of 186,000 miles a second? We accept it on the testimony of men who have investi-

gated the matter. How do we know that a Spanish fleet is lying at the bottom of Manila harbor? Men who were present have told us so. How do we know that Croton water is fit to drink? We rest on the assurance of scientists who have analyzed it. Ninety-nine per cent. of our knowledge comes by hearsay. We receive the testimony of eye-witnesses *unless there is a special reason for rejecting it.*

(2) Such evidence, in favor of Christianity, has a vast cumulative value for us. In Peter's time there were a few witnesses who could say, "That which we have heard, which we have seen with our eyes, which we have looked upon and our hands have handled of the word of life, declare we unto you." We have the testimony of a great multitude, a procession issuing from the upper room in Jerusalem, and increasing along the centuries from hundreds to thousands, from thousands to millions;—passing through the light of fagot-fires and under the shadow of dungeons and gallows-trees, declaring the testimony of Jesus and singing his praises until they disappear amid the glory streaming from the heavenly gates. There are some hundreds of millions of people living to-day who are prepared to testify as to their personal experience in the saving power of the gospel. They all certify with one accord, "We were sinners, troubled with a certain fearful looking-for of judgment. We came to Jesus Christ for salvation, trusting to the efficacy of his blood. He said, 'Thy sins be forgiven thee!' and his peace that passeth all understanding came into our hearts. He is our present help; and as to the future, we are without fear. We have not

followed cunningly devised fables. We speak from experience. We know whom we have believed, and are persuaded that he is able to keep that which we have committed to him until that day." It is submitted that so great a body of testimony is of overwhelming weight. To a reasonable man it must be absolutely conclusive, unless some definite rebuttal is forthcoming. No court of justice would reject it.

The only question is as to the character of the witnesses. Can their credibility be impeached? Peter and his fellow-apostles were men of humble origin but unquestioned honesty, who had everything to lose and nothing to gain by their championship of the crucified Nazarene; and with their blood they sealed their devotion to him. The great body of believers who succeeded them did not claim to be impeccable saints, only sinners saved by grace; nevertheless they showed in their walk and conversation the sincerity of their convictions and the transforming power of the gospel. And what shall be said of those who constitute the Universal Church of to-day? Let a thousand be taken at random from any fellowship of believers, and a thousand from without; and let a just comparison be made between them. We will abide the issue. It was by such comparison that Alexander Pope, himself an unbeliever, was moved to make this historical definition, "A Christian is the highest style of man."

II. *The next line of evidence is Scripture;* of which Peter says, "We have also a more sure word of prophecy, whereunto ye do well that ye take heed as unto a light that shineth in a dark place."

> How precious is the Book divine
> By inspiration given;
> Bright as a lamp its doctrines shine,
> To guide our souls to heaven.

The Scriptures are here characterized by Peter as "more sure," that is, than oral testimony. The word of eye-witnesses is corroborated by divine revelation. This is the court of last appeal.

It is obvious that there must be somewhere a final criterion of truth. There are standards of weight and measure at Washington for the testing of every pound and yard-stick in our land. It cannot be supposed that the Heavenly Father would set his children adrift without a chart for their direction. This is the ground and rationale of the Scriptures. They were intended to be an ultimate and infallible rule of faith. And they are so received, despite all controversy, by the universal church. The man who rejects them is bound, in justice to himself, to find some other court of final authority, where he may seek, amid the noise of conflicting voices, a confirmation of spiritual truth.

The apostle justifies his confidence in the Scriptures by adding that they "came not by the will of man; but holy men spake as they were moved by the Holy Ghost." If this means anything, it means that the men who wrote the Scriptures did not sit down of themselves, with stylus and parchment, saying, "I will write an account of the Creation," or, "I will write the history of Israel," or, "I will write a prediction of the Messiah"; but they proceeded to their work and performed it under the direction and control of the Spirit. The figure is that of a vessel under sail. They were "moved" by the Holy Ghost as a ship is borne onward by the wind filling its canvas. They wrote what they were told to write by the Spirit of God.

Still further, the apostle says that the Scriptures so written are not "of any private interpretation." The word rendered "private" is *idia*, literally "one's own." This means that no man is his own interpreter. When we speak of "the right of private judgment" with reference to Scriptures, we mean to exclude all human interposition; but alas for the man who approaches revelation in the dim light of reason alone. The finite cannot grasp the infinite. "Spiritual things are spiritually discerned." God, who gave the Scriptures, must help us to understand them. The Holy Ghost, by whom the sacred page is illuminated, opens our eyes, that we may wisely read it. The chancellor of Queen Candace, riding in his chariot, with the parchment before him, knit his brows in perplexity as he read the prophecy of Isaiah, "*He was led as a sheep to the slaughter; and like a lamb dumb before his shearer, so opened he not his mouth.*" Philip the evangelist, walking alongside and hearing him, asked, "Understandest thou what thou readest?" He wisely answered, "How can I, except some man shall guide me?" He was then guided by the Spirit; and the truth flashed upon him.

In order to understand the Scriptures, we must put away all preconceptions of doctrine and accept this divine aid. In default of that, they are as if written in an unknown tongue. If we read by "our own interpretation," we read to our own undoing. When Galileo sought to convince his accusers by saying, "Look through my telescope and you shall see Jupiter's moons for yourselves;" they answered, "If we did, we should have no case against you." This is why men so often see nothing in Scripture, or read only to the confirmation of their errors; they refuse the influence of the Spirit, by which the truths of Revelation would be made plain and clear before their eyes.

III. *One more line of evidence is named by Peter; to wit, Personal Experience.* We are like wanderers in the night; voices are heard about us, saying, "This is the way, walk ye in it;" better still, the Bible is given us as a lantern "shining in a dark place"; but when yonder we see the light of the morning, our perplexity is over. Thus personal experience adds final confirmation to oral testimony and Scripture. Peter says we do well to listen to the word of eye-witnesses and to give heed to the lamp-light of prophecy "until the day dawn and the day star arise *in your hearts.*"

O taste and see that the Lord is good! "He that hath the Son of God, hath the witness in himself." All voices, human and divine, are ineffective until by vital appropriation we make the gospel an indwelling fact. Then we know that Jesus Christ hath power on earth to forgive sins. Then we, becoming witnesses ourselves, can testify that his love is an easement of all pain and sorrow. Then we feel his friendship as the great incentive to spiritual growth and usefulness. The truth is put beyond all peradventure when the day star arises in our hearts.

A woman came running into the city of Samaria, saying, "I went out to Jacob's well to draw water; and a wayfarer met me who spake as never yet man spake of spiritual things; he told me all things that ever I did. Is not this the Messiah for whom we have been looking? Come and see." They followed her back to the well and heard him. They besought him to be their guest and he abode with them two days; and many believed because of his word. Then they said to the woman, "Now we believe, not because of thy saying; for we have heard him ourselves and know that this is indeed the Christ, the Saviour of the world." Thus in the last reduction a man is savingly convinced only by personal experience; when he can say, "I have met Christ, have made his acquaintance, have reasoned with him by the way, have learned to love him."

One thing is better, and only one—*to see him in the brightness of his heavenly glory.* The day star itself shall fade in the high noon of heaven. Here we walk by faith; there hope shall be lost in fruition, and faith in sight. We shall behold the King in his beauty; and we shall be like him, for we shall see him as he is.

A native convert in the South Sea Islands gave this testimony: "I listened to the Missionary when he spoke of sin, and he and I were like two canoes going side by side. Then he spoke of salvation, and I dropped behind—mast broken and sail blown away—while he sped on. The sea drove me on a barren coast, where I lay helpless for a time. I arose in blackness and darkness and felt my way like one groping along a wall. Then I seemed to touch a door; I pushed for my life; it flew open, and I beheld my Saviour, the glory shining in his face!"

The fullness of revelation is before us. Meanwhile let us use the light we have and live up to it. Let us listen to the voices of eye-witnesses, follow the gleam of the Scriptures and heed the testimony of our hearts. Here is the secret of peace and moral earnestness. And in due time all shadows will vanish in the Sun's glory. Our path shall be "as the shining light, which shineth more and more unto the perfect day."

THE TOWER OF BABEL.

"And they said, Go to, let us build us a city, and a tower whose top may reach unto heaven: and let us make us a name, lest we be scattered abroad upon the face of the whole earth."—Gen. 11, 4.

Is this a true story? There are those who regard it as a myth or legend coming down from the primitive ages. Others, who hesitate to pronounce any portion of Scripture false, view it as an allegory. This, however, is evasion. Tell a child that the story of Washington and his hatchet is to be taken in an allegorical sense, and his just conclusion will be that you do not believe it.

There are certain facts to be accounted for: One is the Unity of the Race. It is the custom of ethnologists to trace the lineage of nations through a threefold channel, Aryan, Shemitic and Turanian, back to a single source. Another is the Confusion of Tongues. Such philologists as Bunsen, Rawlinson and Max Muller, argue from a multiplicity of cognate words and phrases that all languages sprang from one original. And still another fact is "the Aryan Cradle." It is commonly held that somewhere on the great central table-land of Asia there was a gathering of the clans from which successive migrations went forth to people the earth. These are conceded facts. If the story of Babel is not true, they must be accounted for in some other way. The presumption is in favor of the narrative until something better shall be found to supplant it.

At the subsidence of the Flood the survivors were Noah, his three sons, and their families. In gratitude for deliverance, they "builded an altar unto the Lord" and, gathering around it in prayer, made due acknowledgment to him. They lifted their eyes and, lo! the bow of promise was over them. And God said, "This is the token of the covenant which I make between me and you: I do set my bow in the cloud; the waters shall no more become a flood to destroy all flesh." At the same time he divided the earth among them and commanded them to "go forth and replenish it."

In pursuance of that command they left Ararat and journeyed toward the west. The regions through which they passed were marked by the desolations of the deluge, but presently they came to the plain of Shinar, where nature was now putting on a new garb of beauty and fertility. There they tarried in all probability for some hundreds of years, during which they were greatly multiplied. Why should they go further? They were prosperous and content. Then came the happy thought: *"Go to, let us build us a tower whose top may reach unto heaven; and let us make us a name, lest we be scattered abroad upon the face of the whole earth."* The issue showed that this was a foolish plan. They made some serious mistakes.

Their first mistake was in saying, "Let us make us a name." What right has a man or a nation to "a name"? The difference between greatness and mediocrity is purely conventional; it is a mere measurement of atoms. Plutarch says that Flaminius, on supping with a wealthy friend, complained of the surfeiting and bewildering variety of dishes; to which his host replied, "Give yourself no uneasiness; all are of swine's flesh, differing only in the sauce and dressing." So it is with men whose breath is in their nostrils; great and little, they came from dust, and must return to it. Call the roll: "Cæsar!" "Alexander!" "Napoleon!" What are they? A living dog is better than a dead lion. Comparisons are grotesque. Ambition is tragi-comedy. "The paths of glory lead but to the grave." No name is worth getting which is not possible to the humblest.

> "To serve the present age,
> My calling to fulfill;
> O, may it all my powers engage
> To do my Master's will!"

The same is true of nations. The path of history is lined with ruined thrones and dynasties. *Sic transit gloria mundi.* At this moment we are dreaming dreams of American greatness. We have reached the danger line. Our momentary victory over an effete sovereignty has intoxicated us. We are saying, "This is great Babylon which I have built!" We are aspiring to join the syndicate of Great Powers. We are talking of an Anglo-Saxon alliance. Yes; by all means let us have alliances—alliances with all nations—on the basis of humanity, but not otherwise. God save us from an overweening pride! Why should we join the procession that has marched through the centuries with trumpets and flying banners to dust and oblivion? God has better things in store for us. John Adams said, "I always consider the discovery and settlement of America as the opening of a divine scheme for the illumination of darkness and the emancipation of the oppressed peoples of the earth." Let this be our glory, this our name: to fulfill our manifest destiny as a nation divinely appointed to give shelter to the persecuted and to send forth the evangel. As a Christian people, it behooves us to clasp hands with all other Christian peoples in the great enterprises of humanity and universal evangelization. In this let us content ourselves, and go on singing:

> Our father's God, to Thee,
> Author of liberty,
>   To Thee we sing.
> Long may our land be bright
> With freedom's holy light,
> Protect us by Thy might,
>   Great God, our King!

The second mistake of the Babelites was in their determination not to be "scattered over the face of the whole earth." In point of fact it was God's purpose that they should disperse and possess the earth. It was with this in view that he had made the landed apportionment. They had apparently forgotten the injunction delivered to them under the bow of promise. They were guilty of insubordination in resolving thus to abide in the vale of Shinar.

It is bad policy for a nation to shut itself up within a Chinese wall. At the beginning of our history, we formulated the Monroe Doctrine. This was our

Tower of Babel. The Washington construction of that doctrine forbade the forming of any "foreign entanglements." It seemed, indeed, as if we should find difficulty enough in caring for our own welfare, without concerning ourselves about the affairs of the nations at large. God thought otherwise. A time came when we were invited, not to say divinely instructed, to lend a hand in the overthrow of the unspeakable Turk and the deliverance of a persecuted people. But Armenia was too far away. We reminded the Lord of our domestic policy and insisted that this was a foreign affair, in which we could not entangle ourselves. He then pointed to Cuba, saying, "Behold a desolated and starving people at your door." It was to no avail. Three weary years went by; then, down went the *Maine!* And the spray of that dismal wreck rose like a beacon to admonish us. That was God's way of broadening our theory of national life. It was as if he said, "This is not a question of vicinage. Open your ears to the cry of humanity! Send out your heart to the uttermost parts of the earth!"

It is bad policy for a church, also, to remain in the vale of Shinar. The Master's word was, "Go, evangelize." His disciples, a feeble folk, and terrified by their Lord's tragical death, insisted on remaining at Jerusalem. One day as they were gathered in an open court there was a sound as of a rushing, mighty wind. The power of the Spirit rested upon them, and they began to speak in divers tongues. If this meant anything, it was a plain intimation that with this polyglot preparation they were to go and preach the gospel among all the peoples of the earth. But they were slow to apprehend the great commission; they still huddled at Jerusalem. Then came the stoning of Stephen. They looked into each other's faces, pale, terrified, whispering, "Our beloved deacon is slain!" And in various directions they fled, "going everywhere," and carrying with them the unsearchable riches of Christ. God had endeavored to draw them toward their duty with the cords of a man; but, failing in that, he resorted to the scourge. No church can work in upon itself and live. Far better a plain conventicle with a broad heart than the finest cathedral that ever was reared to be occupied by a people whose wizened souls were walled in by selfish respectability. The currents of ecclesiastical life are centrifugal. "There is that scattereth, and yet increaseth; and there is that withholdeth, and it tendeth to poverty." To go into all the earth is to flourish like a vineyard on a southern slope; to tarry in Jerusalem is to perish of dry rot.

The same holds true of the believer. To work out one's own salvation is the first of duties chronologically; but it is only the beginning of the spiritual life. A man intent upon self-culture, praying for the deepening of his spiritual life, is further on, but still within the bounds of selfishness. A father pleading for the salvation of his household, claiming the blessings of the Abrahamic covenant, has made still further progress; but is yet only "beginning at Jerusalem." Let him not complain if, despite the sureness of the covenant, his sons and daughters go amiss by reason of his selfish insubordination. The old families of

Europe have sought from time immemorial to preserve their estates by entailing the inheritance; yet many of our American parvenus have crossed the sea to take possession of ancient castles. The law of entail impinges upon a law of nature. By the same token, it is impossible to entail the inheritance of grace. As you care for the salvation of your household, send forth your sympathies beyond the domestic circle. Forget not to communicate. Piety is like the fragrance of ointment: it cannot be clasped in the hand. It is like sunlight; you cannot box or bottle it. O God, enlarge our hearts! Help us to go forth and evangelize the earth. We must get beyond all narrow spheres. Our field is the world. No man liveth unto himself. Followers of Christ, disperse your energies! "Go" is the word; go in your prayers and sympathies with the evangel to the uttermost parts of the earth. Thus only can you bring your life into harmony with the divine will.

The third mistake made by the Babel builders was in leaving God out of their reckoning. They made no mention of him. In proposing to build a citadel high enough to avoid all danger of another flood, they had apparently forgotten his bow of promise. Their tower was to reach unto heaven and stand like a finger of defiance pointed at the throne. The story is told in three chapters :

(1). A splendid conception. "Go to," they said in mutual congratulation. The architects were called; plans and specifications were made. Immense! magnificent! The structure was to be two miles in circumference, with a road broad enough for two chariots abreast, rising in seven spiral terraces toward the clouds. When it was finished they would ride in triumphal procession to the top.

(2). Speedy execution. All set themselves with enthusiasm to the task. Here was clay, yonder was bitumen; clay and bitumen would make the best of bricks. The foundations were laid; the superstructure rose, terrace upon terrace. The women and children looked on with admiration. There were plans for the dedication ceremonies. No doubt they would be practising hymns and arranging liturgies for the approaching day.

(3). Sudden frustration. Our best laid plans gang aft aglee. God said, "Go to; let us go down!" He speaks after the manner of men. Indeed, he is always coming down to see. Close your ledger, lock your vault, keep your purposes close in your heart. Still will he search and discover all. One morning there came an effectual stay of proceedings. The toilers presented themselves to the master workman for instructions as usual; but they could not understand. One asked of another, "What is he saying?" What had happened? Were all going daft? The place was filled with a jargon of confused voices. The workmen, perplexed and bewildered, "left off to build." Did you ever try to converse with a foreigner whose language you did not understand and who could not speak a word of English? You were soon tired and must needs get up and go. This was precisely what the Babelites did. This was what God intended them to do : *get up and go.* They gave up their project, they drifted apart by diverse paths; they dispersed to people the earth. It is vain to oppose ourselves to the divine plan. Let the kings of the earth set themselves in array; he that sitteth in the heavens will laugh. I have watched a colony of ants building their home; bright and busy, running in and out, making bricks and raising their ambitious Babel higher and higher. Foolish little people ! How easy it is to discomfit them. You may topple their tower with your foot, and send them scampering hither and yon. So God holds in derision those who plan and purpose against his holy will.

What is our lesson ? You have a purpose. I would not give a farthing for a man who has none. Do you mean to be rich ? Take heed how you leave God out of the reckoning, then, for you belong to him. Heap up your wealth, coin upon coin ; and observe how the image and superscription of the King is upon it. Kneel down by your strong boxes and say, "Here, Lord, is thine own ; what wilt thou have me do with it ? "

Or do you mean to make a name for yourself ? Take heed; you are on dangerous ground. Some of the brilliant names of history—Byron, Robespierre, Philip II, Hildebrand, bloody Claverhouse, Napoleon—are like bombs hissing through the air and discharging corrosive gases as they fall. These names are pilloried before the nations. The centuries hiss at them. But if you mean to make a name for piety and benevolence, to extend your influence for truth and righteousness, well and good. But take God into the reckoning. A name is worth having only so far as he may use it.

Or do you intend, above all, to work out salvation? If so, one caution: hearken to the divine voice. The Lord has marked out the plan: "Other foundation can no man lay than that is laid, which is Jesus Christ." Beware of your own devices; lest, like the Babelites, you be brought to confusion. There is a way which seemeth right unto a man, but the end thereof is death. Take God at his word. He that believeth on the Son, hath life; he that believeth not, the wrath of God abideth upon him.

Do your best. Make your life tell. Achieve a true success. It is said of Æropus that he was a great lantern-maker, but the poorest king that Macedonia ever had. His success was his failure. So it may be with you, my friend. You may succeed in some lower sphere and fall short of the great purpose which God has concerning you. What are you making of yourself? You are pushing on at a tremendous rate; but what for? Life is structural. Build on Christ and build the noblest. Be true to your royal birth, to your divine destiny. Live for your best self, the weal of your fellow-men, and, above all, the glory of God.

THE RENDING OF THE VEIL.

"And the veil of the temple was rent in the midst."—Luke 23, 45.

The veil here indicated was the Katapetasma, or inner veil of the tabernacle. It separated the two apartments, the Holy Place and the Holy of Holies. Josephus says it was sixty feet high. It hung from four pillars of gilded acacia wood. The hooks by which it was suspended were of gold, and its pillars rested in sockets of silver. The fabric itself was of fine twined linen, covered with richly embroidered cherubim. It typified the complex personality of Jesus, in which heaven and earth were interwoven as warp and woof; the attributes of Godhood being combined with the perfect graces of manhood in an absolute harmony of moral beauty. It is by the atoning work of Jesus, accomplished through this complex personality, that we regain our lost estate, as it is written, "Having, therefore, brethren, boldness to enter into the holiest by the blood of Jesus; by a new and living way which he hath consecrated for us through the veil, that is to say, his flesh; let us draw near with a true heart, in full assurance of faith."

The rending of this veil was full of significance, as,

indeed, is every episode connected with the great tragedy. It occurred on Paschal Friday, the fifteenth of Nisan. The High Priest was expected, on the evening of that day, to lift the outer veil, or Kalumma, and expose the Holy Place to the view of the assembled people. They might see there the candlestick, the table of shew bread and the golden altar of incense, and beyond these the Veil of Separation which concealed the sacred reliquary. On this particular day the priest entered the Holy Place to attend to his customary duty. It was the hour of the evening sacrifice; he was probably engaged in lighting the lamps of the golden candlestick, when he saw the great curtain begin to part asunder from the top to the bottom as if rent from above by an unseen hand. He stood amazed and horrified. What could it mean?

It had a deeper meaning than he suspected. We must interpret it in the light of what was then taking place on a neighboring hill. For three mortal hours Jesus had been agonizing on the cross. The heavens had been gradually overspread by the blackness of an Egyptian night. The sufferer had passed deeper and deeper into his vicarious pain, bearing on his great heart the burden of the world's sin, until, passing through hell's door in our behalf, he cried, "*Eloi, Eloi, lama sabachthani!*" Then silence for a time, until the hour of the evening sacrifice, when he cried once again with a loud voice, like a soldier wounded unto death summoning all his strength for a last triumphant word, *Tetelestai*—"It is finished!" It was at this moment that the High

Priest, ministering in the temple, saw the veil rent in sunder. In the light of the great tragedy, and interpreted by that final cry, what means the rending of the veil?

I. *The unveiling of the great Mystery which had been hid from the foundation of the world.* Paul speaks of his preaching as being "according to the revelation of the mystery which was kept secret since the world began, but now is made known to all nations for the obedience of faith." (Rom. 16, 25.) And again: "By revelation he made known unto me the mystery which in other ages was not made known unto the sons of men." (Eph. 3, 3–5.) He speaks of himself as a minister of "the mystery which hath been hid from ages and generations, but now is made manifest to his saints; to whom God would make known what is the riches of the glory of this mystery among the nations; which is Christ in you the hope of glory." (Col. 1, 26–27.) And still further: God "hath saved us not according to our works, but according to his own purpose and grace, which was given us in Jesus Christ, before the world began; but is now made manifest by the appearing of our Saviour, who hath abolished death and hath brought life and immortality to light." (2 Tim. 1, 9.)

We are encompassed by mysteries on every side. Nature has her *arcana*, into which the scientists peer with eager eyes. The Greeks and Egyptians had Isis and Eleusis: the rabbis their *cabala;* the Buddhists their occult doctrines. There are deep problems in philosophy; and as to theology, Milton says the angels lose themselves in the wandering mazes of "free will, fixed fate, foreknowledge absolute." We are born with inquiring eyes. Our search for truth is along the winding path of interrogation. But there is one question which, above all and under all, engages earnest souls; to wit, *What shall I do to be saved?* This is the sphinx that, with dull, devouring eyes, confronts the children of men. For all are sensible of sin; all are conscious of the just sentence, "The soul that sinneth, it shall die"; all feel that the great Father must have made some provision of escape from doom; and all alike are moved to inquire, Where is it?

It is the part of religion to solve this problem. All the false systems have attempted it. This is the *rationale* of the altar and the sacrifice; this is the ground of mythologies and pantheons. But there was one Religion from the beginning, in which God enshrined the Mystery of Life. Judaism began with the protevangel: "The seed of woman shall bruise the serpent's head; and it shall wound his heel." No sooner had man sinned than God thus dimly announced the coming of the Christ, to suffer vicariously in expiation of sin. On this prophecy was reared the Jewish system of rites and symbols and sacred observances; wherefore it was called, *Oikonomia*—the "Dispensation" of the Mystery. In this religion the Hope of Israel was transmitted along the ages. Its elaborate ceremonial served both to conceal and to reveal the coming Christ. The world not being ready either to receive or to understand him, he looked forth as yet from behind this lattice and waited for the fulness of time.

THE RENDING OF THE VEIL. 345

The center of this ceremonial economy was the Ark of the Covenant. The Jews were accustomed to speak of Palestine as "The Holy Land." The holiest spot in Palestine was Mount Zion; the holiest place on Mount Zion was the temple; and the most sacred apartment there was, as its name indicates, the Holy of Holies. Here, behind the great curtain, was the Ark of the Covenant. It was a chest of acacia wood covered with gold, with a golden lid known as "the mercy-seat;" over which hovered the Shechinah, or luminous cloud, in which God was wont to manifest himself. In the ark were three historic memorials: the tables of stone, on which were inscribed the precepts of the Moral Law; a pot of manna, recalling the wilderness journey; and Aaron's budded rod. The ark thus furnished was intended to symbolize the incarnation, with its great attendant truths. On the golden cover were two cherubim bending down with curious eyes; as it is written, "Great is the mystery of godliness, God manifest in flesh": and, again, "The angels desire to look into it."

The most important of Jewish appointments was the 10th of Tisri, called the Great Day, or Day of Atonement. An offering was made in the early morning for the people's sin. The High Priest, filling his hands with blood at the brazen altar, passed through the outer apartment, lifted the Veil of Separation, sprinkled the blood upon the mercy seat, and made his intercessory prayer. He then came forth and, in the presence of the assembled multitude, laid his hands upon the head of the scapegoat, which, bearing its burden, was led away by the hand of a fit man to the land of Azazel or oblivion. The people watched until he disappeared from sight, and then gave themselves up to rejoicing, having received assurance of their deliverance from sin.

Such was the elaborate system in which was enshrined the prophecy of the Lamb of God. This was "the mystery hid from the foundation of the world." It is now an open secret. The rending of the veil was the complement of the death cry, "It is finished!" The fulness of time had come for the disclosure of the mystery within the Holiest of All.

II. It will thus be perceived that the rending of the veil meant also *an end of Judaism*. The law of ordinances was a schoolmaster leading to Christ; its purpose was therefore accomplished when he came." "He took away the handwriting of ordinances, which was against us, and nailed it to his cross." The old economy was a dispensation of shadows; but there are no shadows at noon. The Sun of Righteousness is risen upon us.

God forbid that we should speak contemptuously of Judaism or of its venerable rites. Let us take heed how we say, "I believe in the New Testament," with a fling at the Old; for the Old Testament is the foundation of the New, and both together make one Holy Book. There can be no antagonism between them. As well say, "I believe in the rose, but not in the rose tree"; or, "I believe in the brook, but not in the fountain whence it came." The moral law, being written in the constitution of man, abides forever; but the ceremonial law was designed for temporary use. It passed away by reason of its fulfillment in Christ.

The sacred observances of Israel were all comprehended in oblations and ablutions. The oblations or sacrifices were with blood, since without the shedding of blood there is no remission of sin; the only exception being in the case of thank-offerings which were in grateful recognition of blessings flowing from the altar. The ablutions or purifyings were by water; they symbolized and prophesied the opening of the gospel fountain for uncleanness; as we sing,—

> There is a fountain filled with blood
> Drawn from Immanuel's veins;
> And sinners plunged beneath that flood
> Lose all their guilty stains.

All rites and ceremonies thus pointed forward to Christ and are fulfilled in him. In organizing the Christian Church, our Lord preserved only so much of the ancient ceremonial as should be consistent with the utmost simplicity. All that remains of that elaborate system is our two sacraments: Baptism, the initiatory rite of Christian fellowship, speaks of cleansing from sin; the Lord's Supper speaks of the sacrifice of the Lamb of God.

We are thus brought to see clearly that a highly-developed ritualism is not the religion of the New Testament. It was only fifteen years after the day of Pentecost that the First Council was held in Jerusalem. The apostles were summoned there to determine upon a matter which threatened to divide the church. A party of Judaizers had arisen, who argued that Christ came not to fulfill the ceremonial law, but merely to reform it. They held that candidates for admission to the church must pass through the customary Jewish initiation and afterwards adjust themselves to the ceremonial code. In that Council addresses were made by Peter on behalf of the broadminded Jews, by Paul as representative of the Gentile converts, and by James, the minister of the local church. Their contention was that to insist upon submission to the ancient ritual was to put a yoke upon the neck of the disciples which it was impossible to bear. Out of that Council went forth a glorious manifesto in behalf of the simplicity of Christian worship and the glorious liberty of the children of God.

In view of these facts it is obvious that an elaborate formalism is inconsistent with the genius of the gospel. To insist upon incense and canonicals, the elevation of the mass, fasts and festivals, bowings and genuflexions, is to be some thousands of years behind the times. I pray you, as Paul said to the Christians at Corinth, "Be not entangled again with the yoke of bondage." We are come out of the shadows into the light of day.

I see a man bending at an altar, who makes this prayer: "O God, behold my oblation; I have paid my tithes, I have brought the lamb for sacrifice; what more can I do?" I see another bending at the cross; and thus he prays: "O God, I can do nothing; all my righteousnesses are as filthy rags; but Jesus has died. I believe in him; I can do no more. In his name, I pray thee, forgive my sin." This is the difference between Judaism and Christianity. Thank

God for free grace, for the sweet simplicity and glorious liberty of the gospel!

III. And, finally, the rending of the veil means *Welcome to all.* The way into the holiest is open before us. There are no guards about the door. No priest can interpose between the soul and God. There are no Christian priests. Christ alone is "priest forever after the order of Melchizedek," and he ever liveth to make intercession for us. In him all men alike are invited to be kings and priests unto God.

But what is there to see within the veil? At the overthrow of Jerusalem an officer was deputized to force his way into the temple and discover the Mystery of the Holiest of All. Presently a burst of laughter was heard, and a voice saying, "There is nothing here!" Only a wooden chest, containing two slabs of stone, a pot of aromatic gum, and a leafy twig. For the thoughtless or irreverent there is, indeed, nothing here. "Spiritual things are spiritually discerned." But to an earnest soul the rending of the veil is access to life. The ark of the covenant is a silhouette of God manifest in flesh. Its golden cover sets forth the privilege of prayer, to which we have admission by a new and living way, "that is to say, his flesh."

> O may my hand forget its skill,
> My tongue be silent, cold and still,
> This throbbing heart forget to beat,
> If I forget the mercy-seat!

We lift the golden cover and, behold, here are the tables of the law; not those that Moses brake in anger, but the unbroken tables of the obedience of Christ. As it is written, "What the law could not do in that it was weak through the flesh, God, sending his Son in the likeness of sinful flesh, and for sin, condemned sin in the flesh; that the righteousness of the law might be fulfilled in us." And here is the pot of manna, a sweet memorial of Providence, seeming to say, "Take no anxious thought, what ye shall eat or what ye shall drink; your Father knoweth that ye have need." And the budded rod, eloquent of Him who, bringing life and immortality to light, enables us to say, "O death, where is thy sting? O grave, where is thy victory? The sting of death is sin; and the strength of sin is the law. But thanks be to God, which giveth us the victory through our Lord Jesus Christ?" And over all the Shechinah, the luminous symbol of God's presence. This is our pre-eminent privilege in the gospel, to enter with holy boldness and commune with him face to face. There is nothing beyond. "This is life eternal, to know God and Jesus Christ whom he hath sent."

Thus the way is open, friends, into the Holiest of All. Sin is alienation. Adam trembled when he heard God's footsteps in the Garden. Job was terrified by the Voice from the whirlwind. Moses hid in the cleft of the rock when the Presence passed by. Isaiah dropped his eyes under the great Light, crying, "Woe is me, for mine eyes have seen the King!" John fell before the vision as dead. But faith in Jesus Christ repairs the ravages of sin. Faith is reconciliation. Those that were afar off are brought nigh. Here in the Holy of Holies, is Immanuel, God with us. Enter, O penitent soul, and regain your lost estate! The door is open, the veil is rent asunder, God's hands are stretched out still; he waits to welcome you.

www.ingramcontent.com/pod-product-compliance
Lightning Source LLC
Chambersburg PA
CBHW030301240426
43673CB00040B/1025